Studying for Success

D0048641

This lively and stimulating book offers an enlightening new approach to effective study. Without minimising the importance of good organisation and hard work, the author stresses throughout that study must and can be *fun*.

With characteristic humour and wisdom, Richard Palmer updates and reinvigorates a classic, best-selling book with new sections on computers and the Internet, as well as chapters covering important areas such as:

- memory and review;
- essay planning and writing;
- note-taking;
- time management;
- using resources;
- exam techniques and preparation.

This is an inspiring, essential read for all students who want to find the key to achieving success both in coursework and exams.

Richard Palmer is Head of English at Bedford School and is author of *Write in Style 2nd edn* and *The Good Grammar Guide*, also published by Routledge.

Studying for Success

Richard Palmer

Routledge
Taylor & Francis Group

LONDON AND NEW YORK

First published 2004
by Routledge
11 New Fetter Lane, London EC4P 4EE

Simultaneously published in the USA and Canada
by Routledge
29 West 35th Street, New York, NY 10001

© 2004 Richard Palmer

Typeset in Baskerville by
Florence Production Ltd, Stoodleigh, Devon
Printed and bound in Great Britain by
MPG Books Ltd, Bodmin

British Library Cataloguing in Publication Data
A catalogue record for this book is available
from the British Library

Library of Congress Cataloging in Publication Data
Palmer, Richard, 1947–
    Studying for success / Richard Palmer.
        p. cm.
    Includes bibliographical references and index.
    1. Study skills.   2. Report writing.   3. Research.
    4. Examinations – Study guides.   I. Title.
    LB1049.P355 2004
    371.3'028'1–dc22   2003023812

ISBN 0–415–33818–2

To the memory of Philip Read

and

To Annie – for everything and forever

Contents

Figures

Preface

No profit grows where is no pleasure ta'en;
In brief, sir, study what you most affect.

(*The Taming of the Shrew*)

This book will, I hope, help and encourage students of all kinds, but it is primarily designed for those who have chosen a course of study rather than have had it imposed upon them. In other words, I am assuming that you have reached (or are fast approaching) that pivotal stage when education ceases to be compulsory, becoming *your* business rather than that of the law of the land. You are now able to study the subjects you wish to study and go about that work in ways that suit you; conversely, you are responsible for your methods and progress in a way that does not apply when you're younger. In short, and in the words that form my governing theme:

You are in charge.

I hope to convince you that this unique transformation is a liberating one. However, I am also aware that it also prompts two things that might be said to be the defining words of our time: *pressure* and *stress*.

If you are a GCSE or an A level student, you already know a great deal about both. In these days of league tables, fierce competition for UCAS places, and the ever-increasing importance of grades and certificates, young people are obliged to work in a hothouse atmosphere immeasurably more intense than was the case a generation ago. Moreover, in these testing-obsessed days, your work started to matter in a long-term way very early, which makes demands on your character as well as on your intellect. It is hard not to become anxious, and even harder not to seek some infallible means of banishing such anxiety.

By far the most touted cure is 'hard work'. I know of no educational institution, government department or indeed organisation of any kind that does not trumpet its virtues on an almost daily basis, and it is unsurprising that so many students and their families come to assume that sheer effort is the answer to all anxieties and the absolute key to success. There's only one flaw to this cure:

It isn't *true*.

Needless to say, nobody has ever achieved anything without a great deal of industry, and any approach that is lazy or amateurish is doomed. But quantity isn't everything, and if you imagine that you are working 'well' simply because you're spending a long time on it and ending every day in a state of near-exhaustion, the chances are high that you're deluding yourself. And, mindful that those observations – and my earlier ones about 'pressure' and 'stress' – apply no less to learners who are not mainstream secondary or tertiary students, a brief note on the genesis and purpose of this guide might prove illuminating.

All authors, no matter how grand or how humble, remember their first book with particular affection. Mine was entitled *Brain Train: Studying For Success*, and it was published in 1984 by E. and F.N. Spon. Co-written with a then student, Christopher Pope, it was far from being the first guide to study skills to appear, but the competition was a good deal less populous than it is now. That is partly because study skills has become something of an industry – just think of the profusion of study aids on everything from arithmetic to zoology that swell the shelves of the nation's bookshops – but it is also because the worlds of education and employment have undergone seismic changes in the two decades that followed my baptism into authorship. Study skills are now not just a major issue for all full-time academic students but for all returning students, distance learners, those doing professional refresher or re-training courses, and that ever-growing cohort whose main source of information and instruction is the Internet. Indeed, it could be said that these days we are all students: this is the age of *lifelong learning*.

So, when RoutledgeFalmer suggested that a slimmer and updated version of *Brain Train* might be desirable, I was readily persuaded. All authors like to be commissioned, naturally, but I was spurred on by something other than vanity and greed! I have already outlined some of those considerations, but the key one is enshrined in what was *Brain Train*'s first paragraph:

This is a book about study, and its stress throughout is on enjoyment. You may find that combination surprising; if so, you're wrong. Study is like anything else: the more you enjoy it, the more likely you are to succeed.

It has never been easy to convince students of the truth of those words, and it's probably harder to do so now than twenty years ago. Nevertheless, I stand by them more than I ever have, and by the quotation from Shakespeare that forms the epigraph above, just as it did in 1984. If you've *chosen* to be a student, then no matter what the pressure and inevitable moments of stress, *enjoy* that choice and enjoy yourself. I hope this book will help you achieve those goals and, as a result, a significant 'profit' in whatever you undertake.

Acknowledgements

Concerning the original inspiration for, and incarnations of, this book, I would like to re-voice my gratitude to Bernard Chibnall, sometime Head of Sussex University's Media Service Unit, whose courses for teachers first kindled my interest in study skills, and former Christ's Hospital colleagues Andrew Husband, Tim Kirkup and the late Tom Keeley for their interest and encouragement. I remain indebted to my quondam co-author Chris Pope, my original illustrator John Penny, and Christopher Turk and Bob Eadie for their chapters on computers and study, which appeared in the 1984 and 1996 editions of my book *Brain Train*, and informed this new volume.

I am grateful to London University's School of Oriental and African Studies for commissioning a series of study skills seminars, and to Philip Stott, David Boyd and Phil Jagger for implementing and hosting those sessions. Thanks for analogous commissions are due to Wendy Pollard and the Open University's Regional Arts Club, Jackie Max and Stephen Snell of NatWest's IT Learning and Development Operation, Kevin Dillow of Christ's Hospital, and Bedford School, especially in the person of Philip Young. It is also a pleasure to acknowledge the help, ideas and material provided by dear friends Roger and Helen Allen, Colin Baker, Colin Brizicki, Peter and Fiona Bundell, Rob Kapadia, David Neal, Jane Richardson, Martin Smalley, and Michael and Louise Tucker. I also owe a great deal to my first Commissioning Editor, the late Philip Read, to whose memory this book is co-dedicated. He believed in the 1983 manuscript I sent him, and much of what has been possible for me as an author started with that vote of confidence.

Turning to this present volume, my profound thanks to Jon Down for his excellent chapter on ICT and the new technologies; to friend and colleague Andrew Grimshaw for the 'three-point plan' to be found in Chapter 8; to Anna Clarkson and Jessica Simmons at Routledge; and to all my students past and present. Finally, and above all, I thank Annie, my wife. Her ideas and criticisms have been decisively enabling throughout, and without her good humour and loving tolerance during my countless hours in front of first the typewriter and then the PC, this guide would not have achieved one incarnation, let alone three.

Part I

How to get the best out of your mind

Chapter 1

Attitudes, assets and achievement

1 GETTING SORTED

> I like work; it fascinates me. I can sit down and look at it for hours.
> (Jerome K. Jerome)

Preliminary

What would you say the following had in common:

1 Getting up in the morning
2 Writing an essay
3 Cleaning the car
4 Reading *War and Peace*
5 Re-decorating a room
6 Mowing the lawn
7 Having to practise the piano
8 Sending off thank-you letters
9 Preparing a meal
10 Chatting up someone you fancy

You might answer that – with the possible exception of number 10 – they are all a drag but will have to be tackled sooner or later. Another possible answer, though, is that they are difficult to start doing, but that once you've started they're not so bad, even pleasant. Initially, however, there must be a degree of motivation present for you to be willing to start the task.

Like all things, study requires such initial motivation, and that could be paraphrased as your 'interest' or enjoyment. Indeed, my emphasis throughout is on enjoyment. Few people succeed at anything while finding it dull, and most successful people – whatever their job – derive an enormous amount of good old-fashioned fun from what they do. So just about the worst thing you can do when starting a new course is to dwell miserably on what hard work it's going to be. If you *expect* a course to be difficult, obscure or boring, the chances are that it will be. From the start, therefore, cultivate a sense of enjoyment; believe in the pleasures and satisfactions that await you.

Naturally, it is idle to pretend that any course of study does not involve work – hard work. But the key to that phrase lies in the adjective 'hard'. If you take it to mean 'laborious' or 'tedious', you're going to lose a lot of will power at once. If, however, you can latch on to the alternative meaning, of 'muscular' or 'concentrated', you will be setting up a tough and clear-sighted attitude which will sponsor enjoyment. All success requires care and industry: if you have picked up this book hoping for some smart-alec way to bypass necessary effort, you may as well put it down again right away. On the other hand, effort is not enough on its own: pleasure and enjoyment are vital ingredients too.

That last remark does not always apply to pre-16 study. If you're clever – and in my experience most students are brighter than they think – it is perfectly possible to get a GCSE A* in a subject you detest or at least are heartily glad to give up at the end of Year 11. After that, though, the 'pleasure principle' needs to be present. Once you're 16, you are no longer legally required to attend school or college; presumably you do so because you want to. And since it is just stupid to go on doing something you dislike, I will further presume that you are more or less pleased to be doing the course or courses you've chosen. If not, this book may still be able to help; however, some kind of motivation is essential, even if it's only the pleasure of looking forward to when you stop!

To help you work out your own attitude in more detail, here is an extended questionnaire. It is partly meant to amuse, but it also focuses on most of the things crucial to successful study, and many of the items look forward to matters discussed in later chapters. It may be that you will want to tick more than one answer in certain instances; there may be others where nothing listed matches your experience or view. Fine in both cases. The only 'rule' here is that you should be as honest with yourself as possible.

There are nearly three dozen questions. I've divided them into six 'categories'; a commentary on the issues raised follows each one.

A Your situation

I Are you doing your course:

✔

a	Because you love it?	
b	Because it's important in advancement/career terms?	
c	Because you've got nothing else to do?	

2 Are your study concerns:

✔

a	Primarily academic?	
b	Primarily professional?	
c	Primarily recreational/non-vocational?	

All six options are your affair, your privilege, and therefore equally 'right'. There are, ultimately, as many reasons for being a student as there are students, no two of whom are exactly alike. I hope some of you chose both 1a *and* 1b: pleasure and success are intimately connected, as I look to demonstrate throughout.

I especially hope this book will benefit anyone who chose 1c, which might appear to have been offered as a sardonic joke. It was not, and is not. Nowadays, the pressure on young people to continue their studies as extensively as possible is enormous, and as a result the alternatives are both fewer in number and less attractive than used to be the case. If you're a student because nothing else seems available, or because you're used to school/ college life and don't yet feel sufficiently confident to venture into something unknown, or simply because your parents have more or less insisted that you *stay* a student, you deserve – and have – my considerable sympathy. All I'll add is that you'll need to look on that 'sole option' in an affirmative way if you can: if that's all there is, then don't just get on with it – enjoy! And that friendly command applies whatever your needs and whatever 'type' you are.

B Your attitudes I: Inward

I Do you:

✔

a	Look forward to study/work?	
b	Work sensibly but only when necessary?	
c	Resent having to work?	

2 Are you:

		✔
a	Confident?	
b	Diffident?	
c	Arrogant?	

3 As a learner, are you:

		✔
a	Humble?	
b	Modest?	
c	Fearful?	

4 Is your memory:

		✔
a	Good?	
b	Average?	
c	Poor?	

5 Do you:

		✔
a	Think you're a fast reader?	
b	Think your reading speed is average/okay?	
c	Think you're a slow reader?	

6 Do you take to criticism:

		✔
a	Willingly?	
b	Reluctantly?	
c	Resentfully?	

7 Do you prefer to be:

		✔
a	Enthusiastic?	
b	Critical?	
c	Witheringly dismissive?	

8 As a student do you:

		✔
a	Expect to be taught?	
b	Expect to learn on your own?	
c	See things as essentially a partnership?	

9 If you answered (c) to 8, is that partnership: ✔

a	With teachers?	
b	With texts?	
c	With fellow students?	

All these issues are covered in detail later on, so I will not take up much of your time on them now.

It should be obvious enough that if most of your answers to Questions 1–7 were c, you're in trouble! In most cases, you can do something about those negative waves: slow reading, poor memory, excessive confidence or excessive worry can quickly be put right. I should perhaps add that option 2c is unfair and sneaky of me, since I've met only a handful of truly 'arrogant' students in thirty years.

Four other quick things:

• If you chose 1c I'm surprised you're reading this book, unless you picked it up hoping to find some smart-alec cure. If you did, forget it – and if you *really* resent time spent working, then you can also forget any idea of becoming a successful student.

• Criticism: nobody likes it, *nobody*. The best any of us can do is realise that it is usually – I would like to think invariably – offered in order to help us learn, develop and improve.

• A word about *destructive* criticism. There is (contrary to widespread attitudes) a great deal to be said for it. Indeed, it is one of life's pleasures to perform the perfect demolition job on something that thoroughly deserves it. But it would be unwise for a student to look forward to that too much or too often! Unless you're singularly unfortunate in the course you've chosen and the people who administer and teach it, such occasions will be rare, and you should keep the 'witheringly dismissive' part of your armoury under wraps.

• Concerning questions 8 and 9: ideally, you should have ticked *all six* boxes. There is no end to the ways in which you can learn, and no limit to the people and things you can learn from. However, I'd say 9c is particularly important. In the end, students learn as much from each other as from the more evident 'authorities' they encounter.

C Your attitudes II: Outward

1 You believe teachers are: ✔

a	Always right	
b	Usually right	
c	Sad types who can't get a proper job	

2 You believe: ✔

a	A good memory is a gift	
b	A good memory is a skill	
c	Sorry, what was the question?	

3 The printed word is: ✔

a	Gospel	
b	Suspect	
c	Depends	

4 Study aids are: ✔

a	Essential	
b	Rubbish	
c	Depends	

5 How do you evaluate classes versus private work?:   ✔

a	Classes are more important	
b	Private work is more important	
c	They are equally important	

In questions 1 and 2, only option b will do. 1c and 2c are jokes; if you didn't realise that, one or other of us needs to do something about our sense of humour. More important is the sheer *wrongness* of both 1a and 2a; later chapters will explain why.

The only properly sensible answer to 3 and 4 is the vague-looking c, 'depends'. If 3a and 4a are laughably gullible, 3b and 4b are actually no less naive in their unearned, foolish cynicism. The secret in both cases is to use your own judgment: *you are in charge.*[1]

For nearly everyone, 5c is the attitude that should be nurtured.[2] If that is not clear to you yet, I hope it will be by the end of this questionnaire, let alone the book itself.

D Your behaviour, rhythms and practices I: General

1 Do you work best: ✔

a	In the morning?	
b	In the afternoon?	
c	In the evening?	

2 Is your standard concentration span: ✔

a	10 minutes?	
b	30 minutes?	
c	60 minutes?	

3 If aware of feeling tired or sluggish, do you: ✔

a	Act on that and take a rest?	
b	Keep plodding on with the work in hand?	
c	Feel like that most of the time anyway?	

4 How often do you tackle important work when unfit for it?:   ✔

a	Never	
b	Sometimes	
c	Almost always	

5 When working, do you: ✔

a	Take occasional breaks?	
b	Take frequent breaks?	
c	Take no breaks until you're finished?	

6 When working, do you: ✔

a	Listen to music/have refreshments/be nicely relaxed?	
b	Need silence but also comfort?	
c	Concentrate fiercely and cut out all possible distractions?	

7 If faced with three or four tasks do you: ✔

a	Do the easiest/most congenial one first?	
b	Do the hardest/least congenial one first?	
c	Do the easiest/smallest one only?	

8 Assignment deadlines – do you: ✔

a	Normally get work done with time to spare?	
b	Normally do most of it during the last 24 hours?	
c	Normally need an extension?	

9 Do you: ✔

a	Read a lot?	
b	Read what you have to?	
c	Read under protest?	

10 In classes, tutorials and seminars, do you: ✔

a	Look to contribute often?	
b	Contribute occasionally when you feel like it/are asked?	
c	Think it's the teacher's job to entertain and inform you?	

11 Do you consult the Internet: ✔

a	Every day?	
b	Sometimes?	
c	Hardly ever?	

It may have struck you that those eleven questions form quite a mixed bag. That is as it should be, since the way we behave and go about things is seldom uniform, and our states and rhythms vary too.

Questions 1 and 3 have no 'right answer' – or rather, the right answer is the one that's right for *you*. Be honest about it in both cases, and then act on it, playing to your known strengths.

Questions 2–5 and 7 concern your standard work rhythms and work states. It is, I trust, plain which the 'negative' or 'unwise' options are in each case, and if you ticked more than half of these, you need to do something about how – and especially *when* – you tackle things. If your attention lags after a few minutes, if you feel permanently tired, if you get up from your desk six times an hour and wander away, if you are deterred by anything demanding . . . well, there are two possible remedies. One is to start getting sensibly tougher with yourself. The other is to think hard about changing your course of study, since it's readily apparent that you're doing the wrong one at present.

Questions 8–11 also concern time use and time management. They may seem disparate, but they aren't. Virtually all the students I've encountered who are chronically late with assignments also don't read much and are sponge-like in class; in addition, they spend a lot of time 'surfing' the Internet and pretending that in doing so they're working. Study is like anything else: the more you put into it, the more you get out; curiously but happily, it is also true that the more you do, the more you *want* to do and the more everything starts to acquire shape and clarity.

E Your behaviour, rhythms and practices II: Specific

1 When in class or a lecture do you:

		✔
a	Take regular notes?	
b	Take occasional notes?	
c	Just listen?	

2 When you've finished an assignment do you:

		✔
a	Check it immediately?	
b	Check it the next day?	
c	Look it over fleetingly before submitting it?	

3 How often do you look over your past work?:

		✔
a	Every week	
b	Every term	
c	When exam revision comes around	

4 Exams: their status – do you:

		✔
a	Believe they're reliable?	
b	Believe they're fallible?	
c	Believe they're a lottery?	

5 Exams: your attitude and experience – do you:

		✔
a	Enjoy them?	
b	Put up with them as a necessary evil?	
c	Dread them?	

All the issues at stake are covered extensively in the chapters which follow, and any comment now would be superfluous. Except one: don't sneer at the idea of *enjoying* exams. An exam is your decisive chance to prove just how good you can be, and a successful 'I'll show 'em' operation is always deeply satisfying!

F And finally

1 Do you:
✔

a	Enjoy humour?	
b	Consider humour a vital aid to thinking and learning?	
c	Suspect humour is frivolous and time-wasting?	

You may well think that 'a' was hardly worth asking: *every* reader is going to tick it.[3] The reason I included it was that quite a few students who enjoy jokes, lightness of touch and even the occasional silliness in other areas of life believe that such things have no place in study. That is a great mistake. I have, yes, come across impossibly earnest students who succeeded, but precious few. Solemnity is not the same thing as seriousness; it can indeed become its opposite, substituting earnest endeavour for illuminating enjoyment.

And that leads me neatly to my final question.

2 Do you:
✔

a	Want everything to be relevant?	
b	Want to learn?	
c	Want to have fun?	

I'd be disappointed if the preceding 30-plus questions and my commentaries on them have not led to you ticking all three boxes here. In my view 2b and 2c are inextricably linked. No, of course you won't enjoy every single moment of your study, any more than one can enjoy every single moment of (practically) anything in life. But any and every student is profoundly *lucky* in one almost frightening respect: did you know that 70 per cent of the world's 6 billion population cannot read? Given that, the least students can do is enjoy their good fortune and hence their work, or at least most of it!

Last of all: if you ticked 2a – and, to repeat, I hope you did – it was doubtless because you are suitably impatient with digressions which both lead nowhere and waste time, and rather more than impatient if it turns out that you've been spending weeks on a text or topic that doesn't appear on the syllabus you're (supposed to be) following. Fine and absolutely fair enough; however, guard against literal-mindedness when it comes to 'relevance'. It would be overstating the case to suggest that *everything* is relevant to a hungry-to-learn and engaged student, but not by much. For one of the things that distinguishes the really classy mind is the ability to discern relevance and connections in the unlikeliest things, and to get others to see them too.

Summary

'Honesty is the best policy' – so runs the proverb, which has been both championed and sneered at (in more or less equal proportions) for many generations. So far as the student is concerned, honesty is a priceless asset; unlike that proverb, though, my 'line' is not moral but practical. A degree of self-knowledge is essential to any student, and the title of this opening chapter indicates the fundamental importance of *attitude* or, in that modish phrase, 'mind-set'. No matter how hungry and able you may be, you need to have a clear idea of the kind of student you are or want to be. You also need to be aware of when in the day you work best or worst; how you go about the *physical* activity of working; the silliness of working when you're exhausted, bored, out of sorts or whatever; the comparable silliness of *not* working when you have time and intellectual energy to spare; and so forth. There will be times when you need to be tough on/with yourself; there will also be as many times when you need to treat yourself tenderly, even self-indulgently. Those occasions will be explored in proper detail as we go; but first, we need to address that always difficult time when you've got to start. So let's now look at the launching pad.

II GETTING STARTED

> A body continues in its state of rest or uniform motion unless acted upon by a net external force.
>
> (Isaac Newton)

Preliminary

I opened *Getting Sorted* above by listing ten activities that are invariably difficult to begin; I also pointed out that once you're under way they're not so bad. Just as a car requires more 'juice' to start it than to keep it going, so your brain and body need more impetus to begin a task than to continue it. Ignition in all things demands a lot of energy, and there is a good scientific reason for it:

That which is inert wishes to remain so.

That is a simplified paraphrase of Newton's First Law of Motion quoted above. So is this next sentence, its natural converse:

That which is in motion will wish to remain so.

Imagine yourself straining to shift a boulder weighting a quarter of a ton, in order to get it rolling down a hill. All your muscular effort will be expended on moving it the first few millimetres. Once you've created even a tiny degree of motion, the task becomes rapidly easier – until suddenly it is impossible for those same muscles to *halt* the movement.

The human brain does not operate in quite the same way; however, once started it works awesomely fast too. Indeed, one way to ignite your study energy is to remind yourself that you are the proud possessor of the most powerful and sophisticated machine that has yet appeared on earth – the human brain. As I dwell for a few moments on some of the amazing properties of that small chunk of grey matter between your ears, I hope to show you that, no matter how dozy or stupid you may feel, your mental capacity is staggering!

Your brain – or why you can look down on computers

The human brain weighs between 2.5 and 3lb[4] and is made of microscopic cells. You might be interested to know that:

> If it were possible to unwind the brain's tissue into one single strand, it would stretch from here to the moon and back: it would, that is, be half a million miles long.

I find it hard to grasp figures like that, beyond the vague realisation that they're sensational; still less can I cope with the two overwhelming sets of figures that appear below. However, I can assure you that they are accurate even if they're impossible to imagine.

(a) The number of atoms in our universe:

10 000 000 000 000 000 000 000 000 000 000 000 000 000
000 000 000 000 000 000 000 000 000 000 000 000 000 000
000 000 000 000 000 000

(b) The number of interconnections one brain can make:

10 000 000 000 000 000 000 000 000 000 000 000 000 000
000 000 000 000 000 000 000 000 000 000 000 000 000 000
000 000 000 000 000 000 000 000 000 000 000 000 000 000
000 000 000 000 000 000 000 000 000 000 000 000 000 000
000 000 000 000 000 000 000 000 000 000 000 000 000 000
000 000 000 000 000 000 000 000 000 000 000 000 000 000
000 000 000 000 000 000 000 000 000 000 000 000 000 000
000 000 000 000 000 000 000 000 000 000 000 000 000 000
000 000 000 000 000 000 000 000 000 000 000 000 000 000
000 000 000 000 000 000 000 000 000 000 000 000 000 000
000 000 000 000 000 000 000 000 000 000 000 000 000 000
000 000 000 000 000 000 000 000 000 000 000 000 000 000
000 000 000 000 000 000 000 000 000 000 000 000 000 000
000 000 000 000 000 000 000 000 000 000 000 000 000 000
000 000 000 000 000 000 000 000 000 000 000 000 000 000
000 000 000 000 000 000 000 000 000 000 000 000 000 000
000 000 000 000 000 000 000 000 000 000 000 000 000 000
000 000 000 000 000 000 000 000 000 000 000 000 000 000
000 000 000 000 000 000 000 000 000 000 000 000 000 000

These figures are worth brooding on for a moment. When you consider that your little finger contains several *billion* atoms, you may get a sense of just how large a figure (a) denotes. And then you can gape a little more knowledgeably at (b), which is the number of interconnections and patters that it is possible for you to make, using the ten billion (10 000 000 000) individual neurons of your brain. No wonder Tony Buzan has observed, 'Your mind is better than you think':[5] it is vastly superior to the most advanced computer yet imagined, let alone built.

I am not the cave-dweller that last sentence might suggest. Computers are electronic, and the speed of the electrical impulse is about 100 miles per second – not quite the speed of light (186,000 miles a second), but still pretty nippy. Now, the majority of human brain functions are chemical rather than electrical, and such impulses travel at a significantly slower rate – about 190 mph (miles per *hour*). Sometimes brain response *is* electrical. When a red-hot cinder flies towards your eye, or when a snake appears in your path, the primitive brain doesn't waste time asking the analytical brain what to do: it just does it, with the speed of instinct. Some much more sophisticated thought operates nearly as fast, especially when based on knowledge you are certain about and have used often. But human thought is mainly a chemical process, and as such is noticeably slower than a computer.

That is the strength of a computer; it is also its limitation. No computer can *think* in a fashion comparable to humans. It can perform feats of seemingly limitless recall; in the time it takes humans to blink, it can warn, solve, illuminate and confirm. But it cannot think creatively; it has no imagination. A computer, whatever winsome and amusing episodes one encounters in futuristic films, has no personality whatever. (Anyone who has seen a poem written by a computer will know what I mean.)

Compared with a computer, the human mind is wonderful. Not only do you possess a most extraordinary machine behind your face; you also have a unique personality fashioned out of countless experiences, influences, feelings, desires, and thoughts. So:

Bring that personality in to work for you.

I do not mean that you should be self-conscious in the obstructive sense, smugly watching yourself 'working hard'; nor do I wish to preclude that marvellous experience we refer to as being 'quite lost' in an activity that grips us. But if you stay sensibly tuned in to your reactions, thoughts and condition as you study, you will work more efficiently – and enjoyably – as a result. Polonious, the interfering tragi-comic character in *Hamlet*, may be a pompous ass, but his remark

To thine own self be true

is a wise policy for any student.

Right: now that you know how clever you are and what phenomenal assets you have at your disposal, you ought to be feeling more confident about getting down to work. But a willing mind is one thing; getting the body to agree is another. How do you get off the sofa, out of bed, or away from television, and to your desk?

The uses and pleasures of bribery

It is now generally accepted that most students respond better to the carrot than the stick, and that principle is well worth extending to your own treatment of yourself. If you approach your desk feeling resentful about working, you've lost the battle before you've begun. Instead, set yourself a prize or small indulgence which you can look forward to at the end of your study period – a drink, a programme or video you know you'll enjoy, anything you fancy. This is good sense as well as being pleasant: it proposes a bargaining process between your various (and conflicting) desires. To cite Isaac Newton again:

For every action there is an equal and opposite reaction.

It's not simply nice to look forward to a rest and a treat: it's as natural – and important – as breathing. In addition, it is morally edifying: successful work deserves some kind of reward, so get ready to spoil yourself in some small but merited fashion! And if you adopt this rhythm as a matter of course, you will enjoy your study much more, as well as making it much easier to start it.

How *not* to bribe yourself

Self-bribery is no good at all unless you are tough about it. It is useful only if the reward is postponed: enjoying the treat first as a way of getting yourself into a working frame of mind is invariably unsuccessful. Putting something off (as we all do) is an insidious process: the longer we leave a task, the more difficult it becomes to get round to it. So on no account allow your bribes to degenerate into excuses.

We are exceptionally good at finding excuses for ourselves: it is an area where everyone is remarkably creative and about which all serious students need to be on their guard. If you really do feel ill or exhausted, then it is undoubtedly stupid to attempt any proper work. You need to rest in order to fight whatever is ailing you; to put an extra burden on mind and body at such a time would be unproductive. But don't kid yourself that you're ill if you're merely sluggish or fed up: that feeling will often evaporate as soon as you start working.

Similarly – and this is just as important if less obvious – do not listen to anyone who suggests that it's not worth working for less than an hour. As I'll be showing shortly, the brain's optimum span of concentration is between 20 and 35 minutes, and it is remarkable how much can be achieved in that time. It also explains why virtually all school timetables over the last 100-plus years have been founded on a lesson length of 30 to 40 minutes. Such a period matches the brain's natural activity.

Finally: don't spend too long *organizing* the bribe! The treat you plan for yourself is a trigger – something to fire you into working. If you daydream in too much detail about what you'll be doing afterwards, you'll lose all momentum and be back where you started – doing nothing.

Using your brain's natural facility

I've offered a few basic insights into the awesome instrument that is the human brain; more will appear subsequently. But one is best mentioned at once, although it is fully developed in Chapter 2 on memory. It concerns the brain's remarkable elasticity, and in particular its ability to do several things at once.

There follows a slightly edited version of a speech delivered by the schoolmaster Bartle Massey in George Eliot's novel *Adam Bede*. The passage first appeared in 1859, but in view of its astonishing prescience in matters now known as study skills, it is worth bearing in mind that it is actually set in the year 1799. The italics are my own.

> You want to learn accounts; that's well and good. But you think all you need to do to learn accounts is to come to me and do sums for an hour or so, two or three times a week; and no sooner do you get your caps on and turn out of doors again, than you sweep the whole thing clean out of your mind. You go whistling about, and take no more care what you're

thinking of than if your heads were gutters for any rubbish to swill through what happened to be in the way; and if you get a good notion in 'em, it's pretty soon washed out again. You think knowledge is to be got cheap; but it isn't to be got with paying sixpence, let me tell you: if you're to know figures, you must turn 'em over in your own heads, and keep your thoughts fixed on 'em. *There's nothing you can't turn into a sum, for there's nothing but what's got a number in it.* A man that had got his heart in learning figures would make sums for himself, and work 'em in his head; when he sat at his shoemaking, he'd count his stitches by fives, and then put a price on his stiches, say have a farthing, and then ask himself how much money he could get in an hour; and then ask himself how much money he'd get in a day at that rate, and then how much money ten workmen would get working three, or twenty, or a hundred years at that rate – and *all the while his needle would be going just as fast as if he left his head empty for the devil to dance in.*

And the long and the short of this is – I'll have nobody in my night-school that doesn't strive to learn what he comes to learn, as hard as if he was striving to get out of a dark hole into broad daylight. I'll send no man away because he's stupid; but *I'll not throw away good knowledge on people who think they can get it by the sixpenn'orth, and carry it away with them as they would an ounce of snuff. So never come to me again, if you can't show that you've been working with your own heads, instead of thinking you can pay mine to work for you.*

Set over two hundred years ago, this stern but witty lecture is almost identical in its ethos and advice to contemporary educational thinking and the latest Quality of Learning initiatives. Massey articulates three principles of central value and importance to all students from the age of about 13 (if not even younger):

1   If you're going to be any good at anything – of which study is merely one example – you've got to *care* about it.
2   No matter how brilliant a teacher may be, s/he can only do *some* of the work – less than half. The major part has to come from you.
3   The brain is multi-active. 'Single-minded' may be a good dutiful metaphor, but in human beings it is hardly ever physically

possible. The brain is staggeringly elastic and versatile, able to do three or four things well at the same time. *Use* that facility: you can, in an oblique way, study productively while also engaged upon something (apparently) quite different.

Summary

You can, then, do a good deal to get yourself started. You can take comfort in the knowledge that all of us find it difficult to begin virtually everything. You can cheer yourself up by remembering that your brain is the greatest instrument yet devised by nature or by man. You can further increase your confidence by regarding your personality as a strength, as a powerful force that will help you to understand and master whatever it is you need to learn. You can make all sorts of agreeable deals with yourself to ensure that each time you work there beckons some delightful indulgence to lighten your way. And you can take immense encouragement – and make significant progress – from the brain's ability to study for you when you're away from your desk and giving your main attention to other things. There are, in short, at least five good ways to bring your horse to water.

Mind you, as the proverb goes on to say, the rest is up to the horse/student! Nobody can make you study, not even you yourself, unless you want to – which is perhaps the biggest and most decisive point in Bartle Massey's lecture. Since, however, there's not much point in organising yourself intelligently unless you *do* want to study, I will take it that it is now time to look in detail at how best to continue. You've reached the starting blocks: how can you most efficiently plan the race?

III GETTING GOOD

> We are wiser than we know.
>
> (Ralph Waldo Emerson)

Preliminary

Your brain is ready, but it needs to be harnessed. What are you going to do with all this power? Where do you want to go? And what's the best way of getting there?

There are probably as many answers to those questions as there are students. But there are all sorts of ways in which that formidable energy can be realised sensibly and profitably, and this chapter addresses a dozen of them. If they have a common theme, it is the one with which I began: *you are in charge*. It is you who usually knows best what suits you, what's happening to you, what you need, and what you enjoy. Indeed, we can elevate that into a governing principle:

> **No matter who you are – what age, background, gender and so on – there is one thing on which you are the world's leading expert: *you*. You may feel you're inexperienced, know virtually nothing about the subject you're about to study, and that your teachers not only know much more but also know best. Most of that may well be true; but *nobody* knows you better than you do, and never forget that.**

I am not encouraging you to be smugly aloof, ignoring all advice: if I were, there wouldn't be much point in my writing this book! But study is an intense activity, even stressful at times, and you won't get far if you adopt practices that are uncomfortable and alien. So my first injunction has to be – discover your own best method of working.

Discover your own best method of working

In schools especially, much rubbish is talked about working methods. Anyone who says to you, 'The way to work is this, and only this' or words to that effect is a fool, and thus a very dangerous guide. There are as many ways of working successfully as they are people who work successfully. If you feel you work best lying on a large cabinet freezer listening to Eminem while drinking Ribena and soda, I might say you were pretty odd, but I wouldn't say you were 'wrong'. After all, nobody but you is doing the work: it follows that nobody but you is fully qualified to tell you how to go about it. So find your best method. Not your teacher's; not your friends'; *yours*. And stick to it for as long as it goes on succeeding.

The principle I've just outlined is fundamental, but it is also necessarily general, even a little vague. The next three 'tips' seek to put flesh on the skeleton.

Be honest with yourself, but not puritanical

Many students mistakenly imagine that working requires a spartan environment and attitude. If such an ambience genuinely suits you, fine. But if it doesn't, there is no value in depriving yourself of pleasant working conditions simply because you feel it is 'right' to do so: indeed, it is positively unwise to adopt such a practice. Part of you will be tense and resistant as a result, which will interfere with your concentration.

Therefore, if you like working to music, then work to music, and tell those who nag you critically about it to do something difficult and dangerous with their hair shirt. If, on the other hand, it *is* a distraction, then stop conning yourself and turn it off. Stick to your guns by all means, but only if they're shooting straight! A brief anecdote illustrates both sides of this argument very well.

My father likes silence when he's working, as it suits his temperament and his formidable powers of concentration. In my early teens, however, I discovered that I need to control my aural environment,[6] and used music to do so, as I still do. Dad and I used to argue heatedly about this when I was at school; now we realise that each way works for each of us. We're both 'right' – and we'd both be 'wrong' if we assumed our way to be the only way.

Analogous considerations apply to any wish for a cup of coffee or a stronger drink: if you want one, have one. Of course, it makes no sense to work in the condition sometimes referred to as 'tired and emotional', but a judicious amount of alcohol may assist you. Alcohol relaxes the nervous system, and thus can increase your sense of well-being and enjoyment. As with all these things, the key criterion is your awareness of yourself: if even the slightest suspicion of booze in your system renders you mentally chaotic, then put that bottle down at once!

Learn to be selfish

That looks contentious, even disagreeable. I'm not seeking to turn you into a raving egoist inhabiting a universe of one, nor am I advocating self-righteous confrontation. But I have long been struck by Oscar Wilde's observation that our crowded and complex society gives rise to 'the sordid necessity of living for others' and his converse suggestion that the only immoral kind of selfishness was not that of doing as you want, but of expecting everyone else to live and act as you do. These ideas are worth exploring, for they are particularly relevant to anyone undertaking a course of study.

All human beings are selfish. Intrinsic to our nature is the desire to do, what we want to do and to avoid what we don't want to do.[7] It is as absurd to call this immoral as it is to call a cobra evil because it is venomous or a shark wicked because it is a voracious, mindless feeder. All these things are fundamental to the creatures' make-up, and it makes about as much sense to feel *guilty* about being selfish as it would be to blame rain for being wet or fire for being hot.

Study is a selfish activity. However well organised you and your family are, they are going to have to make adjustments and sacrifices in order for you to succeed. I am not suggesting you adopt a cavalier and insensitive attitude on the lines of 'like it or lump it': that is Wilde's second point. But you will have less time for certain things that were a part of your life before you embarked on your course, and it's silly to imagine that you can somehow expand your day to fit such things in *somewhere*. As well as the time consumed by your study, other circumstances or conditions are likely to require adjustment. I've already said that it is essential to find your own best method of working and to stick to it, and that means that you can't afford to consider everyone else's needs. If you need silence, find it. If you need space, locate some.

I do realise that all this is extremely hard for (say) a home-based student with two small children, and I wouldn't dream of making light of such problems. Nevertheless, if you simply decide to give in and 'make the best of a bad job', that is *exactly* what you'll do: a bad job. All good workers, like all good practitioners of anything, must finally be selfish. The number of people who have triumphed at an activity through altruism can probably be counted on the fingers of one foot.

Now on to a further look at the way the brain actually operates and how to make that knowledge work for you.

If you get bored with something, *stop*

This is not the negative focus it may seem: boredom is a *positive* message. The human brain is no fool. If it gets fed up, there's usually a good reason, and if it gets fed up during study, it's telling you that it needs a change. Nobody performs well when bored – a phenomenon that unites cooks, footballers, interior decorators,

musicians and gigolos. So if you suddenly feel bored, two possibilities suggest themselves: either it's the work's fault, or yours. If
the latter applies, then *do* something about it – stop daydreaming,
start concentrating properly, so forth. If it's the work's fault, then
shelve it, and find something else to do until you can return
refreshed to the original task.

This is important advice: one of the secrets of successful study
is knowing what *not* to do and when not to do it. Any subject, no
matter how interesting and pleasurable in overall terms, will have
some dull parts. It is not dangerously exciting, for example, to
learn those French verbs which take *être* in the perfect tense rather
than *avoir*, but they have to be learnt if your aim is proper mastery
of the language as both reader and writer. Similarly, very few
pianists faint with delight while playing scales, but without such
creative discipline, they will be lost, incapable of interpreting any
composer with beauty and authority, because they can't actually
play the notes.

Now for a detailed survey of arguably the most important skill
an independent student can possess – effective time management.

Effective time management I: An overall strategy

Since I'm talking here about private study, it may seem perverse
to refer at once to something as obviously public as the school
timetable. But that mundane structure provides several valuable
clues as to how you might best organise your time away from the
classroom and the lecture hall. For while the *curriculum* in our
schools has changed out of all recognition in the last hundred years,
the *timetable* which delivers it remains much the same. Lessons aver-
aged 35 to 40 minutes in 1900, and they still do as the twenty-first
century gets fully under way. Why might that be so?

In the last two decades a lot of research has been done on the
brain's ability to retain things. Admirable though these neurolog-
ical discoveries have been, one or two have merely confirmed what
our supposedly more ignorant predecessors already knew from
experience rather than telling us anything truly new. Working
educationalists have known for ages about 'optimum concentration spans' and the brain's 'cognitive capacity', even if they used
different, simpler terms. The school timetable proves it, organised
as it is on the empirical and timeless observation that:

The brain's optimum concentration span is 20 to 35 minutes.

That is not, I admit, a strictly scientific truth; nor is it a constant, as we shall be seeing shortly. But it is at the very least an immensely useful rule of thumb that every student should memorise, especially when it comes to organising an evening's work.

Let us assume you plan to work for about two hours. Let us further assume that you are in good shape for the task – fed and refreshed, alert and reasonably enthusiastic about what you're about to tackle. And let us finally assume that as a good, dutiful and industrious student, you then work for two hours at a stretch, with no breaks, changes of task or focus. If you consult Figure 1.1, you will see in graph form a profile of your likely progress and intake during that time. The main features of that diagram are obvious enough. Retention is high for about 30 minutes, declines steadily thereafter, and rises significantly towards the end. (Incidentally, in the case of a written task rather than an absorptive one, 'Efficiency' can be substituted for 'Retention'.)

If we translate that into your likely experience and behaviour during that imagined two-hour stretch, the diagram stands up very well. Fresh and keyed up, you will find that your energy will last for quite a while; after 30 to 40 minutes, however, you will probably start to feel restless and a little tired. Dutifully ignoring such symptoms, you increase your effort and plough on; perhaps you notice – with some dismay – that those feelings of restlessness and fatigue are increasing. Nevertheless, towards the end of the second

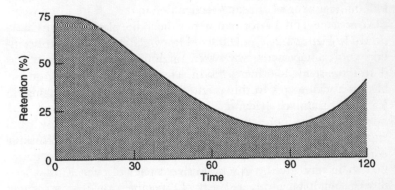

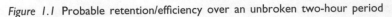

Figure 1.1 Probable retention/efficiency over an unbroken two-hour period

hour you realise that you'll soon be entitled to take a good rest and, somewhat paradoxically, this fires your brain with new energy and focus. Indeed, the extra 'juice' this supplies may well take you slightly beyond the two-hour mark, leaving you feeling rather pleased with yourself.

But you shouldn't be all that pleased; in fact, if you're at all intelligent and eager to do well, on reflection you'll feel aggrieved and frankly fed up. For about 50 per cent of your working period – the second and third half hours – you've been operating at a retention/efficiency rate never higher than 40 per cent and sometimes below 25 per cent. That may not be a complete waste, but it's not very satisfactory. It is even less satisfactory when you realise that a good deal of that particular hour's work will have to be done again.

Educational research – on this occasion in conjunction with and mirroring common sense – does offer some nice surprises as well. The interesting, and most encouraging, thing about Figure 1.1 is that the curve it describes tends to remain roughly the same whatever the span of the horizontal axis. That is actually a 'worst possible' scenario: from experience I would argue that if you divide your work time into shorter, more 'natural' chunks, there is every chance that the retention curve will describe a more heartening rate of retention. With those things in mind, let us redesign your two hours.

Instead of that dutiful, monolithic 120-minute slog, why not divide the time into four sections of 25 to 30 minutes, in keeping with those timetable rhythms? Furthermore, why not take a five-minute break at the end of each one? There are very good practical reasons for doing that, which I'll go into shortly, but for now just look on it as a minor indulgence!

Your time and performance can now be plotted in the way shown in Figure 1.2. You will see, I hope, that the aggregate retention you manage with this system is notably higher than it was during the single two-hour session. Moreover, there are a number of other advantages to this method which are implicit in Figure 1.2 rather than self-evident:

1   By dividing your time, you increase your sense of control over the material which . . .
2   . . . in turn gives your confidence a valuable boost.
3   During that five-minute break after each session, your mind will be 'ticking over' with a clear idea of what it's done and what

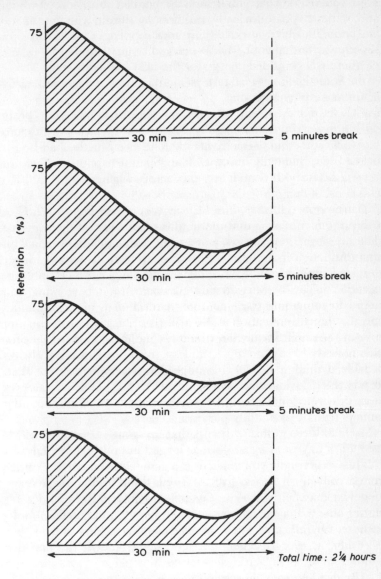

Figure 1.2 How much the brain can retain after short breaks

it's learnt. As you make your cup of coffee, take a stroll round the room, put on a new record or whatever, your mind will automatically review and sift its recent activity without any conscious effort on your part. When you restart, sensibly refreshed, there will be added energy for the next half-hour stint.

Sometimes that restart is characterised by an especially pleasing phenomenon . . .

4   . . . as noted, during your five-minute 'turn-off', your brain keeps working automatically. As a result of such unconscious work, something which was troubling you at the half-hour's end may suddenly become clear. Such a happy step forward will boost both confidence and energy further.

There are two further things to say concerning Figure 1.2. One is that it underlines a point made towards the end of the previous chapter – that it is always worthwhile to work for just half an hour. Although it is doubtless more convenient to have a longer chunk of time, it is not always available, and it is certainly not essential. It can be very irritating to have to stop working and attend to something else, but such a reaction is an encouraging one, for your annoyance at breaking off suggests that you are enjoying yourself. Ideally we would all like to be able to work for as long as we liked – no more, no less; given that this is not always possible, I think it is better to stop while you're enjoying it than to labour on joylessly to 'the bitter end'. One of show business's more celebrated mottoes is 'Always leave them wanting more': the same is true of your study periods.

My final focus in this section is that up-swing of energy towards the end of any working session, as logged in both Figures 1.1 and 1.2. Just to persuade you that this is a genuine phenomenon rather than a convenient fiction I've invented, think back to an average school lesson when you were, say, 13. As covered above, it doesn't matter how old or young you are now: that lesson lasted 35 to 40 minutes. Or rather, it was scheduled for that period of time, but in reality, as every teacher and schoolchild knows, the first five minutes were spent getting everyone into place – including the teacher! – and generally settling down.

Then work commenced. We will cheerfully assume that work continued at a fairly even pace for most of the remaining time. It is likely, though, that the class (and possibly the teacher too) started to feel a little jaded at the 25-minute mark, only to finish strongly as the prospect of the bell loomed nearer. Often lessons over-run because of this final up-swing of energy; moreover, children who ten minutes before were feeling the strain, or who had simply 'turned off', suddenly find all sorts of things to say and ask about as the teacher prepares to leave the room.

The pattern I've just described is virtually identical to the rhythm of the half-hour study period described earlier. The clue to why this up-swing happens so often – and so productively – is to be found in a phrase I've just used, *to finish strongly*. That has an athletic resonance that is wholly appropriate, as I will now demonstrate with an analogy.

This book is published in 2004 – an Olympic year. In the men's 10,000 metres final (which comprises 25, 400-metre laps), the athletes will cover the first 24 laps at around 67 seconds per lap; maybe those down the field will be a little slower, but this is the final, and there are unlikely to be many passengers. They will then cover the last lap in around 50–52 seconds – a staggering achievement after such a punishing prelude, the more so when one remembers that the world record for the 400 metres (i.e. one lap when fresh) is less than ten seconds fewer, at 42.6 seconds. How is this possible?

Well, first, they're very fit, of course. Second, for the winner and medal-chasers at least, fame and money beckon, and of course the heady prospect of winning, which carries its own self-contained triumph, can therefore fire one up to feats that might not normally be possible. But if you watch the event closely, you'll see that the runners who are not in medal contention still manage a startling burst of speed on that last lap. You might argue that they do so out of pride, and I wouldn't disagree. But I think the key reason – for all the athletes – is this:

The sooner they breast the tape, the sooner they can rest.

Even the fittest athlete will suffer a good deal during the race – breaking the 'pain barrier' and so on – and for that reason alone, ignoring more glamorous considerations, he will want the whole thing to be over as soon as possible, so that he can treat himself to a long, cooling drink and a thorough rest.

Study is rather less dramatic than an Olympic Final, but the parallel is nonetheless close:

Whatever the activity, the prospect of stopping soon is almost always attractive, leading invariably to an increase in energy and concentration.

That enshrines the final reason for breaking your work up into smaller chunks: you will benefit each time from that closing up-swing, heightening your retention and your sense of control and progress.

Effective time management II: Devising a realistic timetable

Dividing your *time* into manageable chunks is only part of it; you need to plan out the actual *tasks* as well. You can overdo this: a plan that rigidly accounts for every quarter of an hour is unsatisfactory, for it makes no allowance for discoveries made along the way or for interesting and productive detours. But you should certainly construct a rough overall task schedule.

The previous section spoke of the enabling characteristics of the school timetable; on the other hand, that remorseless programme is one of the things that nearly all sixth-formers and undergraduates are delighted to leave behind. And, of course, it *is* wonderful to say goodbye to a day of eight separate lessons and to evenings of three designated homeworks. But this agreeable departure brings with it new dangers. Sixth-formers are expected to organise their own work, and undergraduates even more so. One (nice) consequence is that you can have more 'free' time than before; unless you're careful, though, this time will become 'free' in the sense of empty. Those apparently fallow slots in the timetable are part of your working week, and if you don't use them, you will soon fall badly behind – and in addition fail to benefit fully from the lessons you do receive. So don't despise the school timetable as something that is now beneath you. Instead, lock on to its basic principles, for they embody the soundest psychological truths.

I have already indicated that for most students for most of the time, a span of 30 to 40 minutes tends to be the most congenial and efficient. It makes a lot of sense, therefore, to go on using the principle of chopping up the day in the fashion you've now formally moved beyond. Work out what you've got to do over the next week, and divide it into chunks you can cope with. It's a good idea to write the tasks down and tick them off as you complete them, thus giving you an immediate record of achievement.

It is also important not to try to do too much, especially at first. I don't want to encourage laziness, but do make sure that the targets you set yourself are realistic. To take an absurd case: it would be insane to read Dickens's *Our Mutual Friend* (some 900 pages) in two hours. Less comic but no less impossible would be an attempt to master in full 30 pages of a closely argued textbook in the same time. You can certainly expect to acquire a healthy sense of the content, its main outline and arguments; but it will be some time before all the material is there 'on tap' in your established, long-term memory. Total understanding is never immediate.

Like a lot of things, timetables are good servants but bad masters; the same is true for advice on work rhythms, such as the concentration-span information I've been peddling. Yes, a weekly study timetable will certainly help you, as will the knowledge that you're likely to work best for a period of about half an hour. But those precepts should never govern you regardless. There will be times when all such pre-planning goes out of the window – and they will tend to define two extremes:

(1) The 'buzz factor'   (2) The 'boredom factor'

The 'buzz factor' and the 'boredom factor'

The buzz factor is the nicest thing that can happen to a student. It occurs when you are so absorbed in your work that you lose all sense of time and all memory of other tasks to be done. In a way, that can cause problems – those other tasks will have to be postponed, and your timetable rescheduled. But if and when this happens, for goodness' sake go with it: the feeling of euphoria that carries you into an hour or an hour-and-a-half's non-stop work is both delightful in itself and hugely productive. It may not happen too often, and when it does it should be totally indulged. As a student of mine said recently after annotating Milton for over two hours without a break:

> **The yardstick is when work doesn't feel like work, but just something you really want to do.**

At the opposite end of the spectrum, the *boredom factor* is just as crucial, albeit much less pleasant. If something that you've got to study really is boring you – and it will happen some time, no matter who you are – then accept the fact. The first thing to do, as noted already, is to stop; the second, trickier thing is to plan out a special timetable and work rhythm for the next time it's likely to occur. You should have a pretty good idea which tasks please you and which don't; when organising the latter, it will prove helpful to do two things:

1 If expecting tedium, reduce your normal timespan.

Set yourself a ceiling of 15 minutes. You may need two or three such periods, but that is much better than trying to do it all in one go in a mood of resentful drudgery.

2 If you can stand it, start any work session with the least attractive task on your list.

This is easier said than done, though I know it's a very sensible principle, I do not by any means always obey it myself. But do not follow my erratic example: try it, for it offers two pleasing benefits. First, it is good to get such things out of the way; second, it is then very nice to move on to something you enjoy more, and which in these particular circumstances you will probably do very well.

You will find further information and advice on devising your own timetable in Chapter 3. For now I close by quoting that fine actor Robert Duvall in *The Killer Elite*. The movie itself was on the dire side, but I shall never forget this one line, which might profitably adorn the desk of any and all students:

I believe in the 6-P Principle: Proper Planning Prevents Piss-Poor Performance.

Think of your brain as the strongest muscle you possess

This may be physiologically inaccurate, but it is an excellent metaphor. There are many parallels between the ways in which body and brain work. And there is no doubt that the mind and the muscles are alike in one central respect: they both work better when they're used regularly.

When you begin a course, your mind will tire quickly; this is especially true if, like many adult students, it is a considerable time since you last did any 'academic' work. There is no need to be ashamed about this: on the contrary, recognise that the symptom is normal and healthy. Just as there are real medical dangers in pushing an unfit body too far, it is unwise to flog a tired and gasping brain. It's not dangerous in the same way, of course; but it's doubly useless, in that such a brain will achieve very little, and that will depress you and create feelings of inadequacy (which, given the circumstances, are unjustified).

However, the more you work, the more active your mind will be, just as your body, as it gets fitter, will be able to take more and more pushing. As I've pointed out, it's awe-inspiring how much the brain can do, and so, while sticking to my earlier advice to take rests when you require them, I can also promise you that a fit brain has a stamina and invention that you need never underestimate.

Keep physically alert as well as mentally aware

High on my list of people I'd like to reserve a cabin for on the SS Titanic are those posturing goons who talk of being 'in tune with your body', and extol the virtues of macrobiotic tomatoes and organically grown turnips. But a degree of intelligent physical awareness is important for any student. Thomas Aquinas wrote:

Trust the authority of your senses.

It is excellent advice. We all have times when we feel stupid, sluggish or out of sorts. Equally, we can all be suddenly overcome with fatigue when only ten minutes ago we were buzzing with energy. Trust these moments. Learn to recognize when to give yourself a much-needed kick and also when to take necessary rest. There is no profit in either watching the day go by from the depths of an armchair, or in flogging yourself into some form of collapse; and your body will be aware of these states before your mind is.

Exercise is important too. The Romans coined a great truth when they defined health as *Mens sane in corpore sano* (a healthy mind in a fit body). If your muscles get slack and unused, eventually your mind will start to copy them. Nothing frantic or even athletic is required, whatever the notorious English Public School

Code may say. But some kind of regular physical activity is an invaluable complement to intensive mental work. If you like paying squash, tennis, and so forth, well and good – provided it is safe for you to do so.[8] But if your ambitions are somewhat gentler, there are many small ways in which you can exercise. Walk to the corner shop rather than drive; run up the stairs two at a time instead of hobbling laboriously; clench and relax your muscles when stationary; you can even try sit-ups, toe-touching, and press-ups (Appendix IV lists some useful relaxation and everyday fitness exercises).

Similarly, you can keep your mind in trim during non-study times with exercises that are also fun and relaxing. Crosswords are first-class in this respect, as are all forms of puzzle and 'brain-teaser'. Reading a newspaper, listening to quiz shows, playing verbal games and many other apparently light-hearted activities are equally useful as mental 'work-outs'.

Rest and recuperation

All work and no play doesn't just make Jack a dull boy: it will make him a lousy student, too. The idea that a student needs to be high-powered and solemnly committed *all* the time is mistaken: it is neither necessary nor desirable. Nobody can be switched-on and continuously alert for 16 hours a day; so accept this as a comforting fact, and build rest and relaxation into your programme.

We all have favourite ways of 'turning off'; indulge yours – though if you find yourself doing so for five hours a day, you're overdoing it! But everyone – especially those who spend a fair time each day concentrating fiercely on academic work – has the right and the need to be an idle moron for a small part of the day. It is, of course, up to you *what* you do. A delicious, lazy soak in a bath may be just right; or a spot of gardening; or a gentle, inconsequential stroll. Whatever it is, you'll know what best relaxes you and allows your brain to refresh itself for the next stint. You should both trust this knowledge and act on it

One curious (but delightful) bonus of such a practice can be the sudden arrival of insights or solutions when you least expect them. The single most illuminating point in my own Ph.D. thesis came to me off-duty, half-asleep in the bath! And many of my friends and students have confirmed how often this kind of out-of-the-blue visitation can happen. You can get inspiration on top of a bus, in a supermarket queue, cleaning your shoes, so forth and so on. The reason for this is clear: if you allow your brain proper rest and freedom, it will, even in its apparently idle moments, be sifting and considering the problems, and working for you unconsciously. There is, of course, a time to worry at a problem *deliberately*; but if you let the brain's automatic rhythms take over for a while, they may save you a lot of trouble, as well as allowing you to restore your energy.

Never be afraid to ask

I am constantly surprised and touched by how anxious many of my students (both secondary and adult) seem to be about 'bothering' me with a question, or request for advice. They don't want to be a nuisance; they don't want to take up my 'valuable' time.

I'm sure I speak for every even half-way decent teacher when I say that being 'bothered' in this way is what we're paid for, and that it is also nearly always a pleasure. Naturally, a minimal amount of tact *is* necessary. I wasn't all that polite, for instance, to a student who, following repeated absence at my classes, phoned me at 6.50 a.m. (not my favourite hour) to say that she was worried about her exams the next day, and could I help! Most of the time, however, teachers are only too glad to be of help to a keen student. Indeed, one of the qualities a successful student most needs is a willingness and ability to ask good questions: the resulting discussion stimulates teacher and student alike. So if you need help, ask for it. Teachers can do their job only if they know what you know, and don't know: if you pretend or 'play possum', he will proceed under false assumptions.

The reason why many students *don't* ask is that they're afraid of looking stupid – if not to the teacher, then to their fellow students. We've all known this feeling, and it is entirely understandable. All I can say is that, in over thirty years as a teacher of both children and adults, *I've hardly ever been asked a really stupid question*. I've been asked questions I've only just answered; I've been asked questions that are irrelevant to the matter in hand; and I've been asked to spell out the obvious for nervy and anxious students. But at no time have I ever felt contempt for anyone brave enough to enquire about something they don't know or don't yet grasp; and very often the questions are so good that they open up a line of thought that I haven't previously considered. So don't be afraid to ask: it is only the student who *doesn't* ask when he needs to who is truly stupid.[9]

Keep reviewing your work

I discuss this fully in Chapter 3, but a few quick guidelines are in order now. If you're reading, make sure you've understood it. Just scanning the words is no good: you must be aware of the structure of the material – i.e. where it starts from, where it's going, how it gets there. Academic reading is intensive; it will require two or three perusals before it is firmly fixed in the mind. Use this fact, and don't imagine you're 'slow' just because you don't pick something up first time. Re-reading will boost your confidence: you'll be able to feel yourself learning and growing. If you're writing, regularly re-read what you've already done. That will keep your target in view, and also prevent flabby repetition. Also, re-read at the end as if you were an outsider – anyone but the writer. Read critically, looking for flaws and errors. I have no wish to turn you into either a masochist or a pedant, but the more mistakes or shortcomings you can spot before the person who marks it, the better will be your work. You will also get a confidence boost when you see how good most of it is!

You should always save ten minutes at the end of a period of study to mull over the work. This can be done as part of the 'winding down' process. The brain, glad to be resting, will be quite happy to run over the main points you've covered; and this will make your return to the work snappier and more fun.

Lastly, you should regularly look over your past work as the course gathers momentum. It doesn't take long: ten minutes a day is ample. There is a double benefit here, too: you'll recognise at once how much you've learned, and how far you're progressing. And when you come to the end of the course, your past work will be familiar to you, so that you can revise, rather than having to do the work over again from scratch.

Remind yourself what your ultimate achievement will be

No matter how much you enjoy studying or how well you succeed, there are bound to be times when you get depressed or just fed up with it all. If such feelings occur *often*, it may be time to ask yourself if you're doing the right course; but the occasional doubt and low moment are inevitable. So don't let these get you down: instead, just look forward to the time when it's over, and when you've got that certificate in your hand.

Sometimes, too, you'll find you get angry – at a low mark, or at someone's implied judgement that you're not as good as you need to be. Creative rage is a first-class study fuel, so use it. Whether your motive is to 'show them', or to prove something to yourself, or (most likely) a mixture of the two, you'll find that some form of gutsy target-concentration is an enormous help. There's nothing like the prospect of a finishing tape to spur you on to greater effort, if only because you can have a well-earned, triumphant rest. And remember also that any worthwhile thing that any human has ever achieved took time, determination, and the fierce belief that it was worth it. It is, too; so keep that in mind.

Summary

A good deal of this chapter may strike you as being no more than applied common sense, and I would agree with you. The trouble is that more often than is comfortable or even comprehensible, common sense – supposedly universal, the only virtue that every-one possesses – is highly uncommon amongst students, from the mediocre to the very brightest. It ought to be obvious, for example, that you know best how you work, or that it's silly to go on working at something that has become jaw-wrenchingly boring. The fact remains that thousands of students pay no attention to these elementary truths, and go on working for too long in a fashion that someone else wants them to or that they've been told to think is 'right'.

With those last two sentences particularly in mind, let me end by saying that I only want you to follow this chapter's advice if it's useful to you. If you always work well for three hours non-stop, then please accept my awed congratulations and ignore my remarks about 'manageable chunks of time'. Remember, the two prime requirements for successful study are a sense of enjoyment and an honest sense of yourself. Nobody – least of all me – should bully or pressure you out of either; all I've attempted to do is tell you about some phenomena I've noticed both as a student and as a teacher, and thereby assist you in working more naturally. We now move on to the student's most important – and most mysterious – piece of equipment: the memory.

Chapter 2

Memory

> O memory! Thou fond deceiver!
>
> (Oliver Goldsmith)

Preliminary

Goldsmith has a point: the memory can deceive, and often does. But we also deceive *ourselves* about our memory. How often have you heard, or indeed said, something like this?

You are lucky, having a good memory.

or

It's not fair: I can't remember half of what I need to.

Luck has nothing to do with it. If you memory is poor, then it's not 'unfair': it's your fault. Happily, and more to the point, you can do something about it.

Of all the myths that surround memory, the most damaging is that it is a *gift*. That is quite untrue. Memory is a *skill* – and like any skill its performance depends on application, on practice, and on regular training. Everyone has potentially a good memory; everyone can train it and thereby increase their efficiency.

Another fallacy is that there is a close connection between memory and intelligence. This notion has been around for a long time, but it has doubtless been fuelled of late by otherwise harmless and enjoyable programmes like *Mastermind* or *Brain of Britain*, whose titles suggest a correlation between great intellectual prowess and the ability to remember masses of unrelated data. In fact, all research conducted so far indicates that memory and intelligence are separate facilities, and it doesn't take more than a moment's thought to realise why. The difference can be clearly expressed by way of two definitions:

Memory: The ability to remember what you know.

Intelligence: The ability to work out what to do when you don't know what to do.

In short, memory is to do with recalling and using things you are *certain* of, while intelligence reveals itself most acutely when addressed to things you are *uncertain* of or ignorant about.

Since your memory is part of you, some personal traits affect it. Your tastes and temperament will determine the kinds of thing you are likely to remember or forget: for example, some people find it easy to remember numbers but very difficult to learn a language, while for others the reverse is true. Such idiosyncracies are hardly negligible matters; however, the key properties required for memory improvement lie within every student's compass, regardless of their personality or strengths:

honesty   care

They go together. I've stressed from the start that successful study hinges on being honest with yourself, and in this case that means you have to decide how much you *care* about learning something that may not come naturally to you. Nobody else can do this for you, but if you can care enough, progress will quickly ensue.

Short-term memory (STM) and long-term memory (LTM)

Everyone's memory is divided in this way. STM is a sort of note-pad which handles all the stuff we need to remember for immediate, imminent, or temporary use; LTM stores all the information we truly *know*. To put it in everyday terms: the STM is like a handbag or briefcase, while the LTM is more like a deep freezer, filled with 'no need to thaw' foods.

Few sane people make a habit of inspecting handbags or brief-cases, but picture one for a moment. In all likelihood, the bag/case you have in mind is pretty full. Most of its contents are useful and needed – but some of them are useless, or rather have ceased to be useful. It's a rare handbag that does not contain a few screwed-up tissues or dead bus tickets; equally, you'd be pushed to find a briefcase that did not house the odd defunct letter or memo.

The STM is a remarkably similar mixture. Most of its load is use-ful and pertinent; yet bits of irrelevant junk often seem to be floating around as well. When, say, you remember that you have to make a phone call at eleven o'clock, it's strange how that urgent reminder can immediately be followed by the fleeting recall of what you had for dinner last night, or how long it is since you washed your hair!

The reason for this is that the STM is neither organised nor fully in charge of its load. There is nothing surprising or amiss about that. Life is too short to organise *everything*, and most people lead the kind of busy lives that render it essential for them to carry in their heads an unrelated assortment of things. For day-to-day matters this is as it should be. I suppose one could devise a system whereby one could remember without writing anything down every single item required on a shopping trip, but why bother? That specific list is a one-off, so it's better to save time, jettison the search for a system, and just use paper and pencil.

However, much of what we do describes a regular, long-term pattern, using information which does not change daily. Study is a particularly strong example – which is where the 'deep freezer' idea comes in.

An efficient deep freezer can store food for a long time. You can ignore its contents for months on end if you choose to, and then raid it for something which can be microwaved at once. The LTM operates in similar fashion. When you've *really* learnt some-thing, it takes up a permanent residence in the mind and is instantly available when you require it, even if you haven't needed or used the information for years. The LTM is, moreover, wonder-fully supple and elastic. It does not have to chuck something out in order to make room for new information: it simply stretches itself a little more. There is also a lot of evidence to suggest that the more you store in your LTM, the better it will work – just as a deep freezer works more efficiently if kept full.

It is, I hope, obvious that successful study depends on the secure transfer of material from STM to LTM. It makes complete sense to compile a list for each trek to the supermarket, but it makes no sense at all to have to look up, say, the date of the Norman Conquest every time you need to mention it. As your course progresses, you will be adding regularly to your store of knowledge and to your growing mastery of the material. Indeed, it is usually essential that you do so, in that most courses are linear: that is, you usually need to master point A before you can tackle point B, or understand concept C before you can progress to concept D. Since you are working under pressure and both teaching time and study time are restricted, efficient LTM storage is a major priority. How best to do it?

As a way of answering that, get a piece of paper and try the little quiz that follows.

1   Write down your name.
2   Write down your phone number.
3   Write down your post code.
4   Write down your mother's maiden name.
5   Write down your car registration number.
6   Write down the number of your credit card(s).

I would imagine that anyone reading this book had no trouble with the first three! I would also guess that, even if you managed numbers 4 and 5 pretty quickly, they came to mind less automatically. And if you got number 6 without needing to look it/ them up, well done, but I suspect you are in a minority.

However well you did, the exercise is highly revealing. The ones you got right came quickly, probably at once. Those that didn't come quickly probably didn't come at all – unless you looked them up. It is a characteristic of the memory that it works very fast or not at all. If you have to 'rack your brains' for something, the chances are heavily against your finding it at the time. But the even more important point is that whichever ones you got right, you did so because you have been in constant contact with the information – in which respect questions 5 and 6 are perhaps the most revealing. If you have had to quote your car registration or credit card numbers more than two or three times, the chances are high that they've stuck in your memory; if not, they almost certainly will not have done so. For example: I can answer question 5 instantly, because I've had to quote it all too often – to insurance companies, motoring organisations and so on.[1] But I would have no chance with 6. That's partly because they consist of sixteen separate digits, yes, but it's also because I never use them over the phone and I've never been asked to quote them in any shop.

As with that little quiz, so with study: the more you keep in touch with information, the more likely you are to retain it. And that does not only apply to the learning of fresh material: it is just as important to revisit work regularly once it has been 'done'. First-time learning – which includes the writing of most essays – requires subsequent confirmation, feedback and back-up. Otherwise, no matter how secure the learning seems to be, or no matter how highly praised the essay, you will find that an alarming amount of its information is gone within a week. It takes very little time to re-read your past written work, and not much more to mull over again reading you've recently completed; it is time unimprovably spent, for its value to you will be both rapid and enormous.

I extend this advice in the next chapter, 'Review'. For those interested in a more detailed account of the short-term and long-term memory, Peter Russell's *The Brain Book* is notably good, being both comprehensive and very readable: Chapters 6, 7 and 10 are especially useful. Another excellent study, if you can get hold of it, is Ian M.L. Hunter's *Memory*, first published in 1957 and revised in 1964. In it he makes the important observation that the activity of memorising is dominated by two broad issues – the role of meaning and the role of repetition – and he goes on to quote from the pioneering psychologist William James in a most illuminating way (the italics are mine).

> Most men have a good memory for facts connected with their own pursuits. The college athlete who remains a dunce at his books will astonish you by his knowledge of men's 'records' in various feats and games, and will be a walking dictionary of sporting statistics. The reason is that he is constantly going over these things in his mind, and comparing and making series of them. *They form for him not so many odd facts, but a concept-system – so they stick.* So the merchant remembers prices, the politician other politicians' speeches and votes (in a fashion) which amazes outsiders, but which the amount of thinking they bestow on these subjects easily explains.[2]

There are close parallels here to the passage from *Adam Bede* discussed earlier (pages 18–20). If anything that truly interests you automatically becomes, in James's term, 'a concept-system', then as Bartle Massey observed, the next step is to *find* a way of making what you need to remember truly interesting, or at any rate an enjoyable and stimulating game. That leads me to the next section, which looks at methods and systems of making things newly fun and memorably connected; there could be few better or more encouraging ways of introducing that topic than quoting another remark by William James:

In a system, every fact is connected with every other by some thought-relation. The consequence is that every fact is retained by the combined suggestive power of all the other facts in the system, and forgetfulness is well-nigh impossible.[3]

Memory and do-it-yourself visual aids

As we've seen, the brain is an awesomely versatile instrument, and there is never a time when it is not doing several things at once. What you are doing now proves that.

As you read these words, you are concentrating fiercely, apparently absorbed in a *single activity*. Yet your brain is doing a number of other things too. Deep in your book, you are aware only of the text itself; yet the motor part of the brain is commanding your physical grasp of the book, the movements of your hand as you turn the pages, and probably several unconscious mannerisms. Various other stimuli and data are coming in as you read. The brain may be getting messages from all over your body – to the effect that you're hungry, want a drink, are shortly going to suffer cramp if you continue to sit on your leg, and so forth. No wonder concentrating seems so hard!

Such a variety of simultaneous brain activity could be most distracting. However, since there's no way of stopping your brain doing all these things, why not get the so-called distractions to work for you? All of us find, for instance, that as we read, a series of images flits across our mind. These may be connected to the material being read, or they may seem irrelevant. It doesn't matter: all are potentially valuable as spontaneous enforcers. I can illustrate the truth of this with a little story from my own schooldays.

I was always a poor scientist anyway, but my biggest hassle was chemical symbols: I found it almost impossible to remember even the basic ones, let alone anything sophisticated. One evening (I was about 12) I was trying to learn 20 of them for a test next day, and having a miserably unsuccessful time of it. Inevitably my mind started wandering as I stared at the page with sullen dutifulness – and suddenly the picture of a very fat woman stuck in a revolving door flashed into my head. Callow, sexist and fattist as I was then, I laughed inanely; but it so happened that as I did so I was looking at the legend

Potassium: K

The test duly arrived next morning, and I did not do well. But I did get 'What does K represent?' right: my fat lady came up trumps, flashing back into my head as soon as I heard the question and re-focusing my memory on that part of the textbook. Okay, I got a censorious look from the teacher when I giggled as I wrote the answer down, but that was a small price to pay!

That puerile reminiscence enshrines an important principle. If something makes you laugh while studying, don't use your mirth as an excuse to break off the learning process: use it by fixing the comic image consciously alongside whatever you were reading when it occurred.

To take another, more homely and altogether unfunny example: I was unable for a long time to remember, when changing a plug, which one of the blue or brown wires was 'live', and I had to look it up or ask someone every time. One day it occurred to me that brown was the colour my hand would end up if I grasped a live wire; I've never again had to think twice about which is which. A somewhat grisly visual aid, maybe, but one where the image was directly relevant to what I was trying to learn. The principle is the same whatever the source of the image: provided you can find a way to link it to the material, it will strengthen and clarify your memory.

The beauty – and the fun – of this technique is that you do it yourself. Auto-suggestion is always powerful, because we are naturally very interested in ourselves; any process which allows us to indulge ourselves while assisting us to do something worthwhile can't be bad! And any kind of picture or image will do, provided it is effective. The most likely to work, however, are those that are one or more of the following:

funny   obscene   dramatic   colourful

These four are strong because they reflect powerful and intrinsic reponses – a principle sometimes called the 'Von Restorff effect', after the distinguished pyschologist's discoveries about the workings of the memory. You do not have to work at or force your images. Indeed, you *shouldn't* do so: their strength lies precisely in their spontaneity, their sudden appearance 'out of nowhere', beyond your conscious control.

The importance of 'play'

You may feel that these techniques are rather frivolous, that 'games' are out of keeping with the serious business of study. I would suggest that such games are utterly natural as well as useful.

Like most animals, mankind is *ludic* by nature: the activity of play is basic to us, especially when it involves a degree of invention or creativity. Over the last generation or so, we have come to realise that a child's love of play is itself a form of learning and that, wisely harnessed, it can accelerate other forms of learning. In this respect, as in many others, we have much to learn from our own childhood; Wordsworth put it very well when observing

The child is father to the man

Patterns of activity adopted when at our most inquisitive and natural should be revered, not dismissed. Besides, games are *fun*, and the more fun you can derive from study, the better you will perform. It's worth repeating that very few people have become masters of their craft by finding it joyless and laborious.

Contemplative learning and intensive learning

No true learning is ever leisurely, because to learn anything requires you to focus and concentrate on it. (This is as true of practical and physical skills as it is of intellectual ones.) But there is an obvious difference in kind between the learning which:

1   leads you to acquire a sound and sensitive understanding of a Shakespeare play;

and

2   characterises the mastering of a list of German verbs.

The first type I have called contemplative learning. By that I mean that your knowledge results from your considered response as a total personality. It does not come from the mere absorption by your brain of the salient facts. This always has to be done, naturally: it's not much use having a sensitive response to Hamlet if you're also under the impression that he lives in Belgium and has a mother named Anastasia. On the other hand, you're never going to get very far as a student of literature (English or foreign) if all you do is memorise the text's external facts and as much of the text, word for word, as you can manage. No: contemplative learning depends on mature understanding and personal response. As it happens, this is hardly less true for physics and biology as it is for something apparently 'subjective' like literature. In this area, therefore, memory would seem to be less important than personality and experience.

Think about that for a moment, however. 'Personality and experience': what is that if it isn't memory? One of the saddest things about amnesiacs is that the loss of their memory causes their personality to disintegrate. Without recourse to stored personal memories, they are as vulnerable and ignorant as small children. They have no guidelines as to how they want to, or should, behave. They become as totally dependent on others as small children are, and even more helplessly 'paralysed' than a wheelchair victim.

So, in fact, memory is a vital part of contemplative learning since in some sense you are your memory. So you should bring as much of yourself to bear on your studies as you can. You will have lived at least 16 years: you have experienced literally millions of things. So use them. I do not mean you should reject as unreal everything you encounter in your studies that has not (yet) happened to you: that would be silly. Neither should you be excessively humble. If something jars on you as wrong or unconvincing (or just inadequate), then explore the reaction. You'll probably find that your dissatisfaction is rooted in something you remember observing, or feeling, or sensing. Such a memory or experience will not, of course, automatically mean that you're 'right'; but it will increase the quality of your thinking and arguing, because you're operating as a whole intelligence rather than as a disembodied brain.

Intensive learning is narrower and fiercer. The central point about it is that it depends on frequency and repetition. The first words you ever spoke were, almost certainly, words you'd heard on hundreds of occasions beforehand. A little later, when you first attended school, I'd bet that among the first things you remember learning were tables – a process that drives most kids into a frenzy of rage and/or boredom while it's going on. But you will probably also admit that when it was over and you had achieved mastery of all your tables, you:

1   were delighted;
2   recognized, if only indirectly, that it was due to the repetition that had so bored and infuriated you;
3   found that the knowledge was automatic from then on.

Twenty years ago now, my younger daughter was in the midst of a campaign of deep hatred against tables; indeed, her comments featured a number of what I'll call 'unidentified flying adjectives' not normally associated with 10-year-old girls. At around the same time the rest of the family noticed that she knew by heart virtually every TV commercial jingle that appeared, even though she despised most of them. Such knowledge was the result of constant exposure: the jingles had registered automatically (which is of course the whole idea). Despite initial resistance, we were able to use a similar 'saturation principle' to accelerate her mastery of tables. We would all, from time to time, fire random questions at her – 'four sevens; eight sixes; nine threes' and so on; within a fortnight her campaign had dissolved. Automatic and unshakable mastery of tables took its place.

This idea worked for two reasons. First, it made a working principle out of the theory that some forms of learning have to be saturative; second, we all made a game out of the process. Not much of one, maybe, but more fun than sitting on her own, trying to do it by rote in a mood of boredom mixed with rage.

In sum: if you have to learn something intensively – i.e. commit it absolutely to memory – get other people to help you by 'testing' you at random and without warning. This semi-playful approach will rob the task of much of its immediate grind, and will also render your study more sociable.

Memory and frequency

I've touched on this already, and more follows in the next chapter. However, one or two important points need to be made here and now. It is generally true that there is a direct link between recall and the number of times the specific thing has been studied or used. This was illustrated by the little quiz on page 41. But it is not always true; or rather, the link depends on circumstances at the time.

Let's imagine you've failed to remember something which, for one reason or another, you feel you should have remembered. There are three possible reasons why this has happened:

1   You may simply not care enough about the item to have logged it firmly (this is the subject of the next section).
2   You may not have looked at it or used it often enough for it to have stuck.
3   You may have looked at it and used it 30 times or more, but never with enough of your mind on it for it to be transferred from the STM to the LTM.

It is the third possibility that concerns me here.

We all have those tantalising moments when the name of something or somebody eludes us, even though we've often heard it. At such times we say, 'the name's on the tip of my tongue'. This charming phrase, however, is not altogether accurate.

There are two possible explanations for this phenomenon. One is that the information is stored in the LTM, but can only be partially or insufficiently retrieved. The reason for such a 'block' may be that the memory is being made to try too hard: as I've said, if you have to 'rack your brains' for something, it's unlikely to be produced at that moment. It's better to turn off and let the information filter through naturally. Sometimes this will take a day or two; at others it may only be a matter of minutes. Of course, when you're under heavy pressure to remember something (as in an exam), it is difficult to relax in this way, if not almost impossible. But it's worth trying – if only because to worry at something in such circumstances is rarely successful in time.

That kind of experience is indeed analogous to having something 'on the tip of one's tongue'. But the second possible cause of such a block is not well summed up by the phrase. There are times when, no matter how frustrated we may feel in being so close to remembering something, we are in fact nowhere near to recalling it. We may say, when someone tells us the answer, 'Oh, yes, of course!'; but we kid ourselves if we confuse such told familiarity with independent, fixed knowledge of our own. In such cases, the block occurs because we've never taken quite enough trouble to lodge the information securely in our LTM. Maybe, while more or less registering the information at the time, we've not been paying full attention to it. Or perhaps we've allowed it temporary residence in our STM, only to evict it a few hours later in place of something fresh. Or maybe it simply didn't seem to matter enough, and we thus allowed it slowly to fade away until it finally vanished.

Pieces of information like this resemble casual acquaintances. We may see them often, but they never become important to our lives. Indeed, they are hardly noticeable, and it makes no difference to us whether we see them or not. They may well be interesting and pleasant, and we may sometimes think we'd like to know them better; somehow, though, we never quite get round to it. Other people and other things seem more important: there just doesn't seem to be room for anything else. In the same way, certain kinds of bits of information may flit in and out of our STM half a dozen or more times, without ever becoming permanent. They don't strike us as important or significant enough, especially when something fresher arrives for us to consider.

We can extend the metaphor. Suppose one such casual acquaintance does become a friend. Then everything changes. That person is now important. As with all true friends, there is an intimacy and automatic confidence between you. It may be that months pass between your meetings; but you think of each other often, and when you do meet up again, rapport is instant and profound. The things we know and are confident about are just like close friends: we are sure of them, and are immediately and permanently at ease with them. How, then, can you help your memory turn 'casual acquaintance' information into 'friendly' knowledge? Well, just think for a moment about the difference between those times when you're reunited with a close friend, and those occasions when you bump into someone you know slightly. In the former case, you are (I imagine) warm, spontaneous and completely at ease, while the latter finds you slightly bemused and full of cliches (I find I'm quite capable of saying such fatuous things as 'Oh, it's you' or 'I haven't seen you since the last time we met'). The crucial difference is self-consciousness, which is absent in the first case and sharply present in the second. My own feelings, when 'caught on the hop' in such a fashion, almost amount to schizophrenia – it's as if part of me has left my body and is watching me with contemptuous amusement, quietly advising me from time to time that it would be a great idea if I shut up.

If you transfer this kind of behaviour, notable for its prickly awareness of self, from the chance social meeting to the attempt to learn, you will see why some things refuse to lodge in your memory despite the number of times you've noted them. You have never truly concentrated on them: they've merely been part of a rag-bag of vague impressions. So if you want something to stick, you've first got to 'glue' your mind to it. Just staring at it time and again is not likely to be very efficient. It can work, but it's more probable that the information will skate across the surface and disappear. Writing it down is much better. For a start, more of your brain will be directly involved, because it will have to work your hand as well as absorb the visual material. Make sure, though, that you focus on what you write, otherwise the memory will vanish.

If you can, make a game out of the information. It's easier to remember a historical date if you can find a way to make the figure mean something else as well Let's take the year of Charles II's ascent of the throne as an example – the Restoration of 1660. You might take the '16' and link it with 'sweet' and re-name '60' as 'hour' (the number of minutes in an hour). You've now created your own puzzle code, 'sweet hour', which is remembered because you invented it and instantly decodable for the same reason. As with nearly all memory aids, it doesn't matter what you use or how you use it: effectiveness, for you and you alone, is the only test. You are trying to work out some way of personalising the information, of making it yours. For as soon as you've made it interesting, you will want to remember it. It's no longer a casual visitor, but someone you've invited in.

Perhaps the most obvious difference between friends and minor acquaintances is how much you care about each, and that brings me to my next topic.

Memory and thoughtfulness: How much do you care?

Hands up all those who have never come out with a remark like this:

I'm sorry about your birthday card/my home-work/that bill: I forgot.

Just as I thought: none of you! 'I forgot' is a classic social excuse, and we all use it at some time or another. In nine cases out of ten, it is accepted – mainly because we know we are all guilty of it. To be unforgiving and lordly about a particular instance seems hypocritical. The fact remains, nevertheless, that the excuse is nonsense; or, to put it another way, the words 'I forgot' are a kind of shorthand for

I couldn't be bothered/didn't care enough/was too lazy to remember.

I don't advise you to point this out too forcefully next time you hear it said: people can lose a lot of friends that way! But I do advise you to take it very much to heart in terms of your study and the efficient training of your memory.

If you have a normal brain, you are capable of retaining a quite staggering amounts of information. To do this you must, however, care enough about each item to hold on to it. For the memory to house something, it has to matter to you: if you don't give a damn one way or another, your memory won't either. For don't forget: your memory is a skill, one of the brain's remarkable tools. It is not a mysterious entity given to you, and therefore somehow independent of you. It will be as good (or bad) as you care to make it.

I've stressed throughout this chapter the need to redesign information, so that it becomes more personal (that's also why, incidentally, Chapter 1 included a section entitled 'Learn to be selfish'). Such practice offers two interrelated benefits:

1   The material becomes more accessible, more 'friendly' and therefore easier to care about.
2   The very fact that you are thinking, and thinking creatively, is itself a way of deepening your response and understanding.

It is no accident that we speak of sensitive, caring people as 'thoughtful'. In precisely the same way, the more you think, the more you will come to care about the information you're studying, and the more likely you are to retain it as a result. It is also no accident that people who do have bad memories can be rather dreary and aloof. They haven't cared enough about too many things, and thus they've little that interests them and even less to offer others.

Mnemonics: The value of do-it-yourself

Mnemonics – creative aids to memory – have a long and distinguished pedigree. The Ancient Greeks were fascinated by them – Aristotle writes at some length on the subject in his *De Insomnis* and *De Anima* – and they were no less absorbing to medieval and Renaissance scholars. Nevertheless, this section will be relatively short, for I am not going to offer you a selection of existing mnemonics and analogous devices;[4] all I want to do is establish a principle.

The reason for this is not laziness, nor am I daunted by the competition! It is that I am extremely sceptical about many of the mnemonics that students are encouraged to use. They are seldom of much help; furthermore, far from easing one's workload, they can actually increase it. Needless to say, the teachers who offer such advice are conscientious and mean well; moreover, many of their ideas are very good. The problem arises because they have not taken note of two fundamental things that together form that 'principle' I want to establish:

1 Mnemonics are as individual as people.

2 The successful mnemonic is one you invent for yourself.

Given that mnemonics are valuable only insofar as they save time and guarantee clarity of learning, they are far better created than imposed – easier, more fun and more memorable. That returns us to the importance of *play* in a student's life; it also returns us to Bartle Massey's observation that there is nobody so uncreative that s/he can't invent games, puzzles, rhymes or just jokes to assist learning and progress (see pages 18–19). Quite apart from the practical benefit you will derive, you'll get pleasure from the fact you have created something. That is always gratifying, and the consequent sense of well-being will also bolster your confidence.

It's time for an example. At least 90 per cent of my students find difficulty at some time or another in spelling the word 'necessary'. It takes a lot of them years to stop wondering if it's two 'c's and one 's', or two of each, or one 'r' or two, or whatever. A pupil of mine once put forward this mnemonic as an aid:

Never eat chips: eat salad sandwiches and remain young

I thought this excellent, and likely to work, up to a point; hence its inclusion here. But the larger point – which by now you might be able to anticipate – is that while it helped a few members of the class, it clearly didn't solve the problem for the majority, who went on writing 'neccesary' or 'neccesarry' and all the rest of it. They were neither lazy nor stupid: the mnemonic simply didn't register with them. When I then changed tack and advised them to devise their *own* sentences based on the same principle, many more made rapid progress.[5]

It is true that occasionally a mnemonic is coined that touches all of us, like the spelling rhyme we are taught when very young:

'i before e, except after c.'

But such instances are rare[6] and best regarded as the exception that proves the rule. As Ian M.L. Hunter says at the conclusion of his own discussion of mnemonic systems:

> [Improvement cannot be] guaranteed by the mere giving of 'rules' for learning. The person must come to understand such rules, not as verbal formulae but in terms of his learning activities; and he can only do this by applying these rules in practice.[7]

Mnemonics are idiosyncratic 'learning activities' best approached as a form of private game. Their distinct character – i.e. *yours* – will enable you to master, quickly and enjoyably, the 'rules' or data in question. Once again, *you are in charge*.

All that said and thoroughly meant, it might in conclusion be useful if I offer a few rudimentary guidelines as to what might work best. First and foremost:

Keep your mnemonics as simple as you can.

Further: the brain will latch on to ideas most firmly if they are:

- **Funny**
- **Obscene/vulgar**
- **Colourful**
- **Connected with something that interests or attracts you.**
- **Dramatic**
- **Bold and sharp**
- **Logical**[8]

The more of these you can work into your devisings, the stronger your mnemonics will be.

Memory blocks

Nearly all of this chapter has, I hope, been positive, albeit tough-mindedly so at times. You can do a great deal to improve your memory provided you're prepared to recognise that it is a skill, not a gift or an art, and that as such it needs to be *worked*. Frequency of contact is probably the key consideration, but it also helps enormously if you care about what you want to remember, or can at least manufacture a way of doing so.

Nevertheless, rare is the person who does not suffer at some stage from 'memory block' – things that one cannot remember, or find it very difficult to do so.

Some very good drivers who have otherwise extremely retentive minds could not possibly think of being a London cabbie, simply because they're hopeless at remembering even the street names in their own neighbourhood, let alone those of the entire London A–Z that comprise what cabbies fondly, and with justifiable pride, call 'The Knowledge'.

It seems to make no difference how hard these people try, or how often they're embarrassed by and about it (and no one likes looking an idiot) – it just won't happen for them. Is there nothing you can do about such 'memory blind spots'?

In Chapter 11 on examinations, I shall be suggesting that the first essential step if one suddenly gets stuck or blank-brained in an exam is to say, 'I am stuck' – to accept the situation and give oneself a couple of minutes to relax into it rather than panic. In the same way, your first duty is to admit, 'I'm blocked', and accept the situation rather than worry at it (see page 207). If none of the advice and devices outlined above have provided a solution, you might try one or other of the following:

1   Recite the information to be learned onto a tape, then play it back as often as you can stand. Once you've got over the usual ghastliness of hearing your voice as it sounds to others,

it may be that the fact that it is your voice will render the material more immediate and learner-friendly.

2   Try to establish (or manufacture) connections between the things to be learnt. It is invariably easier to remember material that is 'grouped' rather than single.

3   Divide the material into smaller sections – single items if need be (the previous point notwithstanding) – and work on them fiercely but briefly. Return to them as often as you can bear: it won't be pleasant, but you may get a result!

4   Write it out for yourself in note form (see also pages 138 and 149–50). The act of writing engages more of the brain than just reading, and – analogous to the voice point in 1 above – the sight of the information in your own hand rather than in impersonal typsecript may help.

If none of those succeeds, there are just two things left to do:

5   Hope that the block will one day simply clear itself, as it were of its own volition.

6   See what sheer stinking vanity will do!

Point 6 is less facetious than you might think. A surprising amount of excellent work is fuelled by either vanity or rage, or both, and if you decide you're determined not to let this stuff get the better of you, the chances are better than even that it won't.

Finally: if absolutely nothing I've suggested works, and if you find too that you have more than the odd memory block in any given subject, it may be that you're somehow temperamentally unsuited to that subject. Some students do come to decide that this is the case, and it's better to know it early, so that you can change to something more in line with your talents and mental strengths. But I would hope that only a few will need seriously to consider such a step.

Summary

The memory is perhaps the most extraordinary of all the many wonderful properties of your brain. If you want to pursue your knowledge of its make-up and function, then all the titles listed under 'Memory' in the Bibliography (page 230) should interest and enlighten you. My own elementary survey has sought to provide a foundation of knowledge about its workings, based on the following principles:

1   Your memory is *your* responsibility, nobody else's. It is entirely within your scope to improve it. If your memory is poor and remains poor, it could well be because you can't be bothered to make it any better.

2   We all have a short-term memory and a long-term memory; and most study skills are designed to shift as much information from the former to the latter as possible.

3   The 'intellectual' or academic memory is not an isolated structure: the more images and prompts you can bring in from the sensory memory, the better.

4   Memory games, especially DIY mnemonics, are excellent aids. They are fun, and harness your personality to your memory, so that *all* of you is focused on the business of recall.

5   If you want to remember things, you've got to *care* about them.

6   There is something compellingly mysterious about memory. It has fascinated scholars for centuries, and there is still much we do not know about it. For your purposes as a student, though, it's best to adopt a sturdy, no-nonsense attitude to it. And as with any skill, a judicious mixture of hard work, play, and sheer *use* will make an enormous difference. If you sincerely want to remember things, it's remarkable what you can do.

The next chapter is closely related to this one. We've seen something of the memory's basic structure and behaviour; we have an idea of why we remember some things but forget others. Now it's time to see how we can keep knowledge fresh and available when we are adding each week to our total store of information.

Chapter 3

Review

And if thou wilt, remember;
And if thou wilt, forget.

(Christina Rosetti)

Preliminary

We have seen that your memory is your own responsibility. Its success depends in large part on two things: how much you want to remember things and how often you focus on them. It's worth repeating that forgetfulness is rarely accidental. People forget things either because they have no real interest in them, or because they do not make enough effort to remember them. As Christina Rosetti suggests, it's entirely up to you.

Let us dispose of one fallacy. A 'photographic memory' is exceptionally rare. You may have seen espionage films in which Agent X or Counterspy Z has only to look briefly at a document, close and open his eyes like a camera shutter, and imprint the material permanently on his brain.[1] Amusing; but reality is less easy. It takes work, not magic, to commit something to memory, and even when the information is securely lodged there, you still need to use it, if it is not eventually to disappear. However, don't be put off by that apparently forbidding observation. The work required will not take much time, although adequate concentration is needed.

Review: Basic principles

A simple quiz in the previous chapter unremarkably suggested that we have no trouble remembering our name, our address, our phone number, and a host of other personal details. The reason is basic enough: they concern ourselves, and all of us are naturally and deeply interested in ourselves. But such interest in self cannot be the only principle governing memory: there has to be a bit more to it than that. See how you get on with *this* quiz. Write down:

1   Your National Insurance number.
2   Your *previous* phone number.
3   The name of your MP.
4   The name of your Euro-MP.
5   The phone number of your doctor and/or dentist.
6   Your timetable/work-schedule *last* year.

It's possible that you remember some of these without having to look them up, but I'd be very surprised if all five come automatically to mind. Numbers 1, 3, 4 and 5 are important, certainly (depending on your view of MPs!), but it's unlikely you need to quote or use them very often; Numbers 2 and 6, on the other hand, were frequently used and significant, but are now defunct, and thus irrelevant.

'Well, so what?' you might ask. 'What has my phone number of five years ago got to do with my current study and all the stuff I'm expected to remember at the end of my course?' Just this: that if you want to log something in your LTM, the key to success is frequency, even more than interest. You can be fascinated by something you learn in week two of your course, but unless you look at it again, several times, in the weeks that follow, the chances are that by week 25 it won't mean very much. The fact is that:

> **The likelihood of remembering something is in direct proportion to the number of times it is used or studied.**

That holds good for short-, medium- and long-term review, and here is an exemplary anecdote to illustrate it.

The benefits of intermediate review

Most readers of this book will, I assume, be studying for a post-GCSE course; however, cast your mind back to earlier school days if you can stand it, and revisit the days of French vocabulary tests.

1   It is Monday evening. You have a French test tomorrow – 20 questions based on about 100 words to be learnt for tonight's homework. You work fiercely at it, and end the evening pretty confident.

2   Next morning, you have a quick consolidatory look, and if you're fortunate you manage a further five-minute one just before the test occurs.

3   You do well; on you go to the next section of work, to be similarly tested next Tuesday.

4   Unfortunately, your French teacher is a sneaky devil. When next Tuesday arrives, the test covers all that previous work, not the new stuff at all.

5   Like everyone else you feel hard done by, moan about 'unfairness', and get a poor score. You may cheer up a bit on discovering that others have done even worse than you; you may even end the lesson in a good mood, vying with your friends to dream up the bitchiest and best phrase to sum up your nasty, devious, cruel teacher!

But your teacher may have done what s/he did not to catch you out, but to prove a point. Please look at Figure 3.1. As with my graphs in Chapter 1 (pages 25–7), this one is a metaphor rather than scientifically based on strict data; nonetheless, it expresses a profound working truth. Even when your brain and memory are at their most efficient (between the ages of 15 and 21), it is highly

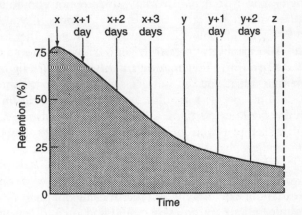

Figure 3.1 Retention curve if work is studied at point x and not looked at again

probable that if you take no further look at material learnt for a
specific task at point *x*, a steep decline in recall will occur over
eight days. Impressive at the time of the test (Monday), it has
halved by Thursday and halved again by the following Tuesday.

There is nothing extraordinary or shameful about this. During
your middle-school years, up to 16+ examinations, a staggering
amount of information and data competes for your attention,
across perhaps nine or ten academic subjects, and many other
things too. You simply cannot retain it all first time around
anyway; furthermore, as the week progresses, more recent material demands retention, perhaps for a science test on Thursday
and a history one the next day. Under pressure, the STM allows
that carefully learnt French vocabulary to fade away: the space is
urgently needed. But although that is understandable, it is not
'good business', and you need to do something about it. That
something is defined by the acronym

RAYL

RAYL is my own variant of the tax system PAYE (Pay As You
Earn) and denotes

Review As You Learn

RAYL is an immensely important principle, one that you should
fix centrally in your mind from the outset of your course. If you
regularly look over your past work, your retention should describe
the pattern shown in Figure 3.2. In other words, if you look at
the work again at points *y* (Thursday) and *z* (the following
Tuesday), you are likely to restore your knowledge to its original
level of 80 per cent. You may even go above that figure, now
remembering things you did not get right in the test. Even if that
'bonus' does not occur, it is still a major improvement on Figure
3.1's levels of 40 per cent and 20 per cent respectively.

For those of you who might be a little sceptical about my
'metaphorical graphs', I am happy to say that there is some significant scientific evidence that endorses all I've said. It is provided
by the work of Hermann Ebbinghaus (1850–1909), who conducted
some important experiments on memorising in the 1880s. The
most telling for our purposes is one based on the learning and
review of eight lists of his own devising.

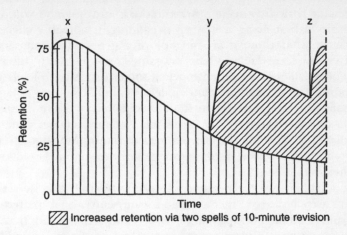

Figure 3.2 Retention curve if work is studied at points x, y and z

These lists in fact comprised nonsense syllables – for obvious reasons, harder to learn than any 'systematic' material and therefore a most stringent test. Ebbinghaus read each list aloud at a steady rate, and continued the readings until he was able to give two errorless recitals of the entire list. He computed the total number of readings required to memorise perfectly all eight lists as the 'learning time'. After a lapse of from 20 minutes to one month (see Figure 3.3), the same set of lists was re-learned in exactly the same way as before, and he duly computed the 're-learning time'. By comparing the two times, he arrived at a measure of the retained effects of the original memorizing. For example, if the original learning required 1,000 seconds, and if re-learning took 600 seconds, then the saving of effort was 400 seconds, or 40 per cent of the original time. This 40 per cent he termed the 'saving score'.

In this experiment he used seven different intervals between original learning and re-learning, shown in Figure 3.3 below.[2]

Time since learning	20 m	1 hr	9 hrs	24 hrs	2 days	6 days	31 days
Average saving score	58%	44%	36%	34%	28%	25%	21%

Figure 3.3 Memory reinforcement through repetition

The steady decline in the 'saving score' might mislead you, as it did me at first. Far from being depressing, it is highly cheering, because what those decreasing percentages actually show is a decline in forgetfulness. The very high 'saving score' after 20 minutes makes absolute sense: when something is completely new to you, it is difficult to remember even half of it straightaway. (Similarly, as we shall see in the next chapter, it is almost impossible to absorb more than 40 per cent of any text on your first reading.) Thereafter, Figure 3.3 almost irresistibly suggests that the more you review your learning, the more you cumulatively remember.

Ebbinghaus was careful not to make excessively precise claims: that's why he logged the 'average saving score'. Such patterns of learning and memorising can never be exactly computed: they will vary according to your temperament and condition, your liking or otherwise for the subject studied, and your natural aptitude in it. Whatever those circumstances, however, I can guarantee that such re-visits will consolidate and thus secure your knowledge much more reliably than if you leave it to chance, and to only one perusal.

The nicest thing about **RAYL** is that is does not – **should not** – take very long: we are talking of

as little as ten minutes a day.

All you are doing is to refresh your memory of things you learnt very recently and with which it is, therefore, readily familiar. Provided you concentrate properly for those ten minutes, such review can be done at the end of an evening's work or at any fallow time. Indeed, such a practice is an ideal way of 'winding down' at the close of a work-session. The brain does not 'turn off' fully and at once: it will welcome a gentle mulling over of user-friendly material.

As Ebbinghaus's experiment implies, this principle can be extended to cover a period of months, not just a week or so. In fact

regular review throughout a course is one key to success.

If you look regularly at your past work, your retention should describe a pattern as outlined in Figure 3.4. By the time you come

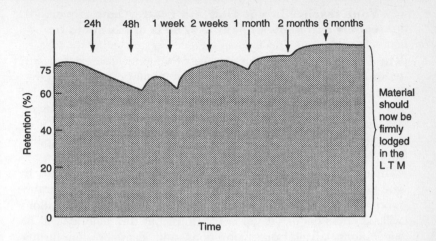

Figure 3.4 The benefits of regular review

to your sixth return to the material, it should be part of your LTM; in other words, you really know it, and it is as accessible and intimate a knowledge as all those personal details which automatically come to mind. (The advice in the last few paragraphs is expanded on pages 65–6 in the section 'Taking the misery out of revision'.)

Feedback

The principle of review becomes even more central when your work runs to more than elementary word-learning and other such basic matters. Any advanced – i.e. post-16 – course has areas which are less matters of fact than matters of interpretation. This is more obviously the case in subjects like literature and history than in science and maths; whatever your subject, however, an advanced course requires you to think as well as absorb information. To put it another way: whereas in earlier years you could succeed by behaving like a diligent sponge, soaking up information in what was essentially a one-way process, your relationship with both the material you study and the teachers guiding you should be a two-way affair, a genuine *dialogue* – and that pre-supposes *feedback*. It also presupposes a sane approach to the business of being taught:

Your teacher is not God, no matter how clever, expert and knowledgeable s/he is or seems to be.

The sooner you stop being in awe of your teachers and regard them instead as wise guides, the better it will be for your study.

An illustration is invariably more telling than any amount of generalising, so let us assume you have completed a long essay on the causes of the English Civil War (1642). Your next task is to consider the reign of Charles II (1660–85), so you start the preparatory reading, allowing the recent essay to recede.

In the mean time, the first essay is marked and returned to you with at least two or three comments – probably considerably more – in the margin and at the end. Some of these annotations will be criticisms or factual corrections, but the majority will be suggestions, talking points, questions, and ideas for your further consideration. Since, however, you are now fully engaged in your other work on Charles II's reign, you may be tempted to do no more than glance at these remarks, concentrating on the grade and any actual mistakes you've made. The *biggest* mistake you can make, however, is to do just that. If you don't use your teacher's comments, you are losing up to 50 per cent of the value of doing that essay in the first place. For remember:

Actually doing a piece of work is only half the job: equally vital is what you do with it afterwards.

Unless your teachers are both lazy and inefficient, they will be only too pleased to discuss their suggestions and comments with you. But it is just as valuable to think them through on your own, using their ideas – and any new ones you may have had in consequence – as a springboard. Whether you discuss these with them or with yourself, such a dialogue is essential, providing three distinct and major gains.

1   Reviewing recent work will help establish it more clearly in your mind, aiding eventual revision.
2   Your understanding of what you've done, and the area of study it covers, will improve considerably. This will increase both the quality of your knowledge and your confidence.
3   Your next task will benefit. Most aspects of a course are organically linked: to return to the example cited, a thorough

understanding of the causes of the Civil War will almost certainly assist you in appraising the reign of the monarch who ruled less than 20 years later.

Taking the misery out of revision

I shall address revision further in Part III, 'Examinations' (pages 188–93), but it is worth a mention here, if only because it underlines the value of Review As You Learn (*RAYL*) as a policy. The word 'revision' is virtually synonymous with 'review': both denote the re-perusal of material that is familiar. Ideally, revision should be somewhat analogous to using a cassette-player. When you insert a tape, the machine automatically reads the magnetic signals and recodes them into music, the spoken word, or whatever. If you've worked sensibly and successfully during the course, past ideas, information, methods and skills should flood back into your mind in a comparably reliable way.

For a great many students, however, 'revision' is a sad and terrifying misnomer. About six weeks before the exam, they return to all their work of the past year or more, and make the appalling discovery that hardly any of it seems remotely familiar. Their 'revision period' is no such thing: it is a frenzied and exhausting time attempting to learn again from scratch. Maybe that's why so many examinees look so dreadful when they arrive at the exam hall – pasty and drained, with bloodshot eyes and trembling hands. It's hardly surprising: anyone would look awful after trying to do upwards of a year's work in less than two months.

If you follow the advice in this chapter, you should never be in that position. When you come to revise, you'll find that cassette-player principle operating hearteningly well. Of course, you may discover that you've changed your mind about some of the things you wrote or thought earlier, or have since discovered new facts or angles that re-colour previous work. This is good: it means you are consolidating your knowledge in a healthily critical fashion that makes a cogent and efficient exam performance much more likely.

Don't laugh, but revision should be *enjoyed*. It ought to be pleasant to dispense with classes in order to work on your own – no matter how well you have got on with your teachers. If you've kept in regular touch with your work over the months, there shouldn't be any need for you to work while battling with anxiety.

You can practise answering past exam questions; you can test yourself or work with a friend; you can concoct little games that sharpen the memory and fully establish the major points you'll want to make in the exam; and, perhaps most important of all, you can

find out in your own time and with no immediate external pressure which areas of your syllabus you like most.

Virtually all advanced exams allow you to choose which questions you do, and it is always wise to pick the topics that you find most congenial. This is as true for maths and physics as it is for politics or English literature: informed enthusiasm is a pleasing quality at all times, and nowhere more so than in an exam paper.

Above all, do not attempt to work all the time during the revision period. If you've reviewed your work regularly, it's unnecessary to adopt such a miserable regime. It is better to have some fun and some rest as well as working. After all, the exams will make major demands on your physical and mental stamina as well as your knowledge: it makes no sense to arrive at the starting-blocks exhausted and fed up. The poet and playwright Ben Jonson expressed this principle unimprovably:

Ease and relaxation are profitable to all studies. The mind is like a bow, the stronger by being unbent.

Summary

At the end of his chapter on Ebbinghaus's work that I made use of earlier (pages 60–62), Ian M.L. Hunter cites four principles or conditions that facilitate learning:

Motivation; Material; Repetition; Maintenance.[3]

Motivation is largely self-explanatory, although Hunter's remarks on it endorse my earlier point about manufacturing interest in a topic if necessary:

Integrate the task into activities which are already interesting.

Material is essentially an extension of that last principle – the need to arrange the stuff to be learnt in ways which clarify and emphasise whatever characteristics are to be memorised. This bears out my earlier remarks about linking, sequencing and the organic nature of most study. Repetition is also self-explanatory by now, I hope. And by 'maintenance' Hunter denotes everything I have said about regular review – at first frequent, and then at progressively longer intervals.

Hunter's conclusion confirms my observation at the beginning of the previous chapter – that there is nothing miraculous about an efficient memory. If you *want* to remember things, that is half the battle; the other half is taking regular and careful looks back at what you've done. This makes your perception of it wider and more detailed; furthermore, the increasing degree of dialogue between the work and yourself transforms it from a distant stranger to an easy acquaintance. Best of all, it shows you that your study is organically yours. It is something that grows and functions as part of you, not some external construct imposed upon you, and that also helps you to enjoy yourself more. Finally, it doesn't take much time. Ten minutes a day is ample, and the benefits of such brief effort are hard to exaggerate. Now that's what I call good time management!

I hope these three chapters have persuaded you that your most formidable resource is your own brain and demonstrated some of the ways in which you can make it an even more powerful asset. The next two chapters look outward rather than inward, concentrating on the host of external resources available to today's student. First, a long and detailed look at computers and related technologies. I'm no more than an interested amateur in this field, so I've engaged a proper professional to write it: Jon Down.

Chapter 4

ICT and the knowledge revolution

Jon Down

Preliminary: Computer can't-do

The phrase *you are in charge* amounts to the governing motto of this book, and it applies to computer-use, email, the Internet and all other aspects of ICT as much as to any other aspect of study. So let us be clear at the very outset about what these technologies will *not* do:

- They will not write your essay.
- They will not carry out your research.
- They will not do your thinking for you.
- They will not instantly make you more intelligent, a better and more successful student. Nor will they reduce by a jot your responsibility for your own work. Never blame the computer when – as almost always applies – 'the fault . . . is in ourselves.'[1]
- They will not, by themselves, supply you with the *knowledge* you need to complete your coursework and pass your exams.

So what *can* a computer do for you?

I COMPUTER CAN-DO: THE ENABLING ARMOURY

Software applications

As I'm sure you know, software is the generic name given to programs that run on a computer. Word-processing programs are the most well-known type of software application. Software will help you order your information and intelligent use of software can help you transform information into knowledge.

One of the reasons for the rapid spread of the use of computers has been the determination of the software companies to ensure their products are used by as many people as possible. As a result, it is possible to get reasonable results out of most software with comparatively little effort – makers of difficult-to-use software soon found that no one would buy it. That said, it still saves a great deal of time and unnecessary effort if you make a point of either getting some training on how to use your software or reading up on it.

It is generally reckoned that most people use no more than 20 per cent of the potential offered by the most common pieces of software. To help you get the most out of the software there is a range of options including:

* taking one of the numerous free or cheap courses offered at your college or by your local learning centre;
* using some of the free training materials available on the Internet;
* if you are using older versions of software, hunting around second-hand and remaindered bookshops for very cheap user manuals.

Whatever you decide to do, you will almost certainly discover quicker, more efficient and effective ways to use the software. You will also discover very many useful things that you never imagined your software could do.

One thing these courses will not do, however, is help you *organise* your work.

Organising and deploying software facilities

Just as you date a set of lecture notes, collate reference notes you make from books, store your papers in different folders with dividers keeping related items together, so you should organise the work you store on your computer. Give files meaningful names: it is very easy to lose a vital piece of information in a series of files called 'biology 1', 'biology 2', 'biology 3', for instance.

Similarly, organise your files into *folders* (the computer equivalent of cardboard ring-binders). However, simply storing all your lecture notes in one folder may mean that you lose that one crucial fact needed to convert your essay from 'good' to 'high quality'.

I have always found that dividing folders up into areas of work (for example 'British history', 'European history', 'Politics') and subdividing each of these into 'Lecture notes', 'Essays', and so forth helps ensure I don't lose too much.

Some software generates larger files, in terms of storage space taken up on your computer, than others. Anything that includes pictures, video clips, sound clips or graphics is likely to be large. If you are using an older computer you may want to keep the storage of these files to a minimum, and even newer machines can fill up quickly. It is even easier to hoard data on a computer than it is to hoard books, CDs or clothes. Just as your room or flat fills up with junk, much of which you can't remember buying in the first place, and swinging a cat becomes a major logistical exercise, when a computer hard disk fills up the computer itself slows down, eventually to a halt. Try to make sure that you delete files you no longer need. You can always copy these files onto a CD before deleting them if you are not one hundred per cent sure you have finished with them.

It is also important to try to avoid sending large files (by which I mean more than 500 kilobytes or half a megabyte) by email. Sending and receiving large files by a modem can be time-consuming and expensive or, alternatively, can strain a school or college network. This will not make you popular either with the recipient of your email or with the staff in charge of the college network. Look in the *properties* of a file (under the *File* menu) if you need to know how big it is.

Caution! Word-processing and planning

Word-processing is the most common software application. It is a fantastic tool for composing, editing and moving paragraphs around essays and reports. What it does not do, however, is get rid of the need for *planning* a piece of written work. You will still need to order your thoughts before using a word-processing package to present them. Failure to plan will guarantee the production of an incoherent jumble of thoughts masquerading as an essay.

For me there is still no substitute for pencil and paper in this planning process. It is far easier to make intuitive leaps, link up ideas and bring themes together when I can see all my ideas in front of me on a single sheet of paper. Word-processors are wonderful tools but a computer screen is simply not big or flexible enough to display all of the ideas coursing around your brain. You can see more information on a side of A4 than you can on the average computer screen. You can draw arrows linking thoughts more easily, put ideas at odd angles and juxtapose opinions in a way that mirrors your thought processes and firms up half-formed ideas. This intuitive way of working is simply not practical on a computer. Only now, having articulated and organised your ideas on paper, can you use a word-processing package to help to express your thoughts.

After completing your planning on paper and composing a first draft of your essay or report, it is important that you print it out and read the hard copy.[2] Scrutinising this printed version has several advantages over scanning the electronic one on screen. Spelling and typographical errors, easily missed on screen, are much easier to spot on the printed page. Spell checkers are very useful for picking out most mistakes but, like all things to do with a PC, it is a facility that has to be used with an 'engaged brain'.

No spell checker can tell that you mean 'it is too hot' when you have typed 'it is to hot'. There is no way your spell checker can recognise that when you type 'thy' what you really mean is 'they'. It is really rather unfair of you to expect it to understand the difference between 'and number' and 'any number'. And for some reason I have never quite worked out, all the spell checkers I have ever used have problems recognising certain words, such as 'liaise'.

Another very tempting feature of word-processing programs is the *Search and replace* facility. Like the spell checker this can be a very useful tool but only if used intelligently. You might, for example, want to replace all instances of the word 'page' with the abbreviation 'pp'. By using Search and replace you can achieve this very easily. However, you are also likely to end up with countless words like 'slippp' when you mean 'slippage' and 'pp turner' when you mean 'page turner'. If you have used Search and replace at all during the course of a piece of work you will certainly want to check a hard copy.

A text reads differently on a computer screen from the way it reads on paper. A phrase you consider the acme of brilliant poetic eloquence on your PC can emerge as meaningless drivel on the printed page. A piece of paper and a computer screen are two different media – you only have to look at the way Internet pages are laid out compared to books in order to appreciate this. The Internet is for short, snappy bites of transient information.

The printed page is more considered, thoughtful and permanent. Be mindful of this difference if your end product is a hard copy.

Word-processing: Troubleshooting and tips

Word-processing packages are prodigiously sophisticated tools and you cannot hope to learn all there is to know about them in a short space of time. So here are my *top ten handy hints*, based on facilities and (legitimate) short-cuts of which many, even comparatively experienced, computer users are often unaware.[3]

1 Even with an English language version of your software, all the characters used by the major European languages (including Greek, Arabic and Hebrew) are available using the *Insert/ Symbol* menu. This facility also has all the main mathematical operators.

2 When you are working on a long document, particularly if you are working on it over a number of days or weeks, the *Insert/Bookmark* menu enables you to mark and quickly find places in your work. You can insert any number of bookmarks and save yourself hours of scrolling up and down your document trying to find the bits you had been working on last.

3 To save constantly switching between the keyboard and the mouse learn the key stroke equivalents to mouse commands. For example, *Control+B* turns on the bold, *Control+Shift +arrow* selects words. This can make typing a piece of work much quicker and it is less likely to interrupt your creative flow.

4 If you are trying to lay out text on a page using columns, tabs and spaces (for a CV, for example), give up and use *Tables* instead. You can format each cell or group of cells within a table to appear just how and where you want much more easily and accurately. Before printing simply hide the borders of the table.

5 Save your work every five minutes or so (*Control+s*) – for me it has become a reflex. You never know when you are going to get a power cut or inadvertently kick the power lead out of its socket.

6 If your work suddenly disappears and you find yourself confronted with an empty document comfort yourself with the knowledge that you have probably pressed *Control+N* (open

new document). Just closing the blank document will, nine times out of ten, reveal all your work to be intact. On the tenth occurrence, don't worry, because you've been following the fifth of my top ten tips.

7 *Control+Z* undoes the most recent key strokes you have made. This is very useful when you are composing directly onto your PC. Even more useful is *Control+Y* which restores anything you have undone using *Control+Z*. Try it and you'll see what I mean.

8 Using the *Insert/Hyperlink* menu enables you to include links to websites or to other files on your computer. I have found this very useful to link sets of related notes. You might, for example, be making some notes on fighting in the trenches in the First World War. By including a link to, say, some notes you made for another module on the poetry of Wilfred Owen will mean that you can open up the related set of notes by clicking on the link, so not having to remember or work out where you stored these other notes. This is an especially useful technique for longer, more complex projects.

9 If you are including quotations in a foreign language then applying *Tools/Language/Set Language* to the quotations enables the word-processor to 'think' in the appropriate language. For example, setting the language to French for the phrase 'Ou est la plume de ma tante?' will ensure that the spell checker recognises the 'Ou est' for the quotation but will pick 'ou' and 'est' as spelling errors elsewhere in the document.

10 Use *Control+S* to save. (Sorry, have I mentioned that before . . . ?!)

Spreadsheets

After word-processing, spreadsheets are the most commonly used software application. Spreadsheets are useful for organising structured information such as columns of numbers, for performing calculations, using formulae and for generating graphs from data sets. They are straightforward to use and excellent at managing small amounts of information that does not need to be changed often. Manipulating mathematical data, financial and other statistical modelling, and carrying out straightforward calculations (such as recording and calculating student grades) are typical uses for spreadsheets.

A spreadsheet can also perform some of the more straightforward *database* functions (see below). For example, a list of British Prime Ministers earlier could be typed into a spreadsheet. The spreadsheet could then be used to order Prime Ministers by date, by party or by name. Indeed, if this sort of task is the limit of your aspiration then you could save yourself a lot of time by using a spreadsheet. On the other hand, if the task in hand demands that you be more ambitious in the size and scope of the information you have to deal with, it is just possible that you might want to dabble in the black arts of the database.

Databases

At its simplest, a database denotes a table of information that can be manipulated in myriad ways. A database can order information, perform complex calculations on specific chunks of information, perform accurate and comprehensive global updates and carry out highly complex searches. While it is easy to set up a simple database, such as a list of names and addresses, it is worth being aware that databases are designed to manage large amounts of continually changing data so you might be better off sticking to a spreadsheet. If you intend to use a database, a degree of training is strongly recommended as databases operate according to relational theory (a branch of mathematics).

I first used a database to record information about the individual parliamentarians of Norwich and Oxford in the fourteenth and fifteenth centuries. As I discovered more and more about these individuals I had to expand the scope of what I was recording. For example, halfway through my researches I discovered a source that revealed which streets many of these men lived in. With a database it is simple to change the scope of the data you are collecting in this way.

Later, as I discovered different lists of the places these men had lived, I was able to use the database to speedily find specific names and associated streets to check against the information in the different sources. Finally, having assembled all the information I was able to perform complex manipulations of the data to reveal trends and patterns across the towns and the centuries. A powerful tool, databases are not for the fainthearted, but, used in the right way for the right job, they can help you achieve results that are impossible with any other piece of software.

Other software

Presentation packages are an excellent way of helping to order your thoughts and, when used effectively, can add an extra dimension to a speech or talk. In addition, these packages are easy to edit (unlike hand-written overhead slides) and can be printed out as hand-outs to save your audience taking notes during your presentation. Video, audio and animation can be included to spice up what you have to say; however, beware of the trap of using your presentation slides as a set of prompt notes for you, the speaker. You may have already heard the expression 'Death by Powerpoint',[4] where a dull presentation is compounded by an unimaginative set of slides or a fascinating talk is disguised by an over-fussy display of computer pyrotechnics. Use presentation software as an aid to understanding, not as a surrogate speaker!

Word-processing, spreadsheets, databases: these, then, are the most common software applications. There are many more specialist applications for desktop publishing (Microsoft Publisher and Quark Xpress are the most well known), drawing and graphics (Coral Draw and Photoshop, among others), statistics (SPSS), managing bibliographies (Endnote, Procite, Reference Manager) and subject-specific activities. The more specialist the software, the more it will cost. If in doubt, do not buy. If you make a mistake it could prove to be an expensive one.

So how *do* you decide?

II BUYING A COMPUTER

Many schools and colleges now have rooms full of computers entirely for use by students. Often, however, demand outstrips supply and you might find it difficult to find a free PC at a time that suits you. It may also be the case that these machines are of variable technical quality and reliability. An attractive alternative option, then, is to buy your own. But how do you see your way through the impenetrable maze of jargon and opinion that makes up the IT industry?

A generally accepted piece of IT mythology, Moore's Law, has it that the capacity and power of computers doubles every year or eighteen months. This makes pontificating about software and hardware a dangerous game, and anyone foolish enough to commit their opinions to print is often open to considerable ridicule in the months and years that follow. Predicting the future of technology is a risky business: whatever happened to Betamax videos and the eight-track cartridge? Even so, there is still some general advice likely to stand the test of time, much of which would I would have found useful when I bought my first computer back in 1989. First, something almost embarrassingly basic, which many eager customers nevertheless contrive to ignore.

What *sort* of computer do I need?

Your answer is your privilege, naturally, but you'd be wise to dwell on the question with due care. Will it be an IBM-compatible Personal Computer (a PC) or an Apple Mac? Apple Macs tend to be used for graphics and design work, PCs for more conventional number crunching with spreadsheets and databases. With PCs making up some 95 per cent of sales there is a wider range of software available for PCs than for Apple Macs and you are likely to find that most of your fellow students run PCs. Apple Mac fans, a loyal and vociferous bunch, will not thank me for saying this, but unless you have a very good reason to do otherwise, it makes more sense to buy a PC.

You might also want to consider whether the portability of a laptop will be more useful to you than the desk-top computer of the sort you tend to find in offices. Libraries are increasingly providing facilities for laptop use, so if you are studying away from home a laptop might be more convenient. However, laptops are significantly more expensive that desk-top computers and the risk of theft or damage to the computer is considerably higher as you travel around. The weight of a portable computer and the length of the battery life are also likely to be key considerations.

Before buying you also need to be clear about what you will want your computer to do. Will it simply be the word-processing of essays? If so, then a cheap, low specification PC will do. Alternatively if you want to do video editing or run Computer Aided Design (CAD) software packages you will need a high specification machine. If you are planning to use a database you may need something in between.

Of course, these deceptively bland phrases beg the crucial question:

How do you tell a high specification machine from a low specification machine?

Price, naturally, is a pretty good guide – you are not going to buy a decent high-specification machine for a small amount of money. Other than price, there are three other measures you need to consider: processor speed; memory; disk space. As this is all getting rather technical, so let me introduce a four-part analogy.

1   I am sitting in my study at home, working on a text (the one that you are now reading, as it turns out) using my brain to pick out and order items from my memory and, where this fails, consulting one of the many books that clutter my apparently ordered existence.
2   That which determines the speed of the brain is comparable to the speed of a computer processor. Processor speeds are measured in *Gigahertz* (GHz).
3   The memory of a computer, like the information that does not have to be looked up in a book but is already lodged in my mind, is measured in *megabytes of Random Access Memory* (MB of RAM).
4   The storage space on a computer, equivalent to the size of my bookshelf, is measured in *Gigabytes* (GB) of a hard drive or hard disk.

Here, unfortunately, the analogy breaks down: it may take me some minutes to locate a piece of information in a book whereas a computer can find the information in a fraction of a second. However, it remains true that when you look at the mass of fine technical detail that sales literature uses to describe a computer, *GHz, MB of RAM* and *GB* are the three key measures of how well it will perform. The higher the numbers associated with processor speed, memory and hard disk, the higher the specification of the machine.

Do some reconnaissance. Make a note of the minimum specifications required by the software that you want to use. As a rule of thumb buy a PC with double the amount of memory (RAM) indicated by the manufacturers of the software and you should have few performance problems.

Further criteria and considerations

Screen size may well be another of your priorities. The standard size for a screen (also known as the *monitor*) is 15 inches but investing in a 17-inch or even a 19-inch screen can make life a lot easier, particularly if you are using a publishing or graphics package. Large screens are also very useful if you are using complex spreadsheets or long word-processing documents. Monitors have traditionally been bulky, ungainly objects but in the last few years reasonably priced flat screens have become available and is it well worth considering the extra expenditure if your work space is limited.

Finally, a couple of extras that, in my view, are close to essential. A *Zip drive* or a *CD writer* make backing up your valuable files as straightforward as possible. If the process is easy then you are more likely to do it regularly. As well as a CD writer, many new computers come with a CD that automatically restores the settings of the PC to those it had when you bought it. So, when you try to reallocate the resource settings for you newly installed scanner and find that your mouse no longer works, and because your mouse no longer works you can't uninstall the scanner or adjust back the resource settings or indeed use your computer in any shape or form, this CD can save hours of heartache and frustration by restoring your original working system.[5]

Research and shopping around

For more detailed advice as to what to buy, nothing beats a chat with a friend or fellow student who already owns a computer that does what you want yours to do. If you are running specialist software, a tutor or technician should be able to give you sound advice, while many university and college websites offer good tips as well. There are also a number of computer magazines aimed at the computer novice which regularly print advice on current specifications and best buys.

Computers manufactured by the big companies tend to be more expensive than the 'white box' machines or 'clones' (i.e. those put together by little-known companies), although with prices continuing to fall the difference in price between the brand names and the white boxes is getting smaller. These white box computers tend to consist of a mix of cheap components, and so are more likely to give you problems. You might also want to bear in mind that the history of computer retailing is littered with episodes of companies going bust and leaving equipment that has been paid for undelivered, and product warranties with no value whatever. If your budget stretches, it is generally safer to buy a PC manufactured by a well-established, reputable, large supplier.

Buying a name brand from the major electrical chains stores tends to be more expensive and, while the computer you buy will tend to be more reliable, should you need technical support this may well be both expensive and not always terribly helpful; the IT supplements of the broadsheet newspapers abound with tales from dissatisfied customers and poor after-sales service. The small, local retailer (a disappearing breed these days) will also tend to be more expensive, but provided s/he comes recommended, you are more likely to get expert, useful technical support without (a) spending several hours listening to Vivaldi in a phone queue and (b) explaining your problem to someone who knows more about washing machines than your computer. A good local store will also be able to give you useful and relatively impartial advice about what to buy within your budget.

Most of the computers I have bought over the years have come from suppliers advertising in magazines or, more recently, from the Internet. This method is generally cheaper and more flexible. You can get extra memory, more hard disk space or other technical refinements made by the manufacturer, and the computer gets delivered to your door.

Shopping like this is fine if you are confident that you know what you are buying. Even so, those broadsheet IT pages abound no less with tales of wrong or faulty equipment being delivered, equipment not being delivered at all, and nightmarish, expensive, Kafka-esque tales of telephone queues, unreturned email requests and non-existent engineers. The computer retail industry has not fully mastered the art of customer service, so once again it is worth asking around to find which suppliers currently run an effective operation.

At this point it is worth saying a few words about *warranties*. To begin with, make sure you get an on-site warranty. This will save you having to return any faulty equipment to the manufacturer, with all the cost and trouble that that involves. As well as the standard manufacturer's warranty, you will be offered additional two, three or even five years' cover. The approach I have always taken is that if a computer is going to break down it will generally do so in the first six months – unless I start taking it apart myself, in which case the warranty is liable to be invalidated anyway! Some of the extended warranty services cost almost a quarter of the computer itself and so you are paying a great deal of money to cover for a very unlikely event. A well-made, well looked-after computer will last you for years, or at least until software upgrades force you to buy another.

The cheapest option of all is to buy from a computer fair, from an Internet auction site, or from shops selling discontinued or second-hand equipment. If you have very straightforward needs and the help of a friend who can give you reliable advice, this can be highly cost-effective. Just as you would buy a cheap, second-hand car to run you around town for a year or so, so this approach can be the way to meet limited needs in the short term – say the odd essay and other bits of word-processing. However, what you are unlikely to get is equipment that can run the latest software, a computer that can easily be upgraded, a warranty of more than three months, or any technical support. If you want to be sure of a relatively trouble-free computer, then the price of new equipment is probably worth paying.

Computer 'peripherals'

This term refers to such things as printers and scanners, and if you are planning to buy your own computer, you'll want at least to consider these. Once again, there is a whole set of choices you have to make. Many suppliers 'bundle' peripherals with a PC or, to put it another way, ensure that when you buy a PC you also buy a printer, a scanner and a digital camera. This has the advantage of simplifying the process of getting kitted out and makes it much more likely that all the equipment you buy will work together. However, are you sure you need a digital camera? Is a colour printer that prints six pages per minute much use when you are going to be printing a lot of long essays? Think about what you *really* need. As with a PC, if your budget stretches, buy new and buy from one of the major manufacturers. By shopping around you may not have to stretch your budget that far.

'Upgrading' software

In an ideal world you'd want to have the latest version of any piece of software. However, software is no different from any other commercial product extant: 'new' does not automatically mean 'better'. So when I observe that the major software packages are 'upgraded' every couple of years, I use that descriptor in the loosest sense. That said, you need to be aware that there is no guarantee that something written on a word-processing package manufactured five years ago will be legible to a word-processing package manufactured this year. If you expect to work on joint projects with fellow students or to be submitting your work to tutors via email, therefore, getting the latest version should ensure that such compatibility problems are minimised.

While the latest versions of widely used software sold on the high street are not always all that cheap, many of the major software suppliers offer discounts to students in full-time education and this can significantly reduce costs. Alternatively, older versions of some software is sometimes available free with computer magazines. Usually these versions do not have all the features of a full version or there is a date beyond which the software will not work. However, for straightforward tasks this can be a perfectly serviceable option. If all else fails, on the Internet there is a whole 'freeware' industry with huge amounts of software available free so, if your computing needs are modest, you may have to spend very little on software.

Adaptive technologies

Both the software and hardware industries are making great strides in the development of products to support people with disabilities. These 'adaptive' or 'assistive' technologies include equipment to help physically (adaptions to keyboards, special mice and other devices to help with putting data into a computer) and visually (software that will read what appears on a screen back to you or magnifies the screen). There are resources for people with hearing impairments, those who have dyslexia and a whole range of modifications that can be made to suit specific needs. Some of this technology can be expensive, but many colleges have some of these resources available on loan, and the Windows operating system (which will come with your PC) has a number of very useful 'Accessibility' options that you can adjust to modify the way your PC functions. With a little bit of research and a small outlay, the use of your computer can be made a great deal easier.

Internet access

Section III, pages 86–90, is devoted to *use* of the Internet and its complementary facilities. Here I'm simply concerned with *connection* to the Internet, which you will certainly want to have if buying your own computer: it will indeed probably be one of your chief reasons for doing so.

In the first instance it is probably best that you simply buy a *modem*, a device that connects your PC to your telephone line, and connect to the Internet via this line. Almost all new PCs will come with a modem pre-installed. You will find the Internet comparatively slow but this is by far the cheapest approach, particularly if you use one of the free Internet Service Providers (ISP), although you should beware of spiralling telephone bills![6] The software that enables you to sign up with an ISP is often given away with newspapers and magazines, or when you buy your PC.

For higher quality Internet access your first port of call should be your college, school or one of several thousand computer centres that have been set up across the country. Here access is generally low-cost or free. Failing that you might want to investigate using ISDN or ADSL, two high speed ways of using the Internet, at home. Currently they are not, however, without cost or universally available and are generally more appropriate for businesses, unless you or some beneficent member of your household is prepared to pay the monthly tariff.

Protecting your computer – and you

If you have gone to all the time, trouble and expense to get yourself a computer, it is certainly worth making sure that you and it are protected. Now, sitting alone at a computer does not, on the face of it, seem the most hazardous of occupations but there are a few things you should bear in mind. Simply staring at a screen for long, uninterrupted periods can easily cause eye strain so, at the very least, make sure you take frequent, regular breaks. An anti-glare filter screen that clips onto your monitor helps. Certain colour combinations can trigger certain conditions; if, for example, you are prone to epilepsy, alter the settings so that instead of word-processing in black onto a white background you word-process in white onto a blue background.

It is equally important that you are seated correctly – position yourself and your computer so you don't strain a back muscle. Foot rests can also help, particularly the lower back, and foam wrists rests for the keyboard and mouse can prevent Repetitive Strain Injury (RSI). This is, take it from me, very painful and can prevent you from using your computer for long periods of time. Sharp, shooting sensations in the lower arm and index fingers are best avoided.

Learning to type properly so that you are not pecking away, two- or three-fingered, will not only guard against RSI but will increase the speed and accuracy of your typing, useful not least if you are using your portable PC to take notes in a lecture. There are several free typing tutorials available on the Internet.

If you use a laptop, be especially careful about how you carry it around. Carrying a laptop around in an over-the-shoulder case for long periods has several disadvantages: it strains the back; it chafes the skin on the top of your shoulder; it crushes the shoulder of any decent jacket you happen to be wearing; and, when you finally put the case down, you have a tendency to list in a rather alarming way. Over the years I have found that a carry-case in the form of a rucksack is not only safer for the computer but is far easier all round.

Apart from physical damage (I can offer no insight other than 'use your common sense' when it comes to spilling tea on your computer or dropping it down the stairs), the biggest threat to your newly acquired machine is from a computer *virus*. Any file that comes onto your computer, whether it be via floppy disk or CD, via email or the World Wide Web, from friend or foe, is capable of harbouring a computer virus. A virus may simply be an irritant that interferes with your word-processor, or it can wipe your entire hard disk, destroying all your work, so make sure you use reputable anti-virus software and that you keep it up to date.

Just imagine, your hard disk has been wiped by a virus. Or your computer has been stolen. Or your hard disk has blown up. No need to worry – you'll have a back up, won't you? *Won't you* ?? Try to get into the habit of copying all your work onto a Zip drive or a CD, regularly. For me, 'regularly' is after every eight hours of work I have done. When disaster strikes, therefore, at least I will only have lost one day's work. If you have a locker at school or college it may be worth using it to store an additional back-up copy. This whole process is tedious and, without a routine, difficult to remember, but it is absolutely essential. The 'my computer has died and I lost all my notes' excuse for failing to hand an piece of work in on time is about as acceptable as the 'my dog ate my essay' alibi.

Talking of excuses, another favourite of the disorganised student also seeks to apportion the blame to technology. Few students have the luxury of using a high quality laser printer at home and so will use college facilities to print out a final version of an essay. However, when an entire class attempts to do this ten minutes before a submission deadline, I can absolutely guarantee that one of the following will occur:

- the printer will run out of toner (ink);
- the printer will get irrevocably jammed with paper;
- the printer will break down altogether;
- the college computer network will crash.

Just as the sun rises in the morning and sets in the evening, your essay will be handed in late.

It will be no good blaming the technology. Everyone – including every tutor – knows that technology is unreliable. This is not news. It is up to you, the student, to take every reasonable precaution against technological failure and ensure you work is safe, secure and submitted by the deadline.

Conclusion: Some further pitfalls

Distraction

Having a shiny new computer (or even a dusty, creaking old one) will not, by the mere fact of its existence, improve the quality of your work. Indeed, it can militate against it. The piece of equipment on which you are writing that essay with the rather uninspiring title is also likely to be home to a whole lot of exciting computer games. It may well also be your gateway to that vast bank of trivia and titillation that is the World Wide Web, of which more follows. Here are two perfect opportunities (i.e. excuses) for you to engage in hours of unproductive displacement activity and fail to fashion any essay whatever. It is difficult when your work tool is also one of your favourite leisure activities. Be disciplined with yourself: if you are sitting at the computer to work, then *work*!

Presentation-neurosis and presentation-wisdom

Once you eventually sit down and write that essay, it is tempting to spend a lot of time using lots of fonts and styles to make it look good. This can be great fun, hugely satisfying and while away many an afternoon. However, despite the best efforts of our politicians, presentation is still no substitute for quality. A poor piece of work, however good it looks, remains a poor piece of work. If you have not already come across the expression 'garbage in, garbage out' (GIGO), then it might be worth committing this handy little adage to memory. Put simply, no matter how long you spend hammering information into your computer, if you have not taken the time and effort to apply your mind then the computer will simply churn out the same old rubbish as you have put in. No amount of fancy presentation will ever disguise that.

Nonetheless, it is worth applying a little thought to how your work looks on the printed page. Find out if your tutor or institution has any preferred styles or bibliographic conventions. Are there preferred fonts? Should essays be double-spaced? Should work be single-sided or double-sided? Just as good presentation will not mask poor efforts, so a brilliant piece of work produced double-sided, single-spaced in a dodgy font will not count in your favour. Remember, your work may have been produced with the aid of a computer but it will be read and assessed by a human being. If an essay is difficult to read it may not receive the justice it deserves.

Plagiarism

Developments in technology, particularly the Internet and email, have made joint assignments and group work more possible. It is also much easier to share work informally with your fellow students. You can often learn a great deal by reading each other's essays or commenting on each other's reports. The downside to these developments has been the increased opportunity it affords for plagiarism, either witting or unwitting. It is so very easy to cut and paste a line, a paragraph or even a whole piece of work into your machine and claim it as your own.

Copying someone else's work is made easy by the technology and is not obviously apparent when you look at the printed pages of an essay. However, the words and expressions used to communicate ideas are very distinctive; indeed, they are unique to every individual. As a result, be advised:

Plagiarism is very easy to spot.

A plagiarised paragraph, page or essay will stand out, being nothing like any paragraph, page or essay you have produced before or after. If you have plagiarised from an authoritative, well-informed source it is highly likely that your tutor will have read (and maybe have even written) the very work you are stealing. If you have plagiarised from a less authoritative, less well-informed source then you are likely to be plagiarising rubbish – there is a great deal of rubbish on the Internet – and if your tutor or institution is particularly concerned about such issues you might discover that your work has been checked by software designed to spot plagiarism.

The ease with which it is possible to use the Internet and email means it is also easy to simply overlook the fact that you must not send copyright material or intellectual property via email unless you have permission to do so. Similarly, you should not use copyrighted materials without permission. If you are quoting or summarising a piece of information from an Internet site then, just as you would refer to a written text in a bibliography, footnote or endnote, you should cite an Internet source. There are various conventions for doing so, all of which contain the web page address, title, author and the date the web page was consulted.

Plagiarism is a moral issue – it is nothing other than intellectual theft – but it is also a practical one whose harvest can be catastrophic. If you plagiarise, you will be at best severely downgraded and at worst summarily disqualified.[7] And the silliest thing about it is that it's so *unnecessary*. A decent student working well is more than capable of producing material that is not only kosher but often better than stuff s/he might lazily be tempted to lift.

III ELECTRONIC LEARNING: THE INTERNET AND EMAIL

The Internet: A new wonder of the world

The Internet is the most extensive, comprehensive and accessible information resource ever produced. There are few areas of education that have not been touched by the World Wide Web and, for colleges and schools, it has become a key learning tool. Increasing numbers of institutions use email, the Web and intranets[8] to communicate, publish resources and course materials, run mock tests and exercises, and use it as a vehicle for collaborative working.

Gone are the days when students were forced to spend hours or days hunting out key text books from denuded book stores or musty second-hand shops. If a book is in print any number of Internet booksellers will deliver it to your home in days. Specialist Internet sites can search in seconds hundreds of *online* (that is, on the Internet) second-hand bookshops across the globe and locate out-of- print texts.

Most further and higher education library catalogues are available online and many archives and art galleries are in the process of digitising or have already digitised (created copies that can be stored on a computer) their collections and published them on the Internet. The Office of National Statistics makes public all manner of government statistical data, while standard works of reference such as the *Oxford English Dictionary* and the *Encyclopaedia Britannica* are published on the Web. Great bodies of human knowledge such as the Human Genome Project and the entire Tate Gallery collection are available through any Internet-connected computer and many major works of literature can be downloaded in full from any number of websites.

While the World Wide Web is by far the largest information resource on the Internet and email (see below) the most commonly used application, there is a range of other widely used resources. *Newsgroups* are places where the informed, the less informed and the simply opinionated have discussions about all manner of subjects. *List servers* distribute messages, requests and information on particular topics to users who subscribe to a service. List servers tend to be popular with Internet users with more serious intent. There are numerous 'news' services that offer continuous information on developments in current affairs. Many academic journals are now available online along with a host of technical and bibliographic databases, and for language students the opportunity to listen to foreign radio stations or watch foreign television can be an invaluable aid.

The Internet: Potential snags

In many ways the Internet resembles some vast, unedited book with no contents page or index. Everything is available but finding what you want is another matter altogether. Search engines are an attempt to make some sense out of the information on the Internet by scanning web pages, newsgroups and databases and either ordering information into directories or producing lists of web pages that contain key words. Common search engines such as Google and Yahoo can, if you learn how to use them properly, be very effective. Used in conjunction with subject specialist, multimedia-specific or country-specific search engines, you can quickly develop skills for hunting out exactly what you want.

If you are using the Internet in your studies, it is crucial that you are able to exercise some critical judgment on the quality of the information you find. If a tutor has recommended a particular site, it is reasonable to assume that its information is good. Similarly, where information is published by a public authority or government agency, generally it can be regarded as official and accurate. However, you are liable to stumble across huge numbers of unofficial sites run by individuals and organisations with a whole range of personal and political agendas. Much of the information on these sites is misleading, spurious or simply wrong, so it is important to understand who is publishing the information and get an idea of their standing. Any credible source of information will indicate the author, the organisation under whose auspices the information has been published and the copyright status of the material. After all, you might happily buy a new car from a franchised car dealer but you would be pretty foolish to buy a car from the first second-hand dealer you happened to come across as you wandered aimlessly around the streets.

Email

Email is, arguably, the Internet technology that has had the greatest impact of all. The ability to send and receive messages across the globe in a matter of seconds has transformed education and the learning process. An example from my own studies might help explain this slightly portentous claim.

Working on a project about the latest developments in database theory, I came across a reference to an article, published by a professor in Singapore, that was not yet available in Britain. Knowing his name and the university he worked in, I searched the Internet and found his email address. I emailed him for details of how I might get a copy of the article and, with the sun now well over the yard arm, retired for the day. The next morning I checked my email to find that not only had he responded but he had also attached a copy of the article for me, which I could now read before my project was due in.

Such, then, is the potential of email. It is cheap and, using web-based email providers such as Hotmail and Yahoo, accessible and usable on any computer connected to the Internet. These email accounts are free to use but limit the amount and size of files you can send. You will almost certainly be given an email account if you attend college, and increasingly these are available to use via any Internet connected computer, regardless of the physical boundaries of the college. There may be restrictions as to the number and size of files you can send; these will vary according to each institution.

A whole subculture has evolved around the use of email. While much of this 'netiquette' is – according to taste – simply fun or vaguely irritating, if you use email a lot, particularly on a formal or semi-formal basis, it is worth being aware of certain conventions. The most obvious of these is

DON'T USE CAPITAL LETTERS: IT LOOKS AS IF YOU ARE SHOUTING![9]

E-learning

The term 'e-learning' has come to mean any activity in which someone uses some form of ICT to help him or her learn. It began with the Open University in the 1960s, with televised lectures being broadcast in the small hours, and gradually progressed, as distance learning, by the 1980s, came to mean the sending of cassette recordings of lectures to students by post.

The rise of the Internet has caused a huge speeding up and development of this approach. Recent growth has been led by the government-funded *Learndirect* programme of vocationally focused learning materials. These materials are available via the Internet or CD for study at home, or in computer learning centres. In addition, the BBC website now houses a huge variety of free e-learning materials catering for both children and adults. All schools and public libraries now have Internet connections and e-learning plays a key role in plans for the development of curricula delivered in schools and colleges. Recently, for example, Sheffield College successfully developed an entirely online distance GCSE

English course. The pass rate for students in the first year was 100 per cent.

E-learning materials encompass a mixture of the written word, music and audio, video, animation, quizzes, games and a host of interactive techniques. Colleges are increasingly adopting these methods, both for students within the college precincts and, using email and video conferencing, to provide tutor support and group activities for students studying well away from the college. The time when you will be able to study what you want, where you want, when you want has, for many students, already arrived and many people, especially older people returning to learning after a number of years, find this flexible approach very appealing.

IV WHAT SHOULD WE CONCLUDE?

Quite simply, the time has almost arrived when it will no longer be possible to undertake any formal learning activity, whether it be GSCE, A level, degree or NVQ, without having comparatively sophisticated ICT skills. With these developments come new ways of learning, new teaching methods and new approaches to assessment. It is not an overstatement to speak of this as a revolution in the way education and learning operate.

If you are so inclined, of course, the technology offers short cuts to producing adequate work. For far less effort you can achieve much the same as previous generations of students. You can subject yourself to distractions, reasons to prevaricate and excuses for poor performance. But you will be missing out and you will soon be left far behind. Instead, invest some time to learn how to use the technology appropriately, looking for ways by which to do better rather than for lazy short cuts. Don't expend less effort but achieve more for the same amount of effort. Don't be distracted, but expand your horizons and increase the breadth of your experience.

For the imaginative student of today it is possible to use tools and resources undreamt of or unobtainable by previous generations. The Internet is now making available to all students resources that were once the preserve of the few; email makes it possible for a student to have direct and instant communication with experts, regardless of institution or location. Technology has never been cheaper, its application has never been more sophisticated and support in using it has never been more available than it is to the current generation of students. Moreover, in many ways the technological opportunities available to students are way ahead ofthose available to people working in industry. Students able to take full advantage of these possibilities in support of their studies will be in a position to be very successful players in the knowledge economy.

And, if all this sounds rather momentous or overwhelming, just remember that, above everything else, the main effect of all of this effort and activity is that it makes learning more *fun*!

For an 'ICT glossary' and a list of 'useful websites', please consult Appendix III (pages 218–21).

Chapter 5

Other sources and resources

> The mark of an educated man is that he's prepared to look things up.
>
> (Kingsley Amis)

Preliminary

I am very grateful to Jon Down for his authorship of the previous chapter, which I was simply inequipped to write, lacking the requisite knowledge and breadth of experience. And he has provided a wealth of authoritative information and advice about what has become the most exciting, wide-ranging and enabling tool of the student's trade. However, for all its immense potency, the PC is not the only resource you will need or find valuable. There are many other, non-electronic sources you can mine – including some human ones!

Kingsley Amis's remark above is as wise as it is humble, but the injunction 'look it up' is much easier said than done. Sometimes, I have to admit, it is the knee-jerk response of a tired, impatient or just ignorant teacher, and as such it is virtually useless as advice. For the obvious point is that no one can 'look something up' unless they first know *how* and *where* to do so. I hope this chapter, elementary in some ways though it is, will leave you better fitted for independent enquiry, and also confidently aware of how to use the full range of resources at your disposal.

I shall be looking at the following:

* reference books;
* libraries;
* bookshops;

- indexes;
- personal indexes;
- teachers.

Reference books

These are best divided into dictionaries and thesauruses on the one hand, and the remainder on the other.

Dictionaries and thesauruses

There is a profusion of such publications available nowadays, and most of them are first-class. But to derive proper benefit from a good dictionary, you've got to know *how* to use it, and that, as with so much else in study, means *thinking sensibly*.

Let's take an example. Suppose you need to find out exactly what the phrase 'professional foul' means. Even a good dictionary (for example, the *Concise Oxford*) will not necessarily spell it out for you, so you've got to think a bit. It isn't good enough to imagine that the two commonest meanings of the adjective – 'engaged in for money' or 'proper to one's profession' – can be applied in this case: to associate 'foul' with the first makes little sense, and to pair it with the second seems outrageously contradictory. The use cannot be grasped until the underlying concept has been at least partially understood – that the foul is committed because there is money or some kind of professional pride at stake. In other words, *both* those two meanings are involved, but dubiously entangled to make an act of cynicism seem somehow more forgivable.

Another example can be taken from a foreign language. It is remarkable how many able linguists commit absurdities to paper, because they haven't worked out what the English means first. Take the sentence:

He has ideas above his station.

The incautious linguist may well translate this as:

Il a des idées au-dessus de sa gare.

This well-known howler is ludicrous, of course. But note that it is not because the translator is poor at French (not necessarily, anyway): it's because not enough thought was given to the English metaphor in question. As a result, the distinct meanings of 'railway/bus halt' and 'social position' are ignored or conflated, with inevitably humiliating consequences.

So the best preliminary advice I can give you is this:

Use dictionaries with intelligence. They are not oracles or magic founts of wisdom: they are *tools* which must always be applied with care and thought.

Naturally, there will be times when your own intelligence, however well applied, is not enough. That is the time to ask – a teacher, a friend, anyone who might know the answer. But if you do keep your mind *in charge*, and not merely expect the dictionary to yield up its secrets like some verbal Slave of the Ring, you'll find the times when you need to ask will be getting fewer and fewer.

Much the same principle governs use of thesauruses – except that there you must be even more careful. A thesaurus, by definition, lists groups of words that have a broadly similar meaning. But it is a valuable aid only if you think very alertly about the possible differences between the words as well as their similarities. Consider, for example, these so-called 'synonyms' for the word *break*:

shatter   demolish   interrupt   crack   fracture

Yes, they all mean 'break'; but look at how idiotic these sentences are:

To make an omelette, first demolish four eggs. He interrupted his leg while ski-ing. We shattered our journey at a motorway cafe.

More seriously, there is a great difference between 'fracturing' a bone and 'shattering' it, or between 'cracking' one's knuckles and 'demolishing' them. Unless you work out beforehand some idea of the strength of word you require, a thesaurus will damage your work rather than help it. To begin with, you may need to use a dictionary in harness with it – admittedly a slow and irksome task. But if you're prepared to endure a little toil at the outset, you'll find that the thesaurus soon becomes a valuable and speedy friend, and not the hidden trap it can be to the non-thinking user.

Successful use of dictionaries and thesauruses hinges on intelligence rather than knowledge. Knowledge is your aim: that aim cannot be achieved unless you apply your intelligence. Of course, someone else can tell you; but someone else won't always be there when needed – and the sooner you apply your own thinking to the search for information, the happier you'll be.

Other reference books

Use of these is less snag-ridden than dictionaries and thesauruses, especially if they have a good index. I find that most students experience problems not so much in using these books as in knowing which one to go to in the first place. There isn't, perhaps, much that a book like this can do about such a problem: knowledge of the most suitable reference books for your particular purpose and subject is probably something you'll learn from your teacher and from the basic information included in your course. However, I can at least list a few admirable reference books that many students seem only vaguely aware of:

* *The Oxford 'Companion'* series: Covers a wide range of subjects. Entries are reliable, judicious and concise.
* *Oxford Specialist Dictionaries*: For example, *Etymology*, *Classical* and so on. Marvellous aids to the non-expert. Terminology and abbreviations take a while to become familiar, but information is clearly and helpfully set out.
* *Whitaker's Almanack*: A rich compendium of 'general' knowledge and information. It may seem eccentric if read through for any length of time – one jumps from anniversaries to maps to tide-times; but invaluable as a wide-ranging occasional helpmeet.
* *Fowler's English Usage*: Still the most authoritative guide to correct and elegant English.
* *Paperback subject-dictionaries*: There's a profusion of these around, of varying quality. In my own experience and opinion Penguin take some beating: I have found their *Art and Artists*, *Politics* and *Geography* issues (all areas where I need a lot of help!) invaluable. By no means comprehensive, but excellent as 'ignition'.

- *Dictionary of National Biography*: Not only full of fascinating factual information, but of great additional interest to history, politics, literature and divinity students, (especially) for the light it throws on the values and beliefs of the time of writing.

Productive use of reference books requires some understanding of how to use an index, which I go into shortly. As for how to find the right one for your needs on any given occasion: well, that will come in time, as you get used to using and broadening your knowledge of them. Meanwhile, teachers, librarians and perhaps most of all fellow-students can help you, and your command and familiarity will soon grow. For there is one delightful bonus about using good reference books: not only do you find the specific information you're seeking but you often learn or suddenly realize other things too. Thus regular and intelligent conference with such aids increases both your knowledge of profitable sources, and your knowledge and intelligence itself: you win on the swings *and* the roundabouts.

Libraries

A good library is a great deal more than a large collection of books and papers; and a librarian is much more than a person who stamps your books and bites into your loose change for late-return fines. Nearly all Senior Librarians are highly-trained graduates, and I have invariably found Chief Librarians to be extremely erudite and, above all, friendly.

The aim of those remarks is not to offer a free commercial for librarians but to point out that they like to be asked to help. Just like teachers, that is what they're paid for, and why they joined the profession in the first place. Nobody's going to die of excitement doing the obvious, mundane library chores: a student with an interesting research request is altogether more welcome. Even if staff can't help you directly, they will almost certainly be able to point you in the right direction, not least because nowadays libraries are fully computerised, with staggering amounts of information on tap.

All libraries will also have a clear and comprehensive index system, both under author and subject; most people, armed with either the name of the book or the author, should have no trouble finding out where the particular volume they need is located. It's also worth 'browsing' through a good index, just as one would browse in a bookshop. Very often you'll become aware not only of where the book you want is to be found, but of other, related books. It was in just such a way, for instance, that I first discovered that Henry Miller had written not only a number of outspoken novels but also a long essay on American life, *The Air Conditioned Nightmare*, which has some claim to be considered amongst his best work.

A library is also a rich storehouse of periodicals and academic papers, material that will eventually be important to any serious student. Indeed, in some subjects (particularly science) it could be said that, for a knowledge of the latest developments and thinking in a given area, periodicals and papers are your best bet. Many academic books comprise material first published in another form; in addition, to be marketable a book can't afford to be *too* far ahead of established thinking. Often an exciting new paper *changes* established thinking almost overnight, thus becoming highly marketable as a book (for example, Crick and Watson's wonderful work on DNA 50 years ago). So browse among the periodicals, too: you'll be delighted to find out how much you pick up.

Lastly, libraries are proverbial as sanctums of quiet in which one can work uninterruptedly. Personally, as I hinted early on in the book, I do not find such an atmosphere conducive to my best work. But many do find it exactly what they want, and if this is true of you, then you're fortunate. For in that case your library can serve you simultaneously as a study, a vast resource, a pleasant place to browse and a source of further enquiry. Perhaps best of all, most of them are free! A library is every student's friend, and if you can cultivate that attitude early on, your student life will be much nicer.

Bookshops

Much the same is true of bookshops as of libraries, but there are one or two additional points worth making.

The best thing about today's bookshops is that they too have been caught up in the computer revolution. Even a small book-shop in, say, a market town will have available a complete record of books in print, plus information about titles that are being reprinted and when they'll be available. That is not only a valuable information service: it means that books can be ordered for you more quickly than used to be the case.

The major benefit of this advance is that it has transformed bookshop assistants into instant mines of information. Gone are

the days when it was possible to encounter stunning ignorance in
even the most famous bookshops in the land.[1] An enquiry will be
answered with comprehensive accuracy within a few minutes: I've
even known bookshops work out from my muddled, half-digested
snippets of information which book I'm talking about, and where
I can get it most quickly (and cheaply).

Bookshops are, in any event, pleasant places to spend time. No
one minds you browsing – most shops encourage it – and it's thus
a good place to dip into books and start your knowledge of them,
even if it's months before you get round to buying and reading
them. And a last word on second-hand bookshops: it really is
amazing what you can pick up. Forgotten but good essays on an
area in your field not only make fascinating reading: they increase
your sense of the development and changes in that field, which
can only be good for your study and its own development.

Indexes

Using an index productively is more of a skill than might be imagined. Obviously, any old fool can look up, say, 'President Nixon' in
the index to a book on US politics, and establish where he is mentioned, or perhaps analysed in detail. But, rather like a reading-list,
you are at the mercy of the compiler. Many indexes are by no
means comprehensive: they simply list the major topics and names
covered – and this may mean that the precise thing you're after is
not mentioned. If this happens, it's unwise to assume at once that
the book doesn't contain what you want. Try another 'heading', or
even a third, before you move on to the next possible source.

Let's take an example, developing one I've just hinted at. We will
suppose you are researching the Watergate scandal in America in
the early 1970s. You look up 'Watergate' in the index, and find to
your dismay that it's only mentioned once. 'Not much use,' you say
to yourself, and prepare to find another book instead. But wait.
Maybe there's a lot of valuable material about the scandal in the
book you're about to discard. Try looking under 'President Nixon'.
Or under 'John Dean' (centrally involved in the whole business).
You might even try under '1972 presidential election' (which took
place just after the original Watergate burglary, from which the
whole scandal snowballed). In other words, don't give up on a book
until you've checked out all the information you've got against
the index.

You see, by the time you're ready to use an index, you'll know a fair bit about what you want to further your knowledge in. People who know nothing about a subject don't start by using the index: there's no point, because it won't mean anything to them. They'll have to read up about the subject a bit before they're in a position to narrow their focus of enquiry in such a way So when consulting an index, stay aware of all the information you've got. If, to take another example, you're working on F. Scott Fitzgerald, don't just try his name, but also 'American novelists'; 'Hollywood'; his various book-titles; even 'alcoholism'. I think you'll be surprised by how often the second or even the third entry that you consult turns out to be very profitable, when the apparently most obvious, first choice disappointed.

Indexes are also very useful tools for rapid cross-referencing. To return to President Nixon: most books about US politics in the 1960s and 1970s will have masses of material about him, and that will be reflected in a massive index entry under his name. If you're researching a particular aspect of his career, you'll need to check out other places in the index and establish a clear 'fix' on which part of the book has what you want. This method is analogous to direction-finding using three bearings, used to establish a precise location for a plane, a transmitter, or something more mundane like a church steeple or bench mark.

Sometimes, using an index can give you an early sense of whether the book is going to be reliable or not. To posit an absurd case: if you pick up a book entitled *Great English Painters* and the index contains no mention of Constable and only one reference to Turner, you can be pretty sure that the book is at the very least eccentric, if not fundamentally ignorant, even deranged. Such short-cuts are perfectly legitimate methods of coping with the vast amounts of potential reading available to you. An index, intelligently read, can establish clearly and revealingly what the author's major preoccupations are, and from that it may well be possible to work out the book's governing 'point of view'. Try out the index in this book, and see if I'm right!

Personal indexes

As I've stressed from the start of this book, there are as many ways of working successfully as there are students who succeed; so there is no need to feel that you *must* adopt some kind of 'personal index' system. To be perfectly frank, I don't use one myself: my mind works in other ways, and finds other methods quicker and more convenient, so I've never persevered with constructing one – there's never been any point. But I do know many students and colleagues who find an index system immensely time-saving and helpful to them; so here are a few basic tips about how to go about establishing one.

As with mnemonics (see Chapter 2, page 52), the precise format and method is entirely up to you, for you know your own rhythms and methods of organisation best. The most obvious overall method might seem to be alphabetical; but you might find you'd rather do it under topic headings or something else. Quite a lot will depend on what subject you're indexing. If it's history, a chronological approach might suit you best, whereas this method is unlikely to be a great help in literature or physics, say.

Although I don't use an index system in my 'day job' as a teacher, I do for all my other work, especially my writing on music. I now own about 8,000 LPs, tapes and CDs: in the past I used an alphabetical system to catalogue and store them, but at present I file classical records according to chronology and jazz under broad stylistic headings or according to instrument. This has a drawback, in that nobody else in the family knows where to find a given recording! But at least *I* know – and that, as with you and your study method, is the real point.

It's a matter of taste and temperament how large and inclusive you wish to make any such system. Some people just log important references (books and page numbers, for instance) that they know they'll want to find quickly and regularly; others extend their system to include summaries of their own essays, listed both chronologically and cross-referring to similar work done at another time. Such an advanced system takes time to compile, especially if you're starting from scratch. But if you find it tolerably enjoy-able, it can be very valuable, for two distinct reasons. First, once you've done it, you'll have a strongly organised, personally logical resource centre that is all your own, and you will rarely have to waste time hunting feverishly for something you know you've read/written but have forgotten where it is. Second, the very act of going over all your work and rearranging it into a new refer-ence system is a kind of intensive revision which will reinforce and probably clarify your knowledge. Even better, the process of systematising it all may well make you aware of connections that you hadn't thought of before, thus broadening and sharpening your knowledge all round.

In sum: you can use a personal index in any way you like, and include in it as much or as little as you wish. The best thing about such a system, be it computerised or compiled in longhand, is that you, and only you, are *in charge*: it is an index (ha ha) of your individual talent and independent mind.

If the information revolution of our time means anything profound – beyond the creation of a new technology and a shift in employment patterns – it is that students and academics of the future are going to be less crucially at the mercy of their memories. This does not, I hope, mean that my Chapters 2 and 3 are about to become redundant! But it is probably true that great success for future students will depend rather less than it used to on their having a super-power memory. Just as important are going to be good organisation and an efficient working knowledge of sources and resources. A remark by Dr Samuel Johnson is characteristically opposite:

> **Knowledge is of two kinds. We know a subject ourselves, or we know where we can find information upon it.**

And one of the best places to go introduces the last, and arguably the most precious, 'source and resource' of all.

Teachers and how to use them

The teacher–student partnership I: Introduction

I would like to think that few lessons anywhere are a complete waste of time – that is, of absolutely no value to every single individual present. Nevertheless, every student has at some time sat in a classroom bored rigid, thinking how much more progress s/he could make if alone. With the ever-growing range of textbooks available and the major increase in part-time and distance learning courses, it is possible to study virtually anything on your own. And indeed there are and always have been a few students who triumph as auto-didacts and who require little or no personal contact with or help from others.[2]

Nevertheless, for the great majority of advanced students

**Truly effective study hinges on a fruitful partner-
ship with one's teachers.**

The respective roles and tasks may differ, but the goal is identical:
your success. And the best chance of that happening is if student
and teacher work together in harmonious honesty and a direction
that is clear to each. In this respect, once again, *you are in charge*:
you need to make the best use of your teacher if s/he is to bring
out the best in you.

It is possible, yes, to master a subject without any kind of help
at all, but the chances are that when you have completed the
course, your knowledge will be less good than if you'd had a tutor
– worse in both quantity and quality of knowledge. For there are
two key advantages teachers have over textbooks:

1   They are flexible and can adapt to your particular needs and
    problems, which a book obviously cannot do.
2   Communication between two human beings is usually better
    – and almost certainly faster – than between a book and a
    human being.

If you genuinely do better on your own than under guidance from
teachers, it's either because you're exceptional or, more likely,
because you're not using teachers properly.[3]

The teacher–student partnership II: Understanding and asking

**'Hear and forget; see and remember; do and
understand.'**

The wisdom of that ancient Chinese proverb is as comprehensive
as it is timeless, and we can first apply it to *note-taking*. To get the
most out of a lesson, it is essential that you retain a *record* of it.
No matter how involved you may be with what emerges in class,
if you do no more than listen and orally contribute, you will in
all probability forget much of what was said by the following
morning, let alone the end of the year. So take regular notes.
Chapter 7 has some observations about how you can overdo this;

it also offers a variety of advice on methods, techniques and how to develop good practice (see pages 128–139). But, however you do it, furnish yourself with something you can *see*. Don't rely on your aural memory – it won't be enough.

Moreover, don't leave it at that. To become truly enlightening, your notes need to be revised and annotated further, preferably that very evening. Such a task will take very little time – maybe only ten minutes – and it won't just consolidate your understanding but will actually advance it. For you are now *in charge* of the information and knowledge which that lesson provided: you have not only progressed from *hear* to *see* but also to *do*. You have made the lesson yours.

That private revision of class notes is important in another way. It goes without saying that you must understand everything you study and note, and it is therefore vital to be honest with yourself about the term 'understand'. Only *you* know if you have truly understood something, when a problem suddenly resolves itself and the penny drops. And it is always preferable to work out any difficulties on your own if you can, away from the fairly intense rhythms of a lesson that is going well and stimulating a lot of response.

All that I've covered so far can be easier said than done. Understanding requires much thought; it can also take longer to dawn than the combined lesson-plus-evening-reflection time provides. Sometimes it does not dawn at all, and the material will need to be revisited later.[4] But no matter how frustrating the process can occasionally be, it is always worth trying to solve a problem yourself instead of merely being told how to do it – or, worse, having it done for you. Not only are you much more likely to remember it next time: you will also be much better prepared for the next step.

Nevertheless, there will be times when you find yourself well and truly stuck/fogged/stagnant, the prisoner of a problem that will not sort itself out. It is at this point that the way in which you use your teacher is crucial – so much so that it can be elevated into a governing principle:

If there is something you do not understand, you must ask – again and again if necessary – until you grasp it fully.

It is almost incredible how many students are prepared to sit in silent ignorance rather than admit to not understanding. What is the point of embarking upon a topic if you're not going to understand it? And what is the point of mutely implying understanding when you have no real idea of what is being talked about? To behave in such a way out of false pride (that most pitiful and damaging of qualities) is the only truly stupid thing a student can do. *Teachers are paid to be asked questions and to answer them.* There is only one thing that really annoys a good teacher, and that is outlined in this 'playlet':

Teacher:	Right. Does everyone understand that?
Class:	*Tacit*
Teacher:	Anyone at all unsure? I don't *mind* – I just need to know.
Class:	*Tacit*
Teacher:	Sure? *[Pause]* Okay, on to the next topic.

(ONE WEEK LATER)

Teacher:	Okay, we covered this last week satisfactorily, and you all understood it, so you shouldn't have any trouble. *[Pause as he sees blank/worried/bewildered/ panic-struck faces.]* What's the matter?
Brave student:	I don't understand this at all.
Other students:	Nor me / Or me / Me neither / What's it all about?
Teacher:	*AAAAAAARRRRRRRGGGGGGGHHHHHHH!!!!*

You can't blame him for screaming, can you? It's partly frustration: a whole week's work has just been shown to be wasted, since it's improbable that the students have understood succeeding lessons if they failed to grasp the original material. But it's mainly a bellow of rage at the sheer stupidity of remaining in silent ignorance when given a friendly opportunity to voice any doubts, problems, or gaps in understanding.

I hope I am always sympathetic to the shy student, and I do recognise how difficult it sometimes can be to admit ignorance and thus risk being 'shown up' in front of others. But if you want to learn, such a wallflower approach is a luxury you cannot afford. So ask your questions – as many and as often as you like. If they are serious and honest enquiries, no teacher will ever get impatient with you. On the contrary, s/he will be grateful – as invariably will the rest of the class – because

**No teacher can help you efficiently unless and
until s/he is aware of what you don't know and
don't understand.**

It's easy to preach to the converted, and even easier to teach the
already knowledgeable. There isn't, however, much point to it:
the teacher's chief function is to help you to master what you
didn't know before.

One last point about student questions. Teachers are themselves
learning as they teach, and questions and ideas from their students
often throw a new light on their subject. Good questions are a
delight to committed teachers: they stretch them, thus expanding
their own knowledge and awareness. So, far from worrying
whether you're being a pest when you raise a query, remind yourself that you are adding to your teachers' enjoyment of the lesson
and their overall insight.

I can summarise this sub-section and set up the next by
observing that the teacher–student partnership is very much 'a
two-way street'. You will greatly help your teachers, in all sorts of
ways, if you make the best use of them; that in turn will make
them more help to you.

The teacher–student partnership III: Teachers
as friends

Many clichés masquerading as wisdom annoy me, but this George
Bernard Shaw item comes very high on the list:

He who can, does; he who cannot, teaches.[5]

It's not just that it's insulting; implicit in it are two notions very
damaging to any student who chooses to regard the remark as
anything other than a faded, cheap witticism. The first is the impli-
cation that any old fool can teach, just like that; the second is the
suggestion that there's something intrinsically inadequate, even
sterile, about teaching as an activity. Those going along with either
sentiment stand little or no chance of getting the best use out of
their teachers, dangerously reducing from the outset their chances
of success and enjoyment.

Not everyone can teach: far from it. For a start, you have to
like children and/or their elder counterparts. No doubt there are

a few misanthropes infesting the odd staffroom here and there – people who dislike schools, students and all term hours between nine and four; they should be pitied as well as despised, because they must have a rotten life. In addition, you have to like your subject, and to know it properly: it is only a matter of time before an intelligent student will ask a question that requires more knowledge than what can be nervily mugged up the night before the lesson.

I stress all that for one reason only: it is essential that you regard your teachers as helpmeets, guides and friends. They are not gods; they are not infallible. Neither do they regard you as idiots, pests, or absolute disciples. They are a few teachers around, yes, who are bored by all students, and there are also a few others who have no interest or even competence in their subject. But there aren't many of either.[6] Most of them are skilled professionals who like what they do and regard it as important; moreover, like anyone with a set of skills, they enjoy using them well, and using their skills well means helping you to learn and grow. Very few good teachers are remotely envious: it is exciting to encounter a mind better than one's own and to help it develop. And once you realise that teachers are on your side, professionally committed to advancing you, and respectful of you as an individual, you will not only be well on the way to achieving the kind of profitable communication that is perhaps the chief benefit of being taught: you will – in a profound and entirely non-maudlin way – have made new friends.

The teacher–student partnership IV: What teachers cannot do

For a start, no one teacher can do it all, no matter how superb. Within their subjects teachers all have particular enthusiasms, fields of expertise, favourite areas; conversely, they all have certain blind spots and – let's not deny it – prejudices, and areas they know less well. This is inevitable and normal, and you shouldn't worry about it. You should, however, canvass other views and ideas whenever you can. Your teachers will encourage this anyway – and they mean it: it's not idle professional courtesy. These days, more and more courses use team-teaching (i.e. two teachers operating in tandem), or at any rate an element of pluralism. This is an enabling development, and you should look to extend it wherever possible. It is pleasing to be asked things by students other than one's own: most teachers are to some extent born show-offs, always happy to increase their audience!

You should also question other students; in the end you may learn more from each other than from your teachers. You all live the same problems and the same learning experience, and therefore share a language that is more immediate and more profound than that which you share with even the friendliest teacher. Read each other's essays; compare notes (literally and metaphorically); work on problems together. You will find it fun and extremely productive.

There is one thing no teacher can do for you, nor is there any reason why s/he should try: to make you *work*. Once you choose to do a course, it is no part of your various teachers' job to chase you for work that you're doing for yourself. If you cannot be bothered to do your assignments and you are not nagged about it, don't ask yourself what your teachers think they're doing, letting you get away with it. Instead, ask yourself what you think *you're* doing, not completing (or even starting) work you've made a free decision to undertake. The following 'gracious apology':

**I'm sorry I haven't done your essay, Dr Palmer, but
. . .**

is uniquely irritating, because:

It is not *my* essay: it is the *student's*.

To put it crudely, I get paid whether students do the work or not. While in the great majority of cases I enjoy reading the essays I mark, it would be overstating the case to suggest that a student essay undone leaves a dismal gap in my life. But it may well lead to a dismal gap in the *student's* progress and success – and that is a cause for sorrow as well as temporary irritation. Once again I must stress *you are in charge* – and that means responsibility as well as freedom.

Finally, however closely you work with your teachers, it is important to stay independent. Up to a point, you are of course dependent upon their skill, their knowledge, their breadth of understanding. Beyond that point, you must be careful to stay yourself. Somewhere along the line you will not see eye to eye with your teacher about an idea, an interpretation, a method.

When this happens it is, admittedly, disconcerting; but it is a good thing. Hardly any teachers are 'Jean Brodie' types. They are not interested in moulding students to an exact specification, and still less do they want their classes to comprise junior clones of themselves. They want you to learn, including and especially learning what *you* like, feel, and consider valuable. That awareness is one of the fundamental characteristics of the truly academic mind, and your teachers will welcome such disagreements and departures as signs that you are developing a mind of your own.

Summary

I've now been teaching for over a quarter of a century, and I still love it; I also continue to like being taught. Nobody is ever so 'mature' that they can't learn something new; one can go further and suggest that the seasoned adult who takes the view that 'You can't teach an old dog new tricks' is not so much mature as stagnating into cretinousness. The business of learning is a lifelong and on the whole delightful one.

Nevertheless, learning *is* a business: important though pleasure and inspirational revelation are, you also need a cool and cost-effective approach. Your teachers may become your friends – I very much hope they will; but first and foremost they are your key *resource*. They are there to be cultivated, tapped and mined in precisely the way that any sensible businessman nurtures a valuable commodity or investment. This may operate in the nicest possible way, but such warmth does not alter the basic truth that you must learn to use your teachers to your very best advantage. Nobody gets very far by being 'the teacher's pet', or by going along with George Bernard Shaw; students give teachers the most satisfaction when they exploit to the full what is on offer.

Part II

Skills and techniques

Introduction

So far in this book I have dealt with the fundamental aspects of study. The first five chapters have focused on approach and basic fact: how the mind works, finding the right attitude and working method, trusting your own instincts, and how best to use the resources at your disposal. By concentrating on how to start, how to adopt a working rhythm that is natural and pleasant, and how to keep in touch with your past work, I have tried to give you a sense of the *overall shape* of study. This feeling is essential to real efficiency and success. I hope by now you have an idea of how good your mind can be, and how much you are capable of. Above all, I hope I have convinced you that a sense of fun is not only possible but desirable: whatever your reasons for doing the course you will do much better if you enjoy yourself. A proper sense of vanity is conducive to all successful study!

It is now time to look in detail at specific skills. The next chapters offer systematic advice on how to take notes, how to plan essays, how to read quickly and efficiently; these are followed by a three-part consideration of examinations. But remember that, as with everything in this book, my ideas are advice, not orders. They are designed to help you, to give you something to think about and experiment with. They are not tablets of stone, so if you find that some of them don't work for you, don't worry: use that discovery and find something else that does. As always

You are in charge.

Chapter 6

Eyes right: Effective reading

Sir, do you read books *through*?

(Samuel Johnson)

Preliminary

Dr Johnson devoted his life to books, learning and words; it is therefore hardly likely that he intended the above remark to encourage mere dabbling in his own books or anyone else's. Quite the reverse: his incredulous question was inspired by the knowledge that if a book is at all worthwhile, it will both need and stimulate several visits.

It needs to be stressed at once that he was talking – as am I – about 'serious' reading rather than 'casual' reading for pleasure. To start at point A and go through to point Z is a perfectly viable way to read a good thriller or a holiday novel; one could argue that such works can only be read that way, partly because one rarely feels the need or desire to return to them. But the reading you do as part of your course is intensive and central – it is material that you have to absorb deeply, and learn. In those circumstances, to rely solely on that 'A to Z' method is rarely effective, chiefly because

> **If a course book is worth reading, it's worth reading twice; moreover, if you want to get something substantial out of it, it must be read at least twice, and probably a lot more.**

Your criterion is mastery, or at the very least intelligent digestion of a book's contents, in terms of both its main arguments and its details. That cannot be achieved at one go – not even in the case of brilliant students reading something they're instinctively and pleasurably drawn to. Indeed, this guiding principle has, I believe, the status of fact:

> **On any first reading, your chances of digesting more than 40 per cent are slim, regardless of the amount of time you spend on it.**

I shall return to that observation shortly. First, however, we need to be clear exactly what is meant here by 'read'. So let us begin by considering a few popular misconceptions about reading, especially those that have a bearing on 'slow readers'.

Six misconceptions

Misconception 1: 'It is essential to read every word'

Though not entirely untrue, this can all too easily become a recipe for painfully inefficient and dispiriting progress.

Like a number of ideas that are unhelpful to advanced study, the notion is a hangover from our primary school days. Please do not think that I am casting scorn on those ideas as such: they are right for the people they serve – young children acquiring completely new skills. A child learning to read must focus fully on each individual word: how else can s/he build a vocabulary and develop a functional sense of grammar?

But once you are into your teens, with a vocabulary that runs into five figures and a by-now automatic grasp of how sentences work, it makes no sense at all to abide by practices which are out of date for you. In the case of reading, this wouldn't matter if such methods were still useful, but they aren't. Consider, for example, this sentence:

> **The man in the wine-splattered raincoat tripped over the sleeping dog and crashed into the dustbins.**

No word is unfamiliar, and no vocabulary problem exists. It is not a difficult sentence: it describes two simple actions, and, though quite dramatic, makes no excessive demands on either our imagination or sense of logic.

However, if you are someone who 'reads every word', you're going to find that sentence fairly laborious: after all, it contains seventeen separate words. Now think of using such a method to read a 30-page chapter, bearing in mind that most books average about four hundred words a page! That is a daunting task: all those separate words – tens of thousands of them per half-hour session – will not only slow you up appallingly but also force you to work doubly hard reconstituting them into meaningful grammatical constructs.

If like most people you've received no instruction in reading since the age of 8, you may be growing somewhat puzzled. The key to what I'm talking about is

an understanding of the way the eye works.

To set up that enquiry, and to demonstrate why 'reading every word' is a poor method, let us consider another misconception.

Misconception 2: 'Fast reading is unnatural/bad for the eyes'

The human eye is an astonishing instrument, but it must focus in order to translate the image for the brain. To focus, it has to come to rest or fix on an object: it cannot track a moving object unless it is able to focus on each stage of movement. You can demonstrate this for yourself via a simple game with a couple of friends.

Get them to focus on your index finger, which you should at first hold in front of their faces at a comfortable distance. Then ask them to go on focusing as you move it slowly to one side and then the other, and watch their eye movement. You will see that it is possible for them to 'track' your finger movement only if they move their eyes at the same rate, constantly adjusting in order to maintain focus.

Words on a page are, of course, static; but, put together in the form of sentences and paragraphs, they occupy a breadth of space which requires the eye to move in order to absorb them all. The laws of its focusing powers, just described, mean that the eye must keep stopping, however briefly, to take in each separate static construct. More comforting is the fact that it has an extremely impressive rate of focusing. All human beings are capable of focusing on four things per second.

That means, if you 'read every word', you can take in four words per second. But that is the least you can do, not the most: there is no reason why each of those four foci per second cannot take in several words at a time. With nothing more gimmicky than alert concentration and a sense of how sentences are actually written, you can make your reading not only faster but much more efficient.

The forthcoming section addresses in detail how to bring that about; first, let's nail for ever the myth that fast reading damages the eyes, which is as worthless as the related old-wives' drivel about the harmful ocular effect of watching too much television.[1] The eye is, first and foremost, a muscle: like all muscles, it is the better for being used often and used efficiently. Speed-reading cannot increase your rate of focus beyond that optimum of four things per second; it can, however, greatly increase your breadth of focus, without putting any additional strain on the eyes whatever. Indeed, because it makes reading more enjoyable and more satisfying, it could be said to reduce eye-strain – if only because you can finish so much quicker and thus give your eyes an earlier rest.

Misconception 3: 'Very fast reading speeds are impossible'

It is said that the late President Kennedy could read state documents and official memoranda (items not noted for the elegance or easiness of their prose) at a speed of 1,200 words per minute. Most people – including the author of a book on reading – have pooh-poohed this as impossible, and concluded that such a spurious claim was the invention of Kennedy's image-building team.

Well, 1,200 words per minute (wpm) is a lot, I agree; but there is no reason to dismiss it as fantasy. I know several people whose reading speed is at least 1,000 wpm and many others who have trained themselves to go far beyond the 500 wpm that is popularly assumed to be the absolute 'ceiling'. How do they manage it?

Remember that sentence I gave you?

The man in the wine-splattered raincoat tripped over the sleeping dog and crashed against the dustbins.

Anyone determined to 'read every word' will, in effect, re-punctuate the sentence as follows:

The. man. in. the. wine. splattered. raincoat. tripped. over. the. sleeping. dog. and. crashed. against. the. dustbins.

That looks ridiculous, of course. But it's precisely what you're doing if you focus separately on each individual word – a method that is, I regret to say, exactly that of the toddler grappling with

The. cat. sat. on. the. mat.

Such a parallel is all the more humiliating when you remember that, unlike the toddler, you now possess a sophisticated sense of grammar. In other words, you know that sentences consist of words that build on each other and make sense as groups or sets. For that is what grammar is, finally – nothing more (nor less) than a system that enables and promotes clear understanding.

Not only is this impressively faster: it is also more intelligent. By reading concepts or intelligible groups of words rather than mere isolated nouns, verbs, adjectives and so on, you are immediately in tune with the writing's basic design and the logic of the writer's thoughts. Thus you will get the point of the writing much more quickly: in addition to the increase in speed with which you cover the text spatially, you are greatly accelerating your understanding.

To sum up: very fast reading speeds are not impossible. You can do wonders to your own speed once you learn to read in 'sets'; indeed, you can increase it sixfold:

• You will cover the print at – conservatively – three times the rate available to you if 'reading every word'.
• You will then double that speed by virtue of a much-improved conceptual grasp of the writing's direction.

To be sure, there will be times when the structure and vocabulary you encounter will be much more complex than the example I have used, and this will inevitably slow your rate down. Even at its least successful, however, I can promise you that the method I've outlined will make a dramatic difference. There is no reason why you should ever be a 'slow reader' again, no need to 'read every word' in a non-literate, plodding fashion. Speed reading is within everyone's capabilities; as an automatic corollary, so is speedier understanding. And for any casual reader, let alone the serious one, that is always the chief goal.

Misconception 4: 'Skip-reading is lazy and dishonest'

It depresses me how often I meet this attitude: it smacks of sterile puritanism, and also displays a basic ignorance of how people learn. Provided it is not the only method you adopt, and provided you do not imagine you can achieve full understanding by it, 'skip-reading' is a sensible and productive practice for any student who has a large reading load. Its charm and effectiveness are twofold:

1   It enables a useful preliminary reconnaissance of new material.
2   It supplies a welcome break from the kind of concentration required during more 'orthodox' or severe reading activity.

'Skip-reading' is a vague term that can mean all things to all men and all women. My use of it is fairly elastic, covering everything from a ten-minute flick through a 300-page volume to the more measured practice of ignoring the odd chapter. In short, I mean any kind of coverage that departs from the A to Z, read-right-through method.

The value of skip-reading is that it allows you to acquaint yourself quickly with aspects of a book and/or its essential territory. Under no circumstances should it be undertaken as a substitute for 'full' reading; as an accompaniment to it, however, it can prove very valuable as a consolidatory exercise or a launching one.

I stressed at the outset that any serious reading is going to have to be done at least twice. It makes sense, therefore, to make your first look at the material a brief and general one. If the volume/chapter/article has an introduction and/or interim summaries, read those first, as well as casting your eye over the rest of the material. This will help you to establish from the start a sense of what the stuff is about. In turn, that will make your eventual 'full' reading more knowledgeable, and thus more confident and alert.

Naturally, you don't *have* to do this. I find it works for me: perhaps it suits my temperament, or maybe it's just that I've always done it, and the habit is now an efficient one. I can also say that it's helped a lot of my students. But if you don't want to skip-read, preferring to get the laboriousness out of the way early on, that's fine: it's no part of my intention to impose unsuitable or disagreeable techniques on you. As I've emphasised from the very first page of this book, you are in charge, and what best pleases you will be your likeliest route to success. But do not despise skip-reading, or, even worse, cultivate a sense of guilt or moral disapproval over it. It is no more shameful than it is useless; and if you find it helpful, then go ahead and do it.

Misconception 5: 'I'd like to read more but don't have time'

I'm afraid that such a remark is, in at least 95 per cent of cases, pure drivel. Nearly all of us always have time to read more. If we don't do so, it's because we can't be bothered, or (more kindly) because we're too tired or sluggish to feel capable of taking on something as demanding as a book. This is normal and not in the least shameful, but it is an excuse, and as such is always suspect.

There are, it is true, some people who genuinely can't read as much or as often as they'd like to. The point is, though, that they are not students! Or, if they are, they must do something about such a time problem. Any advanced study demands a lot of reading – be it science, humanities, languages or more practical courses such as education diplomas or architecture. All the prospectuses I've ever read make this abundantly clear from the start, and if students find that their reading load is getting difficult to cope with, there are only two possible reasons.[2] Either:

1   They're reading unnaturally slowly.

or:

2   They're doing too many other things.

Any attempt to put the blame for your non-reading on your 'impossibly busy life' really won't do. If you're advised to read things for your course and you don't do so, it's *your* fault. 'I haven't had the time' is a classic euphemism for laziness.

Very few teachers or lecturers will give you a bad time if you trot out this stale piffle, because, frankly, they see no reason why they should chase you to do work you've taken on voluntarily. It's your problem, not theirs, and if you advance the absurd claim that you're so vitally occupied that you'd need a 28-hour day to accomplish all you've been advised to, you can't expect more than a weary grimace/grin in response!

Misconception 6: 'Slow reading facilitates memory'

In a way, I've already covered this in my look at the 'reading every word' syndrome. But the fallacy needs separate examination – partly because it seems so reasonable and wise that many can be seduced by it. We've seen, in Chapter 2, that the brain's natural (and therefore most efficient) span covers between 20 and 35 minutes (page 25). We have also seen that recall is usually instant or else not forthcoming at all. In view of this, it is hardly likely that a slow-moving attempt to commit things to memory is going to be more successful than one which is faster and more energetic. But we do not have to rely on such general logic: it can be demonstrated in a clear and concrete way.

Find two pieces of writing, about the same length. They should, ideally, be pieces you haven't read before, although something you've vaguely looked at once will suffice. Preferably, your two pieces should either be about the same subject, or else about two subjects that you feel equally comfortable with (or equally uncomfortable!). If you like, two separate pages or sections of this book will do very well. Then:

1   Read the first piece as slowly as is natural for you. Don't read it more than once; but don't go on to the next sentence until you're confident that you've understood the previous one.
2   Take a few minutes' break.
3   Now read the second piece as fast you can while retaining an intelligent sense of it. Look it over again, once and very quickly.
4   Take another few minutes' break.
5   Finally, get a piece of paper and write down all you can remember about Passage 1, and then about Passage 2 (if you prefer, get a friend/member of your family to 'test' you on each passage).

I would be very surprised if there is much difference between your two performances; moreover, I wouldn't be surprised if you did slightly better on Passage 2 than Passage 1. Most of all, I'd be amazed if the (say) five minutes you spent on Passage 1 resulted in you remembering five times as much of it as you did of Passage 2, which you read in a minute. For, to remind you of an earlier observation:

On any first reading, your chances of digesting more than 40 per cent are slim, regardless of the amount of time you spend on it.

If the material is at all stimulating, your mind needs some time and some room to come to terms with it.[3] You can *imagine* you've understood a sentence, but by the time you've read three or four more sentences, it is likely that, although you retain an *impression* of that sentence which is enough to enable you to understand the subsequent ones, your 'absolute recall' of it will already be partial. You will, with slow, methodical reading, acquire a sense of the overall shape of the material, plus some individual points and ideas. But you can achieve that kind of grasp with the much faster method I've outlined; so why waste time and energy? You're going to have to read all your study material again anyway, however slowly you cover it the first time. Doesn't it seem sensible to deal with the first stage as efficiently (i.e. quickly) as you can?

I wouldn't be writing this book, let alone this chapter, if I were unsympathetic to 'slow' readers. What I do want to banish is the idea that there is anything virtuous or intrinsically profitable about slow reading. As I hope I've demonstrated in principle, it is relatively easy to increase your reading speed. What stops people from trying is that they feel either suspicious of fast reading or cosily orthodox about the funereal rate they adopt, or both. Once you've escaped that trap, once you have acknowledged that slow reading is like a headache – not only does it have a clear cause, but it can be easily cured – you are ready to try experimenting with specific speed-reading techniques, three of which we turn to now.

Speed-reading techniques

'Digital tracking'

This method has been well known for some time, and it is quite straightforward, although not everyone will find it easy. What you do is this:

1 Take your index finger – it will probably help if the nail has not been bitten down to the quick! – and place it directly under the first word of the passage you are about to read.

2   Then read as fast as is comfortable, using the tip of your finger as a 'tracker' – as if it were underlining everything as you read.
3   Continue until you feel your concentration ebbing. Take a short rest, and then go on in the same way, taking rests as and when you wish.

The idea here is to intensify your focus and thereby your speed. Digital tracking increases your attention by physically targeting it, just as underlining or italicising words when writing draws attention to their importance and (presumably) makes them more memorable.

Many people have found this technique a great help, and it is certainly worth trying. I nevertheless have two reservations about it:

1   It can be extremely tiring – just as underlining whole chunks of prose soon becomes arduous. It requires considerable discipline – no bad thing in itself, of course – which can quickly take its toll. That is why my above description mentions the need to rest as soon as you feel the need.
2   Some people – myself included – find such finger-tracing irksome and distracting. For a start, you have to be digitally accurate, otherwise you simply cover up the lines rather than highlight them! More fundamentally, the physical act of tracking can cloud the cerebrum – that part of the brain that decodes signals and makes sense of (among other things) words. In short, the additional motor activity that tracking involves can blur focus rather than assist it.

No single speed-reading technique will work for everybody. If the above is the answer for you, excellent. If not, try this next, which was recommended to me by a very bright Malaysian student I met many years ago.

'The S-plan'

I admit in advance that at first sight this one seems seriously crazy! But try it: I can report that many have found it a remarkably effective method, although I ought to stress that it is best used during the first reading of material to be learnt. In addition, it is entirely unsuitable for the reading of novels, or indeed any kind of creative literature.

What you do is very simple – although, again, that does not mean it is easy! You fix your eye on the top right-hand corner of the page, and then allow your eye to sweep down the page in the rough form of the letter S:

I'll be surprised if you don't get the giggles the first couple of times you try this – I certainly did! But once you've settled down, you should find that a surprising amount of what you take in makes a lot of sense.

Let's assume you're reading a closely-argued article, or a chapter from an academic textbook. As your eye describes its snake-like 'S' pattern, a number of words or concepts are likely to come repeatedly into focus. If this happens – and on average it does so eight times out of ten – the probability is that those instances are *key words*, central to the concerns and arguments at issue (see Chapter 7 for more on this concept). Thus you stand a good chance of picking up a working idea of the territory and its main features – which is all you can sensibly hope for on any first reading. The advantage here is that it will have taken you about a quarter of the time a rapid 'full' read takes, with very similar levels of retention and overall awareness.

As I've just implied, there will be pages that are rendered mere gibberish by such a method – maybe up to 20 per cent. But the 'positive' figure of 80 per cent is not to be sneered at; in addition, as you get more experienced, you can widen the 'band' that the S incorporates, thus increasing the likelihood of hitting upon rapidly intelligible material.

The final 'plus' of this technique is that it's *fun* – hence those initial giggles. And as I've been advocating from the very beginning, anything in study that increases your sense of enjoyment is going to increase your chances of success.

Palmer's 6-point programme

This has nothing to do with the '6P Principle' I outlined earlier (page 32). Instead, it is a system which at its most successful enables you to read a passage six times more efficiently and also actually quicker than one A to Z reading. As with the S-plan outlined above, it is not suitable for any kind of creative literature. Advice on how to speed-read such works can be found in Appendix II (pages 210–12). Unlike the S-plan, however, the 6-point programme is useful at any time – the first reading, the second, and all subsequent ones right up to final revision. It is, I hope, tailor-made for mastering textbooks, discursive essays, articles, and all forms of coursework.

The programme is based on, or approximates, that delightful and apparently casual activity known as 'browsing'. If we pick up a book that looks interesting – in a bookshop, a library, a friend's house – the following behaviour-pattern occurs:

> **Just about the only thing we don't do is start at Page 1 and read from there. Instead, we read the blurbs on the back and inside covers; we look at the index; we flick through the pages once or twice, often stopping if a picture or diagram catches our eye.**

My programme extends that natural approach into a system.

Let us assume you have to read 30 pages of closely argued analysis (the subject matter is more or less immaterial). You:

1 Read the headings, subheadings and (where appropriate) chapter titles.
2 Read the introduction, the conclusion, and any interim summaries there may be.
3 Read/peruse any graphs, illustrations, diagrams and tables.

That will take five minutes at most, and in response to possible questions such as 'So what?' or 'Why bother?' I would observe that:

Those five minutes provide an immediate sense of the overall shape and focus of the material, sketching out the terrain you must later cover in detail.

The text is no longer alien: you are ready to do some real reading – something that is not actually true when and as you pick up the stuff for the first time. Then:

4   Read the first and last sentences of each paragraph.
5   Fill in the remaining gaps: that is, read it through now in the 'normal' A to Z fashion.
6   Review and clear problems.

Let's look at all six points in proper detail.

As noted, strands 1–3 make a virtue and a system out of everyday 'browsing' behaviour, making the initial reconnaissance less random and better focused. After these few minutes, you have acquired a grasp of the author's preoccupations, the direction of the argument, and the broad issues dealt with. You are now ready – and sensibly equipped – to dig deeper.

Point 4 is the oddest and most controversial. Some students have rebelled at it at first, arguing that 'fiddling around' with paragraphs in such a fashion actually wastes time, and is an irritating distraction. This can be the case, I agree; but, much more often, I have found it enormously useful. For if you overcome its initial strangeness, the practice offers two benefits: it is a fine concentration exercise, and it also feeds you a great deal of information at considerable speed.

How? Get hold of a paragraph. (Any will do, provided it's adequately written.) Read it through in an 'orthodox' way. If the writer has any idea what he's doing, you will see that it follows a logical, even predictable, pattern. A paragraph, after all, is an argument in miniature: it introduces a topic, explores it, and then draws a conclusion. So one can assume that if one reads the beginning and end of such a paragraph, it should be possible to make at least an 'educated guess' at the content and direction of the material in between.

That's how the 'fourth strand' of the programme works. Provided you concentrate hard, and are not tempted to scan anything but those first and last sentences, your mind will automatically be drawing inferences and filling in the gaps for itself. So you can flit from paragraph to paragraph at high speed, while your brain estimates the likely nature of what you're missing out.

Of course, there will be times when those 'educated guesses' are inaccurate. At this stage in your reading, you are only getting to know the material, not mastering it, and it's inevitable that you will sometimes fail to take account of a point that appears in the middle. But even that is a help: the surprise you will feel at the subsequent discovery shows how far you've progressed already. For, even before arriving at point 5, where you read the text 'normally', you are now reading it critically. That is, you are reading with certain expectations, a sense of where the writer is going and the 'stops' s/he will be visiting along the way. Encountering an unscheduled (= 'unguessed') stop will be beneficial either way: the writer's detour may be fruitful, or it may be unjustified. Whatever the case, your understanding of the material will have been considerably increased.

I should add, finally, that this technique cannot always be used – for the simple reason that some authors produce paragraphs that only have two sentences altogether! Stinginess of this kind is not neccessarily bad writing: I've seen several excellent science textbooks that use such a method to aid clarity. Usually, though, good professional authors organise their paragraphs in a standard fashion, and that means you should be able to pursue point 4 without undue trouble.

Point 5, as already outlined, restores you at last to the normal A to Z method of reading. But there's a big difference from those times when you have adopted that procedure from the very start. Now you have a strong sense of what you're about to read. This not only means that you will cover the ground much faster: it also means that the various points and ideas will register much more definitely. Furthermore, there's an important by-product: you will enjoy the 'full read' much more. Your confidence will be higher because you know what the stuff is about, and you will also find it pleasant to have a dialogue with the text rather than have to plough submissively through it.

Point 6 is a kind of 'mopping-up operation'. The first five readings should ensure an impressive rate of absorption, but there will be gaps, especially if this is the first session you've had on the material. Now you should read it through again (A–Z style), actively looking for anything you've missed altogether or remain somewhat hazy about.

Using this method, you will spend less time than you would on a once-through 'standard' read. You will still need to return to the material again at some stage, probably more than once; but you will have given yourself an efficient start that will make all future reading more agreeable.

I cannot claim that this system works for everyone, although I can say that it has proved a considerable help to over half the students I've given it to over the years. As implied earlier, some people find Point 4 more trouble than it's worth, and prefer to 'double up' Point 5 – i.e. read the whole thing through twice in an orthodox fashion. However, even when it proves less than fully successful, or even a failure, one benefit almost invariably accrues – a belief that speed-reading is possible, and that a personally suitable technique can be found somewhere or invented some way. As with everything else, you are in charge: if you want to read faster, you will eventually hit upon a productive way of doing so.

As a final incentive, let's take a look at an experience that often characterises the first reading of a textbook chapter. If you're an 'orthodox' or 'normal' reader, I'll be very surprised if you don't recognise this little scenario.

You pick up the book, find the chapter at issue and start reading. All may be well for a while; but by the time you're into the second page, things are getting rather foggy. You struggle on, reach the end of the page – and then, suddenly, you realise about half-way down your third page that you've hardly taken in a thing. Not only have you lost your way: you can't even remember what territory you're in or what the map suggested.

Familiar, is it? Well, be comforted: it happens to every reader sooner or later, and quite frequently too if we're not careful. But it is a dispiriting and energy-sapping phenomenon that is trebly annoying:

1   You've utterly wasted the first five or ten minutes of your study session – all the more galling in that such a time should find you at your freshest and most alert.
2   You will have to do it again – which almost feels like a punishment for 'bad work'.
3   You will feel stupid and inefficient – hardly conducive to the confidence that underscores successful study.

Point 3 is an over-reaction: such an irritating episode does not prove that you're a slow-witted dolt. It is the *system* that is at fault, not your brain: the only stupid thing you've done is adopt such a method in the first place. Much better to use any of the 'skimming' methods outlined earlier, using those first ten minutes to acquaint yourself with the general shape and outstanding features of the material. You will benefit twice over – by making an efficient and confidence-boosting start, and by avoiding all the 'negative waves' that I've just diagnosed!

Summary: Speed-reading and prejudice

A great many people are suspicious of speed-reading theories: I was myself for quite some time. My dislike sprang from those gimmicky and fatuous advertisements that still leer at us from newspapers, whose hard-sell cannot long disguise the inadequacy of the techniques advocated. It wasn't until I read some sensible and honest work on the subject that I was persuaded that anyone can learn to read fast and efficiently and that it's very important to acquire that skill. In conclusion, here's a list of 'key findings'.

1   Surprisingly, moral prejudice has a lot to do with people's suspicions. They regard reading as a serious, even 'holy' activity, and therefore they resist the idea that it can or should be made easier. That attitude has a certain naive charm, but finally it is just silly. If you take books seriously, you surely want to get as much out of them as you can, and in view of that, to imagine that there is one 'correct' way of reading is no more sensible than to fancy that there is a 'correct' way of working. It's just you and the book: nobody else and nothing else count.

2   Speed-reading is physically good for you, whatever old wives may say. The more vigorously and efficiently you use your eyes, the fitter they will be. They will get much more tired if they plod laboriously through a text that the brain finds opaque and joyless.

3   The notion that speed and glibness are somehow synonymous is damaging and false. Ponderous people are rarely bright or interesting: might it not be that their dull superficiality is the *result* of their slowness, rather than the paradox it seems?

4   The brain and the memory work awesomely fast; they also work best for comparatively short periods of time. The more you can do during that time, the more likely you are to retain it. Time and again, our experience shows that it is not necessarily the

people who take the longest over a task who do it best, but those who approach it with energy, enjoyment and a brisk clarity of purpose.

5   Serious reading of any kind is a gradual process, in the sense that full understanding can never be immediate. Speed-reading acknowledges this more sensibly than the narrowly dogged approach. Anything worth while requires several readings before it can be mastered: the decision to make most of them as rapid and pleasant as possible is not a dishonest short-cut but a properly intelligent way of bringing that moment forward.

6   There is nothing virtuous about being a slow reader; more important, there is nothing natural about it either. Slow readers are slow because they lack sufficient understanding both of the material itself and of how eye and brain work best, because they've been poorly trained, because they are imprisoned by certain silly myths, or through a mixture of all those things. If you want to read faster, you can; and I can promise you that you'll enjoy the activity more.

7   Books are going to remain centrally important to our culture in general and student life in particular, whatever further developments there will be in computing, information technology, email and and all the rest of it. Because those latter phenomena have acquired such currency and appeal, however, the skills involved in reading have become, if not sidelined, less high-profile than a generation ago; I would certainly say that students nowadays have an even slower 'orthodox' reading speed than pertained when I first became interested in speed-reading a quarter of century ago. That is not, of course, to argue that today's young are any less bright or diligent than their forebears, but it does suggest that efficient and discerning reading is perhaps a more crucial skill than ever before. In any event, I would argue even more fiercely than I did in this book's original incarnation that:

You will almost certainly need a speed-reading technique that suits you if you are going to cope with your reading load, let alone achieve anything approaching mastery.

I hope the ideas and techniques I've covered go some way to helping you do that.

Chapter 7

Creative doodling
Note-taking for fun and profit

> Notes are often necessary, but they are necessary evils.
>
> (Samuel Johnson)

Preliminary

Very few students, I find, are given early, systematic advice on how to take notes. Some manage to develop a technique that is sound and helpful, but the majority are less fortunate. As a result, their approach to note-taking describes one of two equally unsatisfactory alternatives: the 'grudging' or the 'evangelist'. See if you recognise yourself in either of these portraits.

The grudging note-takers

These students regard note-taking as a pain. They'd go along with Johnson's remarks, except to find him far too tolerant in calling the practice 'necessary'. They buckle down to it eventually, but they neither enjoy it nor find any value or stimulus in what is always and only a mechanical chore. In addition, their method and format are identical to any 'class notes' their teachers may dictate – cautiously and clearly spaced, written in formally correct English, and taking a long, joyless time to complete.

The evangelist note-takers

For these students, note-taking is the magic elixir. They are convinced that all they need do is write everything down, and it will through simple alchemy become fixed knowledge. Their reverence is further demonstrated by their view of the printed word, and of the spoken word of teachers: they are the academic equivalent of the Eucharist, profoundly present as soon as experienced, an automatic and immediate source of strength and wondrous new knowledge.

Such enthusiasm is so uncritical that it becomes self-cancelling at best and a serious impediment at worst. The average student who encounters a joke while reading will laugh; the Evangelist will instead write *'Humour'* in the margin. Such solemn mania can reach alarming proportions, as demonstrated by this anecdote of a colleague:

> I went into the Lower Sixth this morning and said, 'Hello.' Three of them sneered at me, four of them said 'Hello' back, and the other five wrote it down in case they missed anything.

An exaggeration, naturally, but most students, and nearly all teachers, will recognise its essential authenticity.

This reverential approach is *doubly* inefficient, too:

If you attempt to note down *everything*, how can you possibly *listen* properly?

There is a fair chance that, as you write a note, you will be deaf to a remark or point that is more important – and such damage will be repeated and cumulative.

Both 'types' waste nearly all the time they devote to note taking. Grudgers do it under protest, thus deriving little value; Evangelists, over-active and lacking all discrimination, end up with a garbled, non-understood record of the book or the lesson. And both methods fail because no thought has gone into the vital question of *why* we take notes. It is that issue I look at first.

Methods and practice I: Basic strategies and methods

The primary thing to emphasise is:

All notes that are not accompanied by solid understanding are useless.

Unless you have a reasonable idea of what the material you're studying *means*, how can you make useful, intelligible notes on it?[1]

Yet time after time students will, at the start of a lecture, a lesson, or a TV programme, at once launch themselves into a frenzy of scribbling – long before the focus of the argument has been established.

Such a frantic approach is understandable up to a point. One's aural memory can be very short-lived, especially when listening to something as condensed as a lecture, and one is invariably anxious to trap an idea before it evaporates. Even so, it is much more sensible just to

> **listen for a while without simultaneously attempting to record.**

Trying to do two highly intensive things early on can be distracting and unproductive; better to get into the topic first and thus feel comfortable with it when you do start to take notes. All but the most abjectly bad lectures and classes usually ease into their topic in a complementary fashion, announcing their main concerns in advance and repeating each one as and when it is arrived at. So take in the main topics at the beginning, and write only when you reach them later.

The next point to be made is if anything even more vital:

> **Notes are for *you*, nobody else. They are triggers and aids for your private use, and have no status whatever as public documents.**

I stress this so forcefully because a lot of students imagine, when taking notes, that they must present them as if they were going to be *marked*. This is ridiculous. Your notes should not in any way be confused with the class notes your teachers dictate.

- Your notes are both part of your thinking and a reflection of it, done as part of the preparation for a piece of work or as a record and reminder of your reading and research.
- Class notes, though of course valuable, are quite different. The result of months or years of study and teaching, they are as formal as the textbooks you study, and a significant part of your course material.

This means, among other things, that if you want to make your own *private* notes on them, you should feel encouraged to do so – it is an excellent idea.

Now to *methods*. The taking of rough notes is as individual a matter as any other working method: as always, the only criterion is whether it is successful. You will recall what I said in Chapter 1 about working to music, and the many so-called 'distractions' which students often feel they must deny themselves while working. The same is true of note-taking. There is no 'right' way, other than what works for you.

So do your notes *in any way you like*. If it helps you to do them in alternate green and purple biro, do them like that; if you like weaving patterns or funny shapes with them, go ahead; and if it helps and amuses you to do them in a kind of secret code that you can understand easily, that's fine too. The more you can make taking notes a natural and pleasurable exercise, the more vigorously they will assist your study. That is why this chapter is called 'Creative doodling': if you can make note-taking as automatic and 'un-work-like' as the doodles you do when on the phone or listening in class, you'll soon find that you are adding to your knowledge and skills while remaining relaxed and all-but-unaware of 'working'.

For anyone still unsure about what other methods can be adopted in lieu of formal, 'public' notes, and for those 'grudging' and 'evangelist' types in particular, I now look at some specific techniques.

Methods and practice II: Key words

It is a useful metaphor to consider a book, or even a chapter, as a living body. Its basic structure is analogous to a skeleton, and its major points to the vital organs. Other things, which give the work its distinctiveness, are like the flesh and the idiosyncratic features which make us all different from each other.

'Key word noting' is best explained with that metaphor is mind. It aims to isolate the skeleton and the major organs of an argument/episode by focusing on those words or phrases which are clearly central. And I do mean 'clearly'. With a little practice, it ought to be fairly easy for you to register the main drift of a piece of writing, and to see which words and concepts are the vital ones. The added strength of this technique is that it should also be *very fast* – not only saving you time but giving you early, controlling access to the material and so boosting your confidence.

Let us look at an example. I would imagine that most of you are vaguely familiar with Christ's parable of the Sower, but in any event please read the slightly edited version that appears below. I would say that the story hinges on just *seven key words* or concepts. See if you can boil it down in that way, and then check with my list overleaf.

The parable of the sower

1 A sower went out to sow his seed: and as he sowed, some fell by the way side; and it was trodden down, and the fowls of the air devoured it.

2 And some fell upon a rock; and as soon as it was sprung up, it withered away, because it lacked moisture.

3 And some fell among thorns; and the thorns sprang up with it, and choked it.

4 And the other fell on good ground, and sprang up, and bare fruit an hundredfold . . .

5 And his disciples asked him, saying, What might this parable be?

6 . . . [*And Jesus answered*] The seed is the word of God.

7 Those by the way side are those that hear; then cometh the devil, and taketh away the word out of their hearts, lest they should believe and be saved.

8 They on the rock are they which, when they hear, receive the word with joy; and these have no root, which for a while believe and in the time of temptation fall away.

9 And that which fell among thorns are they which, when they have heard, go forth, and are choked with the cares and riches and pleasures of this life, and bring no fruit to perfection.

10 But that on the good ground are they which in an honest and good heart, having heard the word, keep it, and bring forth fruit with patience.

St Luke's Gospel, Chapter 8, vv 5–15; *A.V.* 1611 (edited)

Key words:

seed
fowls

rock
thorns
good ground
sower/God

Those seven key words form a skeleton of the parable. They should be all you need to put together a comprehensive and chronologically accurate version of the story itself and its allegorical meaning.

If, however, you'd feel a little easier with a skeleton that has been a little more fleshed-out, you could add to it as follows:

Seed/the Word of God

fowls seed is devoured/the Word is stolen by Satan
thorns seed chokes/the Word is snared
rock no depth for the roots/the Word cannot 'sink in'
good-ground seed takes hold/the Word is fruitfully absorbed
Sower/God spreads the seed/God spreads the Word

All the other details can be recalled if you have either of the above lists as your base. The only other thing you need to produce an authoritative paraphrase of the tale is the ability to write adequate sentences. Incidentally, the listing of key words in this way is also an admirable method for essay planning, as we'll see in the next chapter.

That first example was an easy one, because the story is so familiar. But the principle holds good for more complex, less comfortable material. I am now going to give you distinct paragraphs, whose gist I think you can pick up remarkably quickly, using the 'key word' method outlined.

Developing key-word noting skills

Passage 1

Here is George Orwell writing about the recent (1946) decline in the use of the English language. Pick out the 'key words' – write them down, or just ring them on the page. You should not have to read the passage more than twice, and the exercise should take three minutes at the most.

It is clear that the decline of a language must ultimately have political and economic causes: it is not due simply to the bad influence of this or that individual writer. But an effect can become a cause, reinforcing the original cause. A man may take to drink because he feels himself to be a failure, and then fail more completely because he drinks. It is rather the same thing that is happening to the English language. It becomes ugly and slovenly because our thoughts are foolish; but the slovenliness of our language makes it easier for us to have foolish thoughts. The point is that the process is reversible. Modern English is full of bad habits which spread by imitation, and which can be avoided if one is willing to take the necessary trouble. If one gets rid of these habits one can think more clearly, and to think more clearly is a necessary first step towards political regeneration.

(Adapted from 'Politics and the English Language')[2]

The secret of the 'key word' method is not to have too many. This can be quite tricky to stick to, for if the writing is good, the prose will be muscular, wasting few words in 'flab'. That means that many words will be doing a fair bit of work, which can make the task of deciding on their immediate relative importance quite hard. Anyway, here's my list – see how it compares with yours:

decline
language
political and economic causes
slovenliness
foolish thoughts
habits
imitation
reversible
think clearly

There are just nine concepts here, involving fourteen words. Plenty of Orwell's argument is absent, including the excellent analogy of the man who drinks. But if those words were underlined, ringed, or written down as I have done, they would form a pretty sound skeleton of the passage. Put another way, they provide nine reliable 'triggers' that soon detonate understanding and retention of the passage as a whole.

Passage 2

This one is harder, I think – mainly because the author defines his central concern, 'totalitarianism', in a way that is far removed from our normal understanding of the word. So be on your guard; and remember that at this stage it doesn't matter whether you agree with him or not – just try to get the shape of his argument. Again, read it through twice, quite quickly, and choose the 'key words' or key concepts.

> Totalitarianism has slipped into America with no specific political face. There are liberals who are totalitarian, and conservatives, radicals, rightists, fanatics, hordes of the well-adjusted. Totalitarianism has come to America with no concentration camps and no need for them, no political parties and no desire for new parties, no, totalitarianism has slipped into the body cells and psyche of each of us. It has been transported, modified, codified, and inserted into each one of us by way of the popular arts, the social crafts, the political crafts, and the corporate techniques. It resides in the taste of frozen food, the odour of tranquilisers, the planned obsolescence of automobiles, the lack of workmanship in the mass; it is heard in the jargon of educators; it lives in the boredom of a good mind, in the sexual excess of lovers who love each other into apathy. And it proliferates in that new architecture that rests like an incubus upon the American landscape. The essence of totalitarianism is that it beheads. It beheads individuality, variety, dissent, romantic faith, it blinds vision, deadens instinct, it obliterates the past. Totalitarianism is a cancer within the body of history, and (as such) obliterates distinctions.
>
> (Adapted from 'Totalitarianism', by Norman Mailer)[3]

The trouble with this passage is not only is it densely written, as was Orwell's, but that most of it is example or illustration. These may be fascinating, but they are not 'key concepts', as anyone schooled in that old-fashioned exercise of precis will remember. Again, compare your list with mine:

totalitarianism
America
no political face
incubus

beheads
cancer
body of history
obliterates distinctions

You will see that all my choices come from either the beginning or the end of the passage. There are two reasons for this:

1   The brain/memory tends to work that way in a piece of inten-
    sive work of this kind – as we've observed (see pages 25 and
    27ff).
2   The author's argument happens in this instance to be designed
    in such a fashion. The middle section develops, illustrates and
    explores an arresting opening statement, which is then
    summarised or confirmed in a number of dramatic definitions.

You may be surprised at the inclusion of 'incubus' – and to be honest, I nearly missed it when preparing the exercise. But, if one thinks for a moment – and this exercise *depends* on one thinking while reading and noting – it is a vital word in the passage, from a number of angles. It evokes sorcery, something insidious, some-thing invisible – all of them ideas that absolutely match the author's theory that totalitarianism has taken major root in America without many being aware of it. It also, of course, suggests some-thing satanic and destructive, which thus establishes in addition the author's prime *value judgement*.

My other choices are, I think, more straightforward. Together, they offer a bald but comprehensible 'map' of the tone and topics of the argument. And again, each word or concept can be seen as a 'trigger' – a means of recalling and organising the direction and overall focus of the passage.

Timing and duration

Key word noting is a highly intensive activity. You'll be only too well aware of that fact if you've just tried to do both the above paragraphs at one go. Indeed, one of the reasons why the Mailer was tougher than the Orwell was precisely because it followed it: you may have acquired a better grasp of the technique by then, but it may have been cancelled out by the fatigue your brain was beginning to feel.

This is entirely normal, and as it should be. Early on in this book we noted that, regardless of the intelligence level of the activity undertaken, the brain performs best for about 20 to 35 minutes at a time. When the activity is as intensive as key word noting, it's to be expected that the brain will want to settle for the lower end of that span rather than the upper. So don't try to do too much in one session; and try to be in a relaxed and comfortable frame of mind when tackling the practice. Key word noting is a form of mental sprinting. The brain is asked to do a lot of work very fast; and, like a physical sprinter, it will perform best if it's nicely 'warmed up' and aware that it will be able to stop soon.

Methods and practice III: Inventing codes and shorthand

I've already stressed that your private notes are for you alone. So it is both sensible and stimulating to adopt any method of abbreviation that suits you.

There are, of course, several established shorthand systems – Pitman's is probably the most famous. If you've been trained in one of these, that's fine. But if you haven't, you can construct your own with a little basic ingenuity. As with the advice I gave on mnemonics, I believe it is better if I *don't* give you much illustration or offer you my own methods – not because I'm possessive about them, but because there's no reason to suppose that because they suit me they will suit you. However, by way of ignition:

1   Use contractions and single-letter abbreviations wherever possible. In an essay it looks both ugly and lazy to refer to, say, Shakespeare's *Henry IV Part Two* as H4ii) but in your private notes such a form is admirable, being both clear and quick.
2   More ambitiously, try to work out a rapid number-reference system, where each digit represents a particular book/chapter/paragraph/whatever. This is particularly useful, because in addition to highlighting specific areas of work, it organises and clarifies your brain's 'filing system' generally.
3   As with mnemonics, the more you can make a game out of time-saving and mind-clarifying methods, the better.
4   I emphasised earlier the potential value of 'doodling'. If you doodle naturally and unconsciously (and most of us do), you

may find it worth while to harness such a practice to conscious, concentrated work. No matter if the alleged 'pattern' looks gibberish to everyone else: you're the only judge that matters. And if you can both have some fun doing this and record things of value, you'll find that the sense of doing 'conscious, concentrated work' fades rapidly, leaving you with the most agreeable feeling of doodling for fun and profit.

Any method that gets you out of the rut of linear, carefully logical response should at least be tried; I'll be surprised if you don't find it valuable. By broadening your approach, such methods broaden your thinking – with the frequent result that you hit upon ideas and a level of understanding that would have remained closed to you under a more 'formal' or allegedly 'correct' method.

Note-taking at different stages

I want finally to emphasise that note-taking is a constant, *fluid* process. Creative note-taking – i.e. for your own benefit – can and should happen at any and all stages of a piece of work. It is worth listing those stages, for many students do not use them all.

1   During initial reading (but probably best omitted during the introduction of a lecture).
2   During confirmatory and developmental second reading, and during the rest of the lecture.
3   Before writing the essay.
4   After writing the essay/attending the lecture. A vital one, this, and one which even conscientious students too often omit.
5   At any subsequent stage where review of existing notes prompts a new, further thought.
6   During final revision, as both a clarifying aid and an ego-boosting demonstration that you do, after all, know/remember quite a lot!

None of these need take much time – especially points 2, 5 and 6. They should, in fact, take precisely as much time, and be done in precisely the form, that you like.[4] Clearly, when using the key word method, your job will be easier on points 2 and 6 than on point 1, since on those occasions the spotting of the key words will be confirmatory rather than identifying.

Summary

Good note-taking is a hugely valuable skill for any student, combining the recording of useful information with alert thinking. Provided these two criteria are met, it doesn't matter a jot how you do them, what they look like, or what use you put them to in the end. Some of your notes will become redundant before the end of your course: this is not proof of wasted time, but instead is the clearest and happiest indication that you've grown beyond them – a process in which they played a vital, albeit temporary part. For, to return to the two 'types' I sketched at the start, you should not 'grudge' the time spent taking notes, nor assume an attitude of 'reverence' about the activity. If you approach note-taking as a task solely for your benefit, you won't ever grudge the time, especially if you liberate yourself enough to employ methods which are lively and amusing. And if you remain alert and genuinely thoughtful, reverence won't be possible: you'll be discriminating and questioning as you note, and will thus move forward in your study far more commandingly. Notes are 'necessary', yes; but, thanks to methods and knowledge that Dr Johnson did not have available to him, there is no need to share his view of them as 'evils'. Nor, indeed, is there any excuse for doing so.

Postscript

The next chapter has a section entitled *Energizing patterns*, which describes techniques that are also useful for note-taking. See pages 145–9.

Chapter 8

Crunch time: Essay planning and writing

> When the day of judgment comes, we shall not be asked what we have read, but what we have done.
>
> (Thomas à Kempis)

Preliminary: Fundamental considerations

However seriously you take your study, the headline quotation is a touch melodramatic. Nevertheless, all proportion being kept, its doom-laden message corresponds to the feeling many students experience when they come to write an essay. It's a moment they dread: they are about to put their work and knowledge on the line, and such exposure cannot be put off any longer.

I am very sympathetic to this feeling – the more so since, to our shame, teachers rarely offer any systematic, fear-allaying advice on the matter. In trying to provide some such help, I want to stress one important point at once:

> **Just as there are different stages in and kinds of note-taking, there are various *types* of essay, each with its own purpose and value.**

In any course, you will write a good many essays.[1] It should be self-evident that they will differ in nature: it would be absurd to expect to produce the same kind of essay at the beginning of a course as those which you do at the end, including the exam. And I'm talking less about a difference in quality than in *type*. Obviously, if your later essays *aren't* better, more assured, tighter and more knowledgeable than your earliest efforts, then something is wrong! No: I have in mind a 'horses for courses' approach, hinging on the need to

tailor your essay to what you most need it to accomplish *at this particular stage of your study*.

Let's specify an example and look at it in detail. Imagine you've been set your first essay of the year. You've covered the work in class and in private; you've read a good deal of the requisite material; you've made various notes; you've allowed time for the ideas to filter through and become tolerably familiar. Now you've got to write about it.

The essential first question to ask yourself is, '*Why?*', or more precisely:

'What am I doing this essay for?'

A number of answers may occur to you, facetious and serious alike:

1 Because we are not brought into life for pleasure alone.
2 Because teachers needs some evidence that they've done the work with, on and for you, and that they're not being paid under false pretences.
3 Because teachers needs some evidence that *you've* done the work.
4 Because you need to find out just how much of the aforesaid work you really do know and understand.
5 Because until you commit yourself to some kind of 'test' on what you've studied, it will be difficult to go on serenely to anything new.
6 Because it's a uniquely profound and naked way of digging into a subject. As someone once said, 'How can I know what I think until I've seen what I say?'

Point 1 is a joke (that's the idea, anyway), and 2 is no more than half-serious – although you'd be surprised how many teachers do feel under such pressure from time to time. Points 3 and 4 are straightforward enough; 5 is less so, but many students will, I'm sure, recognise its importance. Point 6 is rarely thought of by anyone.

Yet point 6 is undoubtedly the most important. It not only – and most obviously – applies to the *start* of a course: it remains a governing truth right up to the time when your chief task is to hone all your past work preparatory to the final exam or submission. For that reason it deserves a sub-section to itself.

The 'exploratory essay'

For at least half any given course, essays are not so much a finished product as part of the learning process. Indeed, essays, or analogous written assignments, are perhaps the central constituent of that process, so wherever possible I would encourage you to look on those early and middle assignments as 'exploratory essays'. The virtues of such an approach are worth listing:

1   If you main aim is to 'find out' through writing the essay, you will feel under far less pressure to arrange your material in an exact display – which is something you probably won't be able to do yet anyway.

2   As a result, the *substance* of the essay will engage you much more than the *format*. This is exactly as it should be for most of the course. Eventually you will want and need to pay equal attention to both, but you can't achieve good structure and style until you're sure of what you want to say, and to establish *that* takes a good deal of time.

3   It encourages you to take risks. This is a creative and invariably profitable experience. Obviously, you have to be *sensible* about this: a wild-but-deliberate dive into a perverse or irrelevant argument is foolishly wasteful. But if you pursue your ideas in an honest and interested way, it won't matter that some of them don't convince, reach a dead end, or turn out to be 'red herrings'. At least you'll know and understand that they are not of value, and why they're not; and others will be highly productive, embody insights and discoveries that the 'safer', restricted approach could never happen upon.

4   Inevitably, you will include more material than is necessary. At this stage, that is an admirable fault. The further thinking and editing that flows from such work will help you to keep in close touch with your work, which as we've seen from Chapter 3 is an essential component of successful study.

5   Some of such an essay's value will reside in its faults rather than in spite of them – an apparent paradox that is best understood by considering the concept of *constructive criticism*.

I know some people who in effect consider the term 'constructive criticism' as more or less synonymous with 'unblemished praise' – where *criticism* means *appraisal* and *constructive* relates chiefly to the building of ego! And in truth there are some occasions when that is the essay-marker's task – and very nice they are too, for student and teacher alike. But the term has another, more muscular application: it consists of telling the student where s/he has gone wrong or somewhat awry. Such criticism is never easy to take, but if absorbed humbly, it allows you to *construct* something better in the future. It is part of the building process that lies at the heart of any good teacher-learner partnership (see pages 101–7).

The key point here is that you cannot construct something out of nothing. One can do a good deal to help improve material logged on a page that has some flaws; one can do very little about material that needs to be there and is wholly absent, apart from point that fact out and advise the student to fill the gap. That isn't constructive in any but the most rudimentary, informative way, but – as I've occasionally had to remind students of mine – nobody can be very constructive when faced with a void.

So it is far easier for a teacher to help students if they've written too much, or if some of what they've done is off-key or unconvincing, than if they've written too little or missed out important matters. In the former instance, one enjoys in effect a detailed and positive 'dialogue' with the student, who is able to make immediate and productive strides forward. In the latter instance, no such dialogue is possible: only two recourses are available to the teacher. The soft option is to identify what is missing and more or less leave it at that, but there is a snag:

One does not know whether the student understands why it's important or whether s/he will cover the necessary additions afterwards.

The tougher route is to say simply, 'Do it again.' Such a suggestion is always depressing and often very annoying, but it is inescapably sound, if only because

It is always easier – whether immediately or at some time in the future – to edit work that is too long, partially unsuccessful or at times flabby than it is to flesh out work that is too thin. Almost invariably, the latter exercise evolves into a complete re-write, starting from scratch.

In short: the exploratory essay allows you to use your teacher in a rich and constructive way; to settle for a bare minimum in such tasks is always an unwise waste.

Essay planning

It may strike you as odd that I have just finished looking in detail at a particular kind of essay before saying anything about basic essay technique and, especially, planning. I have done so in order to emphasise that it is no use trying to plan an essay without first establishing what you're writing it for. The 'exploratory essay', both in its virtues and its problems, demonstrates admirably where your priorities should lie, and how your planning logic should operate. To repeat and expand:

> **The question 'Why?' should be the first word on any and every essay plan.**

Once you're armed with an answer which satisfies you, there's one more question you need to consider before you can safely continue your plan – the question posed by the assignment itself, and specifically the *instructional verb* it uses. Please attempt the exercise below. The answers are overleaf.

What does the question mean?

Below follow fourteen instructional verbs and alongside them fourteen definitions of those verbs. *Not one of them forms a 'match': can you pair them off accurately?* The answers and a brief commentary are given overleaf.

Verb	Definition
Account for	Give reasons; say 'why' rather than just define.
Analyse	Write down the information in the right order.
Comment on	Item-by-item consideration of the topic, usually presented one under the other.
Compare	Point out differences only and present result in orderly fashion.
Contrast	Estimate the value of, looking at positive and negative attributes.
Describe	Elect features according to the question.
Discuss	Present arguments for and against the topic in question; you can also give your opinion.
Evaluate	Explain the cause of.

Explain	Make critical or explanatory notes/observations.
Identify	State the main features of an argument, omitting all that is only partially relevant.
List	Give the main features or general features of a subject, omitting minor details and stressing structure.
Outline	Make a survey of the subject, examining it critically.
Review	Point out the differences and similarities.
Summarise	Separate down into component parts and show how they interrelate with each other.

If that taxed you, do not be downhearted: it ought to have done! But you should now be much better versed in the kind of questions you'll be set, how to decode them and thus how to present your material and arguments to their best advantage. Don't forget, though, that the prime need to work out what you've got to *do* must not, in any circumstances, be taken to mean 'What do they want me to *say*?' That's *your* business, and yours alone.

Answers

Verb	Definition
Account for	Explain the cause of.
Analyse	Separate down into component parts and show how they interrelate with each other.
Comment on	Make critical or explanatory notes/observations.
Compare	Point out the differences and similarities.
Contrast	Point out differences only and present result in orderly fashion.
Describe	Write down the information in the right order.
Discuss	Present arguments for and against the topic in question; you can also give your opinion.
Evaluate	Estimate the value of, looking at positive and negative attributes.
Explain	Give reasons; say 'why' rather than just define.
Identify	Select features according to the question.
List	Item-by-item consideration of the topic, usually presented one under the other.
Outline	Give the main features or general features of a subject, omitting minor details and stressing structure.
Review	Make a survey of the subject, examining it critically.
Summarise	State the main features of an argument, omitting all that is only partially relevant.

Now that you've sorted those two essential preliminaries, how best to continue? That depends. By this stage you should have a sense of a general 'core' of material – what you want to say and where you want to get to. (If you're not thus aware, it's almost certain that you're not yet ready to start writing: you need to do some further preliminary reading or thinking.) If that grasp is already sharply defined, you can probably skip the next section and go on to the one after. But it may be that, though you have a heartening number of ideas and potential points, you're not at all clear as to how they might be most profitably deployed and sequenced. That is where something I call 'energising patterns' comes in.

That term has several aliases, amongst them 'Spidergrams' and 'brainstorming'. On one level, of course, it doesn't matter which one you use: all define a system that has, rightly, come to enjoy a wide currency in the last twenty years or so. But I prefer my own, despite its faint pomposity. 'Spidergrams' doesn't signify much other than, vaguely, the visual form that emerges, while 'brainstorming', with its connotations of frenzied, almost uncontrolled activity, is surely not what you want to be doing as you approach a formal written assignment! If you're not quite ready to begin yet, that's because you need an increased sense of order and shape, plus a charge of 'juice' to get you properly started. The phrase 'energising patterns' captures that combination even if it is rather less snappy than its rivals.

Energising patterns: Reducing the thought gap

One problem common to all students is that their thoughts are so much faster than their writing (or typing) speed. This is a fact of being human, and in crude approximate figures the disparity can be expressed thus:

* Some thought is electronic, and can reach speeds of 100 miles per second.
* Most thought is chemical and therefore slower; even so, the speed involved is around 190 miles per hour (c. 300 kph).
* Even a fast writer will not cover the page at more than five miles an hour.

I call this 'the thought gap'. We've all had the experience of thoughts escaping us before we've had time to 'pin them down' in writing, and very frustrating it is too. But sometimes we fail to register them because we try to write down too much – a whole sentence or logical phrase rather than just a word or even a sign. 'Energizing patterns' by-pass such laborious and wasteful procedures, and narrow the chasm between the respective speeds of thinking and writing.

As an initial demonstration, let us suppose you have been set an essay on 'The cruel sea'. It's probably quite a while since you did a 'composition' of this sort, but no doubt you remember the task well! The 'normal' practice is to think about it for a while until a good idea arrives; to 'chew over' that idea, reflectling on ways in which it could be developed, and then to sit down and start the story/essay.

This can of course be quite successful, but it has one major disadvantage. If you simply wait for an idea to arrive, the likelihood is that you'll use the first good one that occurs to you, and although the first may be the best, it's more than possible that the second or third ideas would have been superior. Better still, you might have been able to combine all three in a rich and satisfying way.

As an alternative to that 'normal' method, why not try trapping your ideas on paper from the very beginning? This may – almost certainly will – stimulate further thoughts very fast. You can do it like this: take a piece of paper, write 'The cruel sea' in the middle, and put a box round it. Your piece of paper now looks like Figure 8.1(a).

'Big deal', you might feel like saying. But just focus on that central box, and let your mind mull over it. As soon as any idea comes, write it down: use a 'railway line' scheme, sending different themes or angles in different directions so as to keep them distinct. Then, if and when you've got to about five 'main lines', look at them in turn and see how many 'branch lines', or sub-themes, you

THE CRUEL SEA

Figure 8.1(a) Energizing Patterns: the start

can get from each one. The emphasis is solely on speed, on pinning down a thought before it vanishes; therefore:

Use single words, or even abbreviations, wherever possible.

Using this method, you'll be amazed how fast you cover your piece of paper. Look at Figure 8.1(b), where you'll find my own effort. Because this is a book, the pattern is quite neat: I can assure you the original was much more of a mess! Tidiness is wholly irrelevant and unnecessary. The only thing that matters is that you should be able to decipher your pattern when you come to consider it more sedately. While *doing* it, you should simply try to get down as much as crosses your mind as fast as you can.

The marvellous thing about this technique is that after just five minutes or so, you have a lot of ideas on which you can now brood as slowly as you like, and you have a large, rich choice. No longer is there any danger that you'll settle for the first decent idea that occurs to you: having worked so fast and productively, you

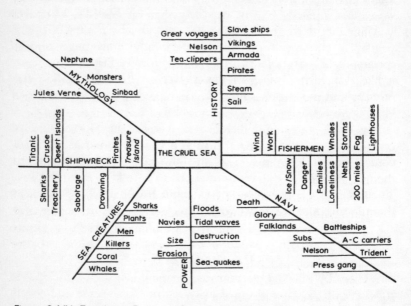

Figure 8.1(b) Energizing Patterns: five minutes later.

can now afford to decide which 'angle' you most like. Moreover, you're in a position to see connections between the themes. In Figure 8.1(b), for example, there are links between various 'branch lines'/sub-themes in 'SHIPWRECK' and 'HISTORY', 'SEA CREATURES' and 'FISHERMEN', and so on. The links are elementary, agreed; but they visually suggest ways in which you can combine and enrich your material, be it for an essay or a story.

'Energizing patterns' are equally valuable in advanced essays. Again you put your chief concept (perhaps the essay's title, reduced if possible to one word) in the central box, let your mind wash over it, and record as many of the resulting ideas as you can. When you peruse the pattern afterwards, you'll not only have a lot of potential material, but a clear visual signal of the connections you can make. With such a visible reminder, your subsequent essay should be more fluent as well as more substantial, its points related to each other in a comfortable and persuasive fashion.

The greatest value of such patterns is that they start you off quickly and enjoyably. They will not solve problems, but they will almost certainly identify what the problems are. They have other major benefits too. Because the method is so simple, it is also very versatile – a pattern can be used for whatever you like, whenever you like:

1   *During a lecture.* Put the title/central concept in the 'box', and see where the lecturer takes you. Using just one-word – 'triggers' you should have no trouble keeping up with him, and the 'railway line' method should allow you to distinguish both his main arguments and several specific points/pieces of evidence for each one. These can later be listed in the form of notes, and thus ensure an impressively high recall of the lecture's substance.

2   *During private note-taking.* I don't myself find it works very well during the first reading/note-taking; but on all subsequent occasions it is most useful. If you look again briefly at Figure 8.1(b), you will see that it looks very much like a 'creative doodle' such as I advocated in the last chapter.

3   *When key word noting.* You can adapt that method to include lines or any kind of visual linking; this will endorse and clarify the key words' importance.

4   *At the start of a revision session.* Do a quick 'energizing pattern' on as much of the material as you can recall, and you will shortly have a definite picture of what you know, and therefore of what you need to refresh your memory about.

5   *As a skeletal plan for an exam answer.* You haven't got time to do the kind of detailed planning I describe in the previous section, but you can afford the few minutes needed to do a pattern of this kind. This will get you confidently started, and also serve as an invaluable reminder of what you want to say – something easily forgotten when under exam pressure.

'Energizing patterns' could usefully be rechristened 'useful mess'. Out of their apparent chaos, your mind makes order and purpose. Such a transition cannot but boost your confidence, and thus makes the subsequent tasks more fun and more successful.

Whether you needed this sub-section or not, you should now be almost ready. However, before we address the matter of writing in earnest, there is one more planning issue to consider.

The psychology of planning – and how *not* to do it

All my observations thus far exemplify the conviction that you should

> **Bring your planning into line with the way essays are conceived and written.**

Any plan – or part thereof – that does not do this is going to create problems rather than solve them. To demonstrate that, let me propose an essay question that is applicable to all disciplines and about which everyone involved in education will have opinions:

> **'Argue for or against examinations'**

If possible, dwell on that for a few moments before reading on: you might even attempt an energizing pattern using *Examinations* as your nucleus-box. Whatever you come up with, it's likely to be better than the 'model' below, which is a pastiche of the kind of planning I've seen and heard advocated for over thirty years:

FOR

1 Introduction.
2 Exams as a necessary test.
3 Exams as outside, 'objective' assessment. Standardisation.
4 Exams as an opportunity to shine under pressure.
5 Conclusion.

Or – perhaps more likely in view of many students' views!:

AGAINST

1 Introduction.
2 Exams as unfair pressure.
3 Unjustified and/or distorting emphasis on speed.
4 Hostility of examiners.
5 Conclusion.

Writing about classical drama, Aristotle famously remarked that to be effective a play must have

'a beginning, a middle and an end'

and the same holds true for an effective essay. In the above model, the middle sections look fine: there are some good ideas in both plans, and no doubt you could think of a number of others.[2] But neither is much use as a way of igniting or indeed fuelling the essay. Consider those bald words *Introduction* and *Conclusion*. What help are they? Do they show you *how* you're going to launch or finalise your argument? Do they give any idea of what they're going to say?

No, of course they don't. I've seen a lot of plans like these, and they won't do: most of them preface essays that, while often interesting and talented, have no real structure. They do not 'mirror' the alleged plan at all; they invariably begin with a couple of vacuous sentences that merely 'mark time' in a frustrating way. Sometimes it will be half a page or more before a point of any substance is made: all the previous material will have been not for the reader's benefit but the writer's – a way of 'winding oneself up' into an argument just as one winds oneself up into a long throw of a ball.

In such essays the conclusion is invariably just as vapid. Rather than summing up the argument or, better still, producing its most telling point as an exhilarating exit, it merely repeats points already made, often in exactly the same words. Thus the reader starts and ends with a yawn – not a happy state of affairs!

Essays planned in such a fashion end up resembling a sandwich whose delicious filling is neutralised by the two pieces of stale, tasteless bread housing it. *Don't* do it like that. Instead, go for something which reflects your strengths and is in line with how the essay will actually be composed. It is to that 'virtual reality' that we now turn.

Writing the essay I: How and where to start

I begin with an apparent paradox:

> **The best place to start an essay is in the middle, or even, if you're sure enough of your material and argument, at the end.**

That will, I hope, surprise you less than it might have done had you not just read my scathing remarks about vacuous introductions.

Of course, you won't present the essay in this form when you hand it in: that would be ludicrous. But an essay is a complex piece of work. While writing you have to focus on the title, marshal ideas, arrange them attractively, attempt to write crisp, pleasing English, and remain constantly alert to the threads of your argument, remembering what you've said and where you're heading. This adds up to a tough task, especially early in a course. So it is wise to begin where you are at your strongest – in the middle. When you've got some points down on paper, and the shape of your argument begins to unfold, *then* you can start thinking about your eventual introduction.

This method is what a 'rough draft' *ought* to be like – a kind of 'scissors-and-paste' job, comprising various sections and sentences which can be properly arranged once they are written down. You can inspect the material at leisure, 'shuffle' it, strengthen it, and begin to tie it together. At all costs you should try to avoid the commonest type of rough draft that students do – that is, writing the essay in an 'orthodox' way in pencil or biro, and then copying out a 'neat', almost-word-for-word version to hand in.[3] This is virtually useless, combining two dismal qualities that lack any fringe benefit: you learn nothing between drafts one and two, and it takes a long, joyless time.

Naturally, you haven't got time to use my suggested method *in an exam*. But if you've used your course time properly, you won't need to anyway. Over the years you'll have learnt how to structure and write an essay under pressure. If you've experimented with techniques of the kind I'm suggesting, and used earlier essays sensibly as part of a review programme, you will by the exam be sufficiently the master of your material to adjust very fast to whatever question/title is thrown at you. I cover exam essay-writing in detail in Part III.

Introductions

I gave you one paradox just now; here's another.

The best time to write your introduction is right at the end.

'The man's a loony,' I hear you muttering. But let me quote you an introduction I read in an Open University assignment. The question was 'Is religion indefinable?', and the student wrote:

In order to answer this question adequately, it is first necessary to consider what religion is, and then to ascertain whether or not it can be clearly defined.

I was sorely tempted to write in the margin a sarcastic 'very good thinking indeed!'. In the end, I simply drew the student's attention to the fact that it *says absolutely nothing*. All it does is offer an empty and unnecessary paraphrase of the question. It may be – *is* – an excellent idea to think for a moment about what the question involves, but it is *not* a good idea to make such preliminary sorting-out the first thing your reader encounters.

Furthermore, it's most unwise to clutter up your style *at any time* with empty blocks of words such as 'it-is-first-necessary-to . . .' or 'in-order-to-do-*x*, we-must-first-do-*y*'. These may have a methodological strength in something like a maths theorem, but in an essay they are simply boring. And it is particularly important not to allow your readers' first reaction to be a yawn or a groan. They may forgive (or even not notice) the odd clumsiness or empty phrase later; but at the beginning they will be at their most alert, their most hopeful and, conversely, their most severe.

If, however, you write your introduction after you've completed the main bulk of the essay, you'll be in a position to produce something vigorous and arresting. One of the finest essays I've ever marked was on Jane Austen's *Emma*, in response to the title, 'Examine Jane Austen's qualities as a social critic'. The material was excellent, with many crisp and invigorating insights. But what made it was the introduction. The student hit me right between the eyes with:

> **Jane Austen knew a great deal about people, but nothing about sex. As a result, her social and moral vision is essentially conservative: ignorance of passion leads to a view of society that is founded on and celebrates order and good sense.**

Admittedly, he was a very bright student, but the real point about this introduction is not its textual intelligence so much as its *calculated* success at grabbing the attention. He knew exactly what he was doing and the effect he wanted to achieve. He knew that even if readers turned purple with rage at such an opinion, they were nevertheless hooked and he was sure enough about the soundness of his material to feel confident that he could demonstrate his argument clearly.

I asked him afterwards if (as I suspected) he'd written the introduction last; he had. He knew that the majority of his insights and judgements in the essay's core pointed to such a view, and so he chose to launch the essay with it. If you adopt the same method you'll be surprised how immediately effective you can make your own work. At the very least you won't ever waste your time and the reader's patience by taking half a page to make your first remark of any weight or purpose.

Conclusions

Similar considerations apply to conclusions as to introductions. What you want to avoid is anticlimax; so, for a start, cut out all such phases as:

In conclusion we can say that . . .
Thus it can be seen that . . .
By way of conclusion I would like to say that . . .
Thus, to conclude . . .
**Thus, in answer to the question, we can safely say
that . . .**

and so on. They say precisely nothing; they fall dully on the eye;
they are quite unnecessary anyway. In most cases, it's perfectly
obvious that you've reached your conclusion – the writing stops
a few lines down! So concentrate on saying something punchy
instead.

How you achieve *that* is less straightforward, of course. You are,
after all, summing up: it is not a good idea to introduce a
completely new point at this stage (though, frankly, such a policy
is to be preferred to the kind of dull obviousness listed above). On
the other hand, you want to avoid merely repeating things you've
covered already, and you should especially avoid using the same
words. Ideally, your conclusion should sum up your ideas and
argument by 're-visiting' them in a fresh and economical way.
Perhaps I might quote again from that *Emma* essay to show you
what I mean:

> **Jane Austen seems to have been serenely confident
> about the values in which she was brought up. Unlike
> her near-contemporary, Emily Brontë, there is in
> Austen no sense of inner conflict about what is right
> and true: the strength of her books and their moral
> outlook lies in her certainty. This confidence is never
> righteous, because of her compassion and humour;
> but it does mean that her social criticism, for all its
> authority, is based on a belief that, at root, her
> society was a just and good one. Radical alternatives
> never occurred to her, because they lay outside her
> experience and imagination.**

Let's list the virtues of that conclusion:

1   It is contentious (as was his introduction): it could cause violent
    disagreement. But that is its strength: it engages readers' full
    attention, and assumes a kind of dialogue with them.

2   It is logical and true to itself. In no sense does it repeat the introduction, but it does match it impressively.

3   The use of a comparison (Emily Brontë) is invigorating, inviting the reader to consider the book in a broader context, and thus extending the debate beyond the essay.

4   It is tautly written and freshly phrased.

5   It is short: long, rambling conclusions are always a mistake, no matter how much interesting material they contain.

6   It is, according to your point of view, stimulating or challenging – it asks the reader to think a little.

You might be fearful of producing such a conclusion, in case it was read by rabid Austenphiles who'd regard any implicit criticism of their heroine as a major heresy. All I can say is that, however much a reader might disagree with or even dislike such an argument, it would be a harsh and stupid one who would 'mark it down' as a result. Bear in mind that few students are ever penalised for being interesting. So try to make your conclusions muscular and compelling, using the principles I've listed above. Anything is better than a tired rehearsal of points and phrases the reader has already digested.

Writing the essay II: Further considerations and guidelines

A good essay is ultimately unique: it reveals the mind, the emotions and the personality of the writer. Beyond a certain point, therefore, it is both undesirable and impossible to lay down the law about what an essayist should do. The finished product will depend on any number of things which neither I nor anyone else can predict or offer advice about. Moreover, given my governing insistence that *you are in charge*, I abominate the idea (touted by some) that successful essays can be effected by following some kind of comprehensive blueprint.

That said, I would hope that any essayist, regardless of subject or discipline, will find these further general principles of value:

Trust your voice

As just noted, the essay is a very personal form. *Use* that fact. There is no need to adopt a disguise or ape others' views and style. Make your language appropriate, yes, but above all make it *yours*.

Start in plenty of time

This is a very boring instruction: I'm sorry about that. But I'm also sorry to say that a sizable number of students ignore it, tediously obvious though it may be. They end up having to dash off the essay the night before the deadline (sometimes a day or two after it!) and the result is invariably unsatisfactory. That figures: the writer will be panicking, resentful and unconfident – hardly conducive to the clarity of focus that writing even a decent essay requires, let alone a good one. More perhaps than any other aspect of study, hefty written assignments require proper *time management*.

Pay full attention to mechanical accuracy and sentence structure

I consider these matters in some detail in the section *Pleasing your reader* at the end of this chapter (pages 160–72). All I'll say here is that such properties may *seem* minor but they aren't. They matter in and of themselves – basic errors and muddled expression always detract, however impressive in other ways the work may be – and because they are often symptomatic of other flaws. Those who can't be bothered to get the little things right often can't cope with the big things either.

Pause before embarking on a fresh argument

This has two benefits. It allows you to reflect on what you've covered already, possibly leading to valuable additions or edits, and the slight rest or change of activity will do you good, thus sharpening up the next stage of your work.

Read as many essays/articles as you can

Reading others' work will allow you to learn from their strengths, but also from their weaknesses or shortcomings. It is intriguing how often one improves not by copying the excellent but by learning to avoid the mediocre or the poor.[4]

On now to the final two sections, both newly written for this edition, which address *Analysis* and *Pleasing your reader*.

Analysis: The three-point method

In the 1840s Edgar Allan Poe wrote what many consider to be the first detective story – 'The Murders in the Rue Morgue'. In it, an orang-utan escapes with a cut-throat razor, climbs to the top of a house and in a frenzy butchers a woman and her daughter. The screams of the women and, most importantly, the shrieks of the ape as it kills attract the attention of a group of people who rush to the top storey of the house. They can't get in through the locked door and hear the commotion on the other side. The ape swings out of the rear window leaving everybody baffled, once the door has been finally forced, as to what exactly was in the room committing such an atrocity. The eccentric but brilliant detective C. Auguste Dupin examines the evidence given and homes in on a vital area. Printed below is an extract from the story, as he explains his deductions to his somewhat less intelligent partner. Please read it now.

My apologies if the decision to use three different type styles proved somewhat disorienting: I set it out in that way because it dramatises the method Dupin followed and which you should emulate, whichever your academic discipline and whatever your analytical task:

1   State your idea/hypothesis   [Text in ordinary type].
2   Use evidence to support your idea – in the form of quotation/ close reference/observed phenomena   [*Text in italics*].
3   Explain how the evidence supports what you say and attempt some analysis   [**Text in bold type**].

If we look at Dupin's explanation of the way none of the witnesses could make out the nationality of the shrieking voice on the other side of the door, we see first of all that he states his *idea*: each witness thought the voice that of a foreigner. Then he goes on to use the *evidence* – the various quotations from the witness statements. Finally he *explains* what is decisive: no words were distinguishable.

Dupin is using a technique that is valid for *all* academic disciplines. Lawyers use it, writers use it, judges use it, scientists use it and you should use it. Once you get into the habit of using it, it will serve you for the rest of your life. It is as old as conscious thought and as new as this morning's newspaper. So try always to bring the three points into your work:

The Orang-Utan and the Cut-Throat Razor

Yet there *was* something to be observed . . . in regard to the shrill voice, the peculiarity is – not that they disagreed – but that, while an Italian, an Englishman, a Spaniard, a Hollander, and a Frenchman attempted to describe it, each one spoke of it as that *of a foreigner*. Each is sure that it was not the voice of one of his own countrymen. Each likens it – not to the voice of an individual of any nation with whose language he is conversant – but the converse. *The Frenchman supposes it the voice of a Spaniard, and 'might have distinguished some words had he been acquainted with the Spanish'. The Dutchman maintains it to have been that of a Frenchman; but we find it stated that 'not understanding French this witness was examined through an interpreter'. The Englishman thinks it the voice of a German, and 'does not understand German'. The Spaniard 'is sure' that it was that of an Englishman, but 'judges by the intonation' altogether, 'as he has no knowledge of the English'. The Italian believes it the voice of a Russian, but 'has never conversed with a native of Russia'* . . . **Now, how strangely unusual must that voice have really been, about which such testimony as this could have been elicited! – in whose tones, even, denizens of the five great divisions of Europe could recognize nothing familiar! You will say that it might have been the voice of an Asiatic – or of an African. Neither Asiatics nor Africans abound in Paris; but, without denying the inference, I will now merely call your attention to three points. The voice is termed by one witness 'harsh rather than shrill'. It is represented by two others to have been 'quick and *unequal*'. No words – no sounds resembling words – were by any witness mentioned as distinguishable.**

(Edgar Allan Poe)

1 State   2 Support   3 Explain

All three are important, naturally, but it is the third that is crucial. In my experience a host of students are adept at stating their (good) ideas and finding evidence to support them, but frequently do not provide enough in the way of *explanation*. And that last is vital if you are to convince your reader (especially an examiner) that you are able to think intelligently.[5]

Pleasing your reader

You might wonder why this final section has taken so long to appear. After all, whether your readers are going to enjoy your work or feel impelled to hurl it through the window would seem to be a fairly fundamental matter. I have delayed it until now for two reasons.

First, for all its importance, *reader pleasure* will hardly ever be the uppermost consideration in the minds of students under pressure to submit an assignment. Writing an essay gives them quite enough to do, including the important matter of pleasing *themselves*, or at any rate producing something that satisfies them. In fact – a point to which I shall return – that *private* pleasure can prove the key to pleasing one's audience; however, it is not surprising if it takes most students most of their course to realise that and act fully on it.

Second, siting it here means that it forms a bridge between Part II and the forthcoming focus on *examinations* which comprises Part III. Pleasing your reader is always important, but it is especially so in an exam, when so much is at stake. By ending this chapter with a detailed look at how you can make life more comfortable and enjoyable for your audience, I aim to consolidate all the advice offered so far and also help get you in the right frame of mind for those final weeks and days of the course.

I shall be considering seven factors:

- handwriting;
- word-processor etiquette;
- mechanical accuracy/word-processor practice;
- sentence structure;
- paragraphing;
- some potential irritants;
- tone.

Handwriting

This and word-processor etiquette go together in several important ways, and if in our computer-dominated world it seems a touch perverse to begin with the pen rather than the PC, I do so because:

- At present virtually all timed exams require you to answer in longhand. The time when candidates sit exams online may not be very far away, but it isn't here yet.
- Handwriting is, obviously, very personal. That is its strength; it can also become a source of anxiety and thereby variously problematic.

Apart from those (rather sad) people who go to calligraphy classes and drool over finely manicured copperplate script, very few of us like our own handwriting, do we? Over the years we get used to it, naturally, just as we eventually become accustomed to the sound of our voice on a tape or the sight of our movements on a video. But all three retain an at least vestigial ability to embarrass us. As a result, some writers – especially teenage ones – are tempted to 'play around' with their natural handwriting, trying to disguise what they have come to regard as ugly, clumsy or insufficiently stylish. This is unnecessary but harmless – unless and until it damages clarity.

By that I do not mean chronic illegibility, where it is impossible to decipher what the writer is talking about, even after three head-throbbing attempts. Candidates like that invariably fail, and rightly so. However, such cases are very rare: speaking as an examiner, I reckon to encounter just one every three or four years, or one in a thousand scripts. But I do come across a considerable number of answers which, though essentially legible, are unpleasurable hard work, for one or more of the following reasons:

- *Handwriting where individual words are illegible.* Depending on what the word is, that can be very important; even if such instances are not crucial to flow or argument, it is still annoying and distracting – two highly reader-unfriendly qualities that you don't want to perpetrate.
- *Very small handwriting* – the kind that makes you wonder if the writer is some kind of loony miser who regards the use of more than one piece of paper as the height of ruinous extravagance.[6]
- *Swanky, precious handwriting* awash with loops, curls and smart-alec adornments.
- *Handwriting that slopes notably,* either to left or right; in extreme instances, this can induce dizziness in the reader.
- *Handwriting that regards lined paper as a challenging affront,* veering all over the place on a random basis; sometimes one can wonder if the writer was drunk.

- *Sprawly, energetic handwriting* that may look superficially pleasant but where letters are badly formed, incomplete or ambiguous.

And perhaps most enraging of all:

- *Handwriting that consists solely of block capitals.* I have never understood why anyone favours this ghastly practice: it is very laborious to *do* and excruciating to read.

All that's the bad news – or, if you prefer, the bossy pedant in me. The good news is that nobody is going to think your hand-writing inadequate or questionable in any respect provided

you make sure it is *comfortably* legible.

A good way of guaranteeing that is to look over your handwriting from time to time as if you were someone else. This is difficult to begin with, naturally, but if you can so scrutinise your hand, looking actively for things which might not be clear or which might irritate, you'll quickly find yourself putting them right. Conversely, if your writing pleases *you*, it's likely that it will please your readers too, or at any rate be no problem for them.

Word-processor etiquette

Aside from all its awesomely sophisticated properties, the PC is a marvellous *toy*. Great; also very dangerous. Toys are almost magical things; hence their enduring appeal, not just for children but grown-ups too. But that magic resides at least partly in their being *private* things: we may like to show them off but we don't like sharing them for any length of time. Needless to say, students cannot afford to operate like that: their success, even their exist-ence, depends on sharing. And amongst all else that means you must be just as aware of your audience when glorying in the facil-ities of you word-processor as when you have a pen in your hand.

Or *more* aware, if anything. The growth in IT literacy over the last ten years has been prodigious, yet it bewilders me (especially in view of the above observations about magical toys and awesome facilities) that hardly less prodigious is the number of students who suffer from 'TNR-FS10-SLS Syndrome' – the apparent belief that Times New Roman, font size 10 and single line spacing are the only, or the most desirable, options available. Try reading the text in the box below as an illustration of how that dismal trilogy that can test the patience and absorptive powers of even the fittest.

- *Handwriting where individual words are illegible.* Depending on what the word is, that can be very important; even if such instances are not crucial to flow or argument, it is still annoying and distracting – two highly reader-unfriendly qualities that you don't want to perpetrate.
- *Very small handwriting* – the kind that makes you wonder if the writer is some kind of loony miser who regards the use of more than one piece of paper as the height of ruinous extravagance.
- *Swanky, precious handwriting* awash with loops, curls and smart-alec adornments.
- *Handwriting that slopes notably,* either to left or right; in extreme instances, this can induce dizziness in the reader.
- *Handwriting that regards lined paper as a challenging affront,* veering all over the place on a random basis; in extreme instances, one wonders if the writer was drunk.
- *Sprawly, energetic handwriting* that may look superficially pleasant but where letters are badly formed, incomplete or ambiguous.

That wasn't too comfortable, was it?! And I made life easier for you by using text that you've just read (pages 161–2 above). Imagine, first, what it would have been like to encounter such text 'cold', and, second, what it would be like to read 3,000+ words in the same format.

Fonts are not as personal as handwriting, obviously; on the other hand, your PC gives you an enormous choice, and it's both fun and profitable to experiment until you find the one that suits you. And as you go about that exploration, bear in mind those who will read what you produce: try to settle on a 'package' which pleases you and is also reader-friendly.[7] As a student, remember that nearly all who will peruse your work are older than you: they may not be positively ancient, but their vision will probably fall a fair bit short of 20–20. Be kind to old eyes!

That is neither mawkish nor facetious. Most of your work is going to be *marked* – and, let us hope, in considerable, helpful detail. It is very difficult for a marker to find any real space to annotate and comment if your prose is squeezed tight through tiny fonts and Scrooge-like spacing. As a result, you not only make life uncomfortable for your markers: you make it almost impossible for them to assist you in the way they want and you need. Moreover, while an examiner will not annotate your work in the same way – i.e. offer advice for you to consider and act upon – the principle still applies. Most examiners like to comment as they go, partly to get a 'fix' on what they're assessing, and partly to offer their Chief Examiners/Team Leaders/Awarders some chapter and verse on why they arrived at the eventual mark given. And hard-pressed examiners don't appreciate microscopic prose anyway: it is not in your interests to put their backs up![8]

Lastly – and this has as much to do with the forthcoming discussion on word-processor practice as with etiquette – the 'TNR-FS10-SLS Syndrome' often claims another casualty: *you*. Very small handwriting or typescript is not only hard to mark: it is equally difficult for the writer to *check*. It is, I think, not just laziness or a deluded belief in computers' power to think for you that causes so many students to submit word-processed work riddled with errors and glitches: often they simply cannot *see* them. Greater generosity with text size and line spacing will benefit your composition and editing as well as ensuring your work a much warmer welcome when it becomes 'public'.

Mechanical accuracy/word-processor practice

This is not the place to offer a full-scale crash course on how to spell and punctuate properly or, to look ahead to the next section on how to write competent sentences. That would be uneconomical in a book of this length; it would also be inappropriate for a book of this *kind* – i.e. a guide for sophisticated students. I have assumed from the start that you are bright and competent, and it would be crassly patronising to imagine that you don't think it's a good idea to get things right or to express yourself clearly.

However, we all make mistakes, we are all at times delinquent about checking our stuff properly, and the likelihood of both increases the more time pressure one is under. It fascinates me, for example, how many emails are riddled with inaccuracy. I am sure this has to do with the senders feeling obliged not to waste phone-time – even if they're not paying for it! That may be good-hearted but it's still bad practice, and if you're not careful, such sloppiness can spread from emailing to other modes.

As in so many other aspects of study, good *time management* will allow you to check all your work carefully before submission. But don't leave it to chance: designate a precise slot in your personal schedule for such a task. And if your time management goes awry once or twice – and again that happens to us all – you must still find such a slot.

Of course, it is best to check your work *as you go*. If you're not sure about a spelling, don't guess: look it up, at once. If unsure how to punctuate a sentence, either re-cast it in a way that restores your confidence, or ask advice. However, unless you're very unusual, more often than not you won't do this: you'll shelve such minor things until you've accomplished the major ones – like getting the essay finished!

That's understandable, and it's okay provided you do *shelve* rather than *abandon* those enquiries and corrections. Moreover, when you do come to edit and check, you'll need to be very alert: it may be days since you did the original work, and your sense of it will inevitably have faded somewhat. It is also a good idea to be ruthless:

Read your stuff over as if you're somebody else – and a fairly hostile somebody else at that, someone itching to catch you out.

Deal with all those uncertain spellings, subtleties of punctuation and grammar, and of course all overlooked slips of the pen/keyboard as if gleefully determined to frustrate that hostile somebody!

Next:

Make sure your *facts* are right.

That doesn't just mean historical dates, chemical symbols, or GNP figures: it means anything that forms part of your source work's 'data base'. In an essay on *King Lear*, for instance, you may have spelled *Edgar* correctly, but are you sure you don't mean his half-brother *Edmund* instead? If so, that isn't a spelling mistake as such (no spell-checker on earth will pick it up, for a start) but it's still a mistake, still a question of mechanical accuracy. Look fiercely for such things.

Finally:

If using a word-processor, *stay in charge.*

Jon Down has already given you much eloquent advice on this. Here I'll just say that a typo is every bit as much *your* fault as a hand-written error – don't blame the computer – and repeat my observation in Chapter 1 that a computer cannot *think* as a human does. It cannot identify context, and it's no good at puns, whether intentional or otherwise. So if you write *bred* when you mean *bread*, *weather* instead of *whether*, or *phalluses* where you intended *fallacies*, the computer won't – can't – help: that's your job and your job only.

Don't despise these 'minor things' because they're little and unexciting. So are the cells in our bodies, but that doesn't mean they don't matter: when any of them goes wrong, the whole body starts to suffer. And that's as true of your essay work as it is of your being.

Sentence structure

You won't have got this far – either as a student or in my book – without being able to recognise and write decent sentences. So here all I want to do is offer three injunctions and comment on them briefly.

Don't ramble.

Naturally, nobody *sets out* to do this.[9] The flaw occurs because one gets so involved with the material that one loses a sense of direction and of one's goal. Good, tough punctuation will help – or rather, a good, tough *awareness* of how you're punctuating: if you're about to use your eighth comma in succession, or if you haven't used a single punctuation point for four lines, you're rambling, bet on it. If you suspect your awareness of such practice has been vague, *stop at once* and look back on what you've just written, amending it as you go.

The tendency to ramble will be greatly reduced if you:

Only start a sentence when you know how it's going to finish.

You don't have to prefigure every last word or its exact place in the sentence, but you should have a clear overall 'map' in your mind of the path your sentence will follow.

This requires considerable discipline, and it won't be at all easy to begin with. But it's one of those very good habits that is also quickly acquired. Soon you won't have to adopt such a policy consciously: it will have become virtually instinctive.

Vary your sentence length.

Obvious advice, yes, but in the heat of composition the point is easily forgotten. As my 'don't ramble' observations doubtless imply, I would say that *the* most unpleasing style from a reader's point of view is a succession of 60-word, five-clause sentences that seem to (indeed *do*) go on and on and on. Yet too many short sentences can be almost as irksome. In extreme cases it's as if one's reading multiple variants of 'the cat sat on the mat', but even truly muscular material can lose impact from such a jagged stop–start rhythm.

There is no need to be arithmetically obsessive about ensuring variety. An approach based on something like 'short, long, long, short, short, long . . .' may seem *theoretically* effective, and if you're currently in the habit of writing two hundred and six short sentences per essay or thirteen very long ones, I suppose it might have its virtues. In all other instances, however, it doesn't begin to match the way people actually write once under way. Just be sensibly aware of how your sentences are coming out as you go, and the requisite variety should ensue automatically.

Taking care of the second and third suggestions in particular will increase your awareness and mastery of shape, clarity and rhythm. As a bonus, that will almost certainly spill over into your handling of the sentence's 'big brother', the paragraph, to which we now turn.

Paragraphing

A fair number of students who are otherwise highly competent writers let themselves down through poor paragraphing. Again, this is usually the result of pressure – brought on by the time constraints of an exam, the intensity of composing a complicated, subtle argument, or both. But, however sympathetic one may be to the reasons for such neglect, the results can be critical. Poor paragraphing harms a writer in two interlocking ways. First:

Poor paragraphing greatly irritates any and every reader.

Often that irritation will set in *within seconds*. Most markers/examiners instinctively 'scan' a script as they pick it up, and their hearts will sink as they note an amorphous block of text with no shape, no variety and above all, no 'breaks'. Minuscule though the relief may be, the eye appreciates coming to a stop and then starting again; the lack of such provision will not endear you to its author, and you already be resentfully preparing for a long, arduous read. Unfortunately, too, such suspicions are rarely unfounded: two or three paragraphless pages *is* a long, arduous read, even if the material is of high quality.

That last rarely applies, though, for the failure to paragraph not only irritates the reader but also harms a writer because, second:

It blunts the thinking of the writer.

Instead of being shaped, dramatised and sharpened, successive points become increasingly blurred, even directionless.

In my view paragraphing is finally an art, not a science. But if you're a bad – or non-existent – paragrapher, a little science in the form of elementary arithmetic will serve you very well. Whenever you write an extended piece, be it in your study or in the exam hall:

Aim for two or three paragraphs per page.

That does not require you to be metronomic or wooden: occasionally your argument will benefit from a long-ish paragraph, and at other times a short one may be equally effective. But if you mentally file it as a rule of thumb, your writing will improve – as will your relationship with your readers.

Some potential irritants

Contrary to many student myths, academic readers and examiners are by no means intolerant, unimaginative, stuffy or mean-spirited. However, they do – either by nature or instruction – tend to be *conservative*. That means you have to be careful about certain practices which strike you as natural and normal, but which may go down less well with your readers. So here's a quick 'hit list' of things you might wisely remember:

- Never use *etc.* or even the full *et cetera*. It looks – and indeed almost always *is* – vague, lazy, or both.
- Never use *incredibly* as a synonym for *extremely* or *very*.
- Never use either *basically* or *definitely*: both are invariably meaningless, having about as much weight as *sort of* or *er*.
- *Literally*: if tempted to use it, be sure you know what it means.
- Use *quotation*, not *quote*, if you intend the noun use. This may be very pedantic, and it may also be a dead issue in ten years' time. It isn't at present, though, so be strict with yourself!
- Use *abbreviations* with the greatest caution. Yes, it may be a drag to write out, say, *A Streetcar Named Desire* in full throughout your essay, but blithely to substitute *ASND* might cost you more than the time you save. Similarly . . .
- . . . Avoid anything that resembles *code*, and keep *jargon* to an absolute minimum. In most subjects, there are technical terms which are both necessary and productive, but in the main readers will bless you for keeping things as uncluttered as possible.

That rather breezy – and selective – list nevertheless identifies most of the things that I and many other examiners frequently complain about, or which at any rate dull one's pleasure in students' work.[10]

The issues aimed at pleasing your reader discussed so far are not always easy to attend to, but they are ultimately uncomplicated, even straightforward. My last focus is a very different matter.

Tone

Speaking as a teacher of literature, *tonal considerations* cause my students more difficulty than any other aspect of a text, be it poem, novel, play or non-fiction prose; consequently, tone is also the hardest of all concepts to teach. There is nothing surprising about that. Assessing tone brings into play a multitude of things – amongst them voice, attitude, rhythm and other musical characteristics, register of language and historical, political and social context. Furthermore, the absorption of tone depends on the mood, personality and mind-set of the *audience* as much as those of the writer. What may impress Reader A as skittish humour can strike Reader B as vinegary sarcasm, while Reader C may detect limpid tenderness in a piece which Reader D considers posturing sentimentality.

A prime reason for this decidedly slippery state of affairs is that one is dealing solely with words on a page. It's hard enough at times to determine someone's exact tone even if you also see the twinkle in the eye, the down-turned mouth, the aggressive thrust of the jaw, or any other physical clues. When one peruses a text the writer is invisible; nor is it possible to deduce *with certainty* what the writer's 'voice' is like, including such matters as volume, accent and intonation. And that is true of all texts, not just literary ones. The latter may tend by their nature to be richer, more complex and multiply demanding than others, but it is not just students of literature who experience the kind of difficulty I allude to above. Evaluating tone is a challenge to everybody.

Fortunately, as an essayist the only tone you need concern yourself with is your own, and however forbidding that two-paragraph preamble may seem, my chief reason for including tone as a topic is to strengthen and encourage you. For if you're now as aware as I hope you are about how crucial matters of tone can be and how alert you must stay to them, the chances are high that you'll hit the right note yourself. We have already looked at a number of things that affect tone and the reader's impression of it. Let me offer some further guidelines.

Avoid both arrogance and coy diffidence.

Most guides – be they in book, style-sheet or lecture form – warn students about the dangers of arrogance, and here am I doing the same. In fact, arrogant student essays are extremely uncommon. *Arrogance* denotes aloofness and the conviction that one knows better than anyone else, and rare is the student who even feels that, let alone trumpets it on paper. Nonetheless, be careful when censuring something. Your right to do so is unquestioned, but you will win few friends and no marks with a response on the lines of 'This is a load of rubbish' or 'a child of 8 could do better'. There are more dignified and likable ways of indicating disapproval.

A more frequent problem than arrogance is its 'innocent cousin', *incaution* – particularly any claim to a breadth of knowledge that the reader may doubt. You may, for example, have read somewhere that the unravelling of the structure of DNA was the greatest scientific achievement of the twentieth century, or that *Mansfield Park* is the finest of Jane Austen's novels. Both are perfectly tenable views, but if you assert them baldly, your marker is likely to respond on the lines of 'How do *you* know?', adding either 'Aware of all the major scientific discoveries across a hundred years, are you?' or 'Deeply versed in all her books already, huh?' That may be unfair, especially if you *are* that conversant, and even more so if the reader infers arrogance on your part, but I trust you can see why such sweeping claims are unwise. Stick to what you *know*: it is unlikely that there won't be enough such real knowledge to serve you admirably.

By *coy diffidence* I mean the 'These-are-only-the-views-of-little-me' approach which may be intended as fetching modesty but can instead seem mere wheedling. It is not arrogant to assume that people will be interested in what you write (especially as they're paid to read it!) so there's no need to be apologetic. Further to that, use 'in my opinion' and the like only when you suspect you're arguing something that is at variance with others' views; to pepper your work with such phrases damages flow and can also seem hectoring.

The strengths – and dangers – of humour

I have tried to make this guide entertaining and amusing throughout, and even if I've failed, that doesn't alter my belief that humour is not only one of the great joys in life but without equal as a means by which to instruct and enlighten. Not everyone agrees with me on the latter, however, and so, much against my will, I must also urge caution when it comes to jokes, wit and even irony when writing essays. That does not mean abandoning them on principle and just like that, but if tempted towards the humorous, ask yourself what the effect is likely to be. Will it please or just seem facetious? Will it strengthen your point or undermine it? Will you come across as witty and urbane, or a smart alec? If in the slightest doubt about the answer, *don't do it*. Eloquently relevant here is a remark made by a poet whose tonal qualities are multiply rich and challenging, and who was also, in the words of a friend who knew him very well, 'the funniest man I ever met' – Philip Larkin:

> **One uses humour to make people laugh ... The trouble is, it makes them think you aren't being serious. That's the risk you take.**[11]

As a student under assessment – especially in an exam – that is a risk you can't *afford* to take.

Summary: Be natural as well as sensible

I've concentrated on 'don'ts' and 'be carefuls' so far; let me end on a more positive and cheering note. I've been stressing from the start that *you are in charge*, and that applies to your tone and style as much as anything else. Yes, beware of the traps I've drawn attention to; on the other hand, the worst thing you can be – even more damaging than arrogant – is *toneless*, whereby your prose reads as if you were taking minutes for a council meeting. Neutral, deliberately uninflected writing of such a kind has its place, but that certainly isn't an academic essay.

Last of all: you will capture your natural strengths and avoid most of the dangers I've identified if you can get into the habit of *listening* to your writing, even to the extent of reading it out loud when and where you can. *Voice* is a major constituent in all good writing: it is no accident that an elegant essay sounds as good on radio as it reads on the page, and vice versa. Staying sensitively alert to your own voice will virtually guarantee an unaffected and impressive tone.

Now on to exams!

Part III

Examinations

Introduction

Examinations have always been a built-in part of nearly all vocational courses. The overwhelming likelihood, therefore, is that you will face an exam at the end of your course – be it after one, two or three years. And no book on study would be complete without a section investigating their purpose, the attitudes they inspire, and the techniques that can help you to succeed at them.

The first point to make is that the majority of students dislike exams. Indeed, student unease about them is far and away the greatest and most frequent problem that teachers encounter. As a result, a lot of teachers dislike exams too. This was always the case, but never more so than now: with the advent of National Testing, League Tables, Ofsted Inspection at all levels of our educational system, and other highly public modes of scrutiny, teachers feel under considerable pressure on their own account, since results reflect nearly as much on them as on the students themselves. In addition, given that we live in a world where qualifications have never seemed so important, teachers become disturbed and anxiously protective about the intensity with which some of their students worry. And this can create a vicious circle, whereby teacher and student simply aggravate each other's suspicions and fear.

I hope that the following sections will help you to relax somewhat about exams and lead you to regard them as just another part of your course, not some horrific and undermining ordeal. Above all, I want to persuade you that taking exams is just as much a *skill* as all those areas covered in Part II. Examinations are not a lottery, an Act of God, or an evil game run by a secret society: they are a perfectly rational method of assessment whose techniques can be comfortably mastered. Naturally, as with any skill, you have to possess some aptitude, and work at it. There can be little doubt that you have the aptitude: were this not the case, you probably wouldn't have lasted the course long enough to get anywhere near the exam. The application, as always, is up to you; I hope the discussion and advice that follow will make such work both worthwhile and congenial. And it is again worth repeating this book's regular refrain: even though other people will of course set and mark your exams, *you are* – or should be – no less *in charge* during a public performance (which is what an exam is) than is the case in private study.

Chapter 9

Psychology and attitudes

Everything in life, including marriage, is done under pressure.

(Isaiah Berlin)

Preliminary

In the first incarnation of this book, I spent some time listing and then answering *objections to exams*. Two things governed the decision to omit that material here. First, it ran to well over 1,000 words, and considerations of space made me take a hard look at it anyway. But second and more important, such a 'debate' is now a philosophical matter only. Twenty years ago there were moves afoot to reduce the dominance of examinations and introduce more continuous assessment, coursework and the like; there were even those (though I was not amongst them) who thought the days of timed papers were numbered.

The picture is now very different. Yes, continuous assessment remains a significant factor in our education programmes; at the same time, the number of timed examainations, far from diminishing, has increased. There has never been a greater incidence of testing in the UK's educational history than pertains now, and whatever you and I may feel about it, that state of affairs will continue for at least a few years yet. So, although I believe that the 'for' and 'against' cases I originally explored retain their psychological and philosophical validity, in practical terms they have been become dated and superfluous. The best thing I can do now is help you to feel as serene as possible about the system you're stuck with and about what lies ahead.

First, let's accentuate the positive.

The virtues of exams

Provided they are sensibly set, and provided that they are not the *only* mode of assessment, timed examinations are a sound and illuminating method of discovering a student's overall ability. They test three central things which no other format yet devised can truly evaluate:

1 They establish whether students' knowledge is actually their own. All other methods of assessment leave room for plagiarism, collaboration, or mere parrot-like regurgitation.

2 Is this knowledge available at short notice, or indeed more or less instantly? Or does the student require three days' preparation? I wouldn't be very happy hiring or working with the latter kind of mind: would you trust someone that slow or uninformed?

3 Can this knowledge be transformed into rapid and intelligible communication to others?

If you've done your own good work, are mentally fit and agile, and have stayed *in charge*, all the answers to those questions so far as you're concerned will be affirmative, healthy ones.

That is an entirely sincere argument. Like virtually everyone in UK education, I am concerned about how much pressure is put on today's students from the age of 7 onwards; I am also aware of the horror stories that have surrounded A levels over the last three years; it is more true now than ever it was that exams must themselves continue to be closely examined. But while I do not pretend that exams are perfect – injustices do occur, there are occasions when papers are poorly set – no one has yet come up with a superior alternative, one that achieves what exams try to do and in a 'fairer' way.

Let us move on to consider more closely some matters of exam psychology. To begin with, a look at examiners.

Examiners: Friend or foe?

First and foremost, get rid of that identikit model of Examiner-as-Monster that every student has constructed at one time or another. There are not miserable old hacks who detest the young and are looking gleefully to humiliate them. They are not incompetent amateurs who couldn't run a bath. They are not morally bank-rupt mercenaries cynically indifferent to your future. They are not soulless failures cursing the fate that condemned them to this drudgery and who are now looking to take it out on you.

They are, in fact, ordinary human beings who for a variety of reasons are inherently on your side.

1 They've all done exams themselves, and so have a sympa-thetic awareness of what it's like for you.
2 They are clear about the limitations of the whole business, and will approach your work with a professional friendliness that allows you the benefit of the doubt more often than not.
3 They want you to do well, for two sturdily practical reasons:
   • A good paper is more pleasurable to read than a mediocre one . . .
   • . . . and its obvious quality means they earn their money faster!
4 They do this work in their spare and/or holiday time, which means that amongst all else they are committed to education, playing their part in ensuring the system works properly and rewards those who should be rewarded.

In addition, never imagine you are at the mercy of the whims of just one marker. By the time the final mark and grade have been determined, the majority of scripts will have been closely assessed by several people. Extreme care is taken to ensure that candidates get a thorough and fair deal. Any unusual circumstances (illness, dyslexia, recent bereavement and so on) are taken fully into account. All examining bodies canvass schools and colleges prior to the exam for an estimate of each candidate's likely perform-ance, and any major disparity between estimate and actual grade leads to all his/her papers being looked at again. Universities are no less thorough; I always found the Open University notably caring and generous in its attitude to examinees, and I've heard nothing to suggest it is any different anywhere else.

To summarise:

• Examiners are just people; so are you.
• They are hired to do one job – to find out if you can do what the exam asks you to do. If you do that well, you will score well.
• They *like* you to do well: it makes their job nicer and faster.

And most important of all:

- Forget all ideas of 'them against us': in truth, it's them *with* you, working in harness to ensure, wherever possible, your success.

So whatever anxieties may attend your view of exams, I hope I've persuaded you that fearful hostility to those who will mark your work should not be amongst them. If I haven't, you can still use that obdurate scepticism in a positive way; after all, a great deal of achievement in life is based on a healthy degree of rage, on an 'I'll-show-'em!' determination. Whichever your stance, you will benefit from adopting this governing principle:

> **Try to look on exams as a stimulating challenge, the chance to shine. Negative thoughts are not only unnecessary: they are self-fulfilling passports to failure/disappointment.**

Changing gear and approach

Going beyond mere regurgitation

One of the nice things about being a voluntary student – the kind for which this book is primarily designed – is, obviously, that you're doing something you want to do. There is, however, a rather more stringent corollary to this pleasing advance.

During your 'elementary' schooling, which in most Western countries means up to the age of 16, it is likely that you have to study a number of subjects you find less than riveting, including one or two you are then profoundly grateful to give up. But one of the built-in advantages of these early days is that a great deal of your work is directly taught, even pre-digested for you, which in turn means that:

> **Up to the age of 16, you do not necessarily have to think creatively or independently to succeed.**

Most of your work at this level is a question of absorption and subsequent regurgitation. Of course, you have to understand the work properly for that regurgitation to be effective, but your progress is largely dependent upon how sound your technical ability is to digest and reproduce pre-packed information. It is for this reason that many dutiful, well-taught and alert students can get an A* in a subject they detest.

I am not sneering at such work and qualities, nor suggesting that they are unimportant. However, from sixth form onwards they are not enough on their own. They may remain the *basis* of everything, but unless you learn confidently to do some independent thinking of your own, your career as an advanced student will be somewhat humdrum. You need to think of yourself and behave as a sophisticated individual with opinions and the capacity to 'wonder'; your days as an efficient sponge are over.

Accuracy versus correctness: Exams and 'the right answer'

Only a fool or a charlatan would deny the importance of accuracy. It is the basis of everything, and without it anything is just a shambles. If a recipe tells you to cook a dish in a moderate oven for 30 minutes, your guests aren't going to be over-delighted if you submit it to furnace-like temperatures for an hour and a quarter. In the same way, if a petrol-pump gauge promises you ten gallons, and you find out later that it was fixed/on the blink, so that all you actually received was ten litres, you aren't going to be terribly happy. Analogously, no student can expect to get away with (say) the proposition that 4 x 6 is 257, or even 25, any more than you can expect leniency in your submission that the Battle of Hastings took place in 1382, or that the French for 'man' is 'Le bloke'.

Nevertheless, the point about all those examples is that they are *rudimentary* – in the sense of 'fundamental' rather than 'easy'. Yes, you need to obey oven temperatures and time, and you need to be able to trust the pump gauge. But it's a matter of choice, taste and subtle debate whether you add a little sour cream or some extra seasoning, or whether you select Q8, BP or Esso. The same is true for academic matters. You must ensure your maths is accurate and your spelling correct – you must, in short, get all your *facts* right. But their use is up to you: the key now is *interpretation*, whether your subject is physics, history, economics, or anything else.

Of course, many students do realise this, as no doubt you do. At least, they realise it in principle, but nevertheless fail to act on such theoretical awareness, as could easily happen to you too. There are, I think, two main reasons why this is so.

The first is the constraints of the exam itself. It isn't easy to relax in an exam[1] and, because of this, one is often more cautious than normal. The temptation is to 'play safe' – and that can mean shutting out most of the things that have made you a talented and successful student in the months before. It is important that you try not to 'tighten up' in such a way: stay yourself and *in charge*.

The second reason returns me to the innately conservative nature of your elementary schooling. In pre-advanced exams, there is little obvious difference between 'accuracy' and 'correctness': the name of the game is, 'Do you know your stuff?'. It would be silly to suggest that this actively prevents you from thinking in an independent, creative way, but the point is that there is no pressing need for you to do so. As a result, many able pupils deduce that there is apparently little value in trying to be different or stimulating. They gradually get the central message – that if they trot out their facts in a well-organised fashion, and do precisely what they're told, they pass. It's virtually as simple as that. And that is more the case now than when I wrote the original edition of this book. The entire tenor of National Curriculum Key Stage 4 has become dismally conformist, pivoting on drab correctness; I sometimes think it's now a disadvantage for students at this level to have any true personality or individual quality of mind. Greyness is all.[2]

Fortunately, that last pseudo-epigram does not apply beyond age 16. But many such newly advanced students do not grasp that fact: they take 'getting things right' to be a permanent law. And I cannot emphasise too strongly that, in advanced study, there is no such thing as *one* right answer. In exams, many advanced students ignore this. Instead of answering questions in a natural way, they convince themselves that they must search for what the examiner thinks and wants them to say.

This is very bad policy for a number of reasons. For a start, it's self-evidently doomed, because you'll never know what an unknown examiner's opinions/tastes are! More subtly, and more importantly, you thus turn your back on the qualities that have made you a good student. Once you start thinking in terms of what you *should* say rather than what you feel and *want* to say, you're turning yourself into a studious zombie rather than a vigorous academic. Edgar's lines at the end of King Lear are a splendid model for any examinee:

> The weight of this sad time we must obey,
> Speak what we feel, not what we ought to say.

Those who regard an exam as a 'sad time' will find the 'weight' of the occasion lessens considerably if they rid themselves of all extra constraints. Assuming that you have learnt well, been taught well and prepared yourself well, the simple and cheering truth is that

> **If you apply your knowledge, and have a sound methodological and factual base, you will be fine.**

Take a tip from something we've all had to study for at least several years – maths. Anyone who has taken this subject from Key Stage 2 through to GCSE will remember being told time and time again that one gets more credit for the 'working' than for the solution. The same is true for all advanced work. The credit – which, crudely, means *marks* – is earned by your method, your approach, *you*. Such things are far more vital than any notional sense you may have of 'correctness'.

Do you sincerely want to do well in exams? Then enjoy them!

I have argued throughout that successful study will be fun. This is as true for exams as for all other aspects of your work – arguably more vital, since the pressure on you is greater. I believe it is essential for you to cultivate a long-term attitude that grows to regard the exam as a natural and exciting climax to a pleasureable course.

I'm not so insensitive as to imagine that all exam fears can be cured by a few minutes' 'positive thinking'. Exams require a number of strengths and qualities – including sheer stamina – that do not materialise overnight. However, if you can think of the exam in the terms I've outlined from an early stage, it will prove very fruitful. If you've worked successfully during the course, no exam should hold any terror for you. And you might also find it valuable to reflect on something I've noticed throughout my teaching career:

All good students are humble, but hardly any of them are modest.

Humility means a proper awareness of all the things under the sun that you don't know; *modesty* can very easily cost you a proper awareness of all those things you do know. Jean Paul Sarte was spot on when he defined the latter as 'the virtue of the half-hearted'.

The belief that exams will be a nice release, a chance to show everyone how good you are, is certainly preferable to working ourself up into an induced panic, whereby the exam seems about as attractive as being on the wrong end of a thumb-screw. It is to that opposite approach, which can be disastrous and has no compensating factors whatever, that we now turn.

Negatively charged

Posturing excuses

How often have we heard a candidate aged 10, 30 or 50, just prior to entering the exam room, announce to all within earshot:

I'm dreading this – I haven't done a stroke of work for weeks.

It is an apparently straightforward, throwaway remark. But consider the number of powerfully implicit messages that such an offhand disclaimer sends out:

- It protects the speaker from failure, or at least the humiliation of failure. If s/he does fail, it won't be through inadequacy but because s/he didn't do 'a stroke of work'.
- Conversely, kudos is being added to any possible success. If s/he passes, s/he will seem naturally gifted – someone who had no need to do 'a stroke of work'.
- The casual, what-the-hell tone creates an air of bravado and cool style, establishing an immediate superiority over all those who are quietly wrecking their fingernails.
- The impression created is one of lofty boredom. The underlying idea seems to be that only an idiot would bother to work for an exam.

• There is even the suggestion that s/he has had much better, more exciting things to do than study!

It seems almost a shame to pour cold water on such a blaze of virtuosity. But the fact is that all those implications are annihilated once it is realised that

It is all splendidly, utterly *untrue*.

Examinees who really are 'dreading this' will have been up most of the night working, don't you worry. On the other hand, if they genuinely haven't done 'a stroke of work', then they won't be dreading it at all – the whole exam ceased to have any meaning for them weeks ago. After all, 'dread' is not boring!

Such a syndrome can equally apply to able students who know they've made a 90 per cent effort rather than a 100 per cent one. Public disclaimers of this kind protect you from the narrow failure to achieve a distinction just as winningly as from the dramatic failure to secure a pass. It is frightening how ingenious we can be when it comes to making excuses. If we expended just half that mental energy on doing the actual work, results would be remarkable!

False pessimism and self-fulfilling prophecy

Unjustified, unearned confidence is not a happy or attractive quality; however, there is nothing more devastating than false pessimism. The shock that awaits false optimists can be salutary, showing them what has to be done in future. Their self-esteem will be bruised, but it won't be obliterated at one go. The appalling thing about false pessimism is that it can destroy your real ability and its future potential long before they are tested. If you work yourself up into believing you're going to do badly, then I'm afraid the odds are that you will.

A sporting analogy usefully demonstrates this point. If you go into a rugby tackle expecting to be hurt, it is distinctly likely that you will be. Your body will be awkward and vulnerable, making injury much more probable. Similarly, if you are frightened of a cricket ball and imagine it will hurt you if you try to catch it, then it probably will: your fingers will be stiff and angular, and your palms will be wincing well in advance of receiving the ball. Result:

the ball will probably hit the fingers rather than the soft cushion of the palm, causing sharp pain at the least.

Exams are much the same. If you go into the room in a muck-sweat of panic, your brain ablaze with feverish anxiety, and your memory straining to remember everything you've ever been taught, you will be:

• more or less exhausted by the time you read the paper;
• already conditioned to think in terms of failure and the impossible difficulty of the whole exercise.

False pessimism is an insidious cousin of modesty: it can take all the heart out of you – and invariably for no reason. You can guard against it by cultivating an attitude that is far more cheerful ...

Si tu veux, tu peux

The ideal mood in which to enter an exam room is keyed-up but expecting to do yourself justice. The best analysis of this positive approach that I've read is by the thriller writer Adam Hall:

> I subscribe to Coué, Maltz, and the Frenchman who said, 'Si tu veux, tu peux.' They all make the same point, but Coué put it quite well: in any contest between the imagination and the will, the imagination always wins.
>
> An example would be: if the ship's been sunk under you and it's a ten-mile swim to the shore, you'll stand more chance of getting there by using imagination instead of will-power. You can grit your teeth and will yourself to do it, but the command is conscious, and your *subconscious* is on board for the trip and it can be a lead weight if left to its own little games: once it starts brooding about the black silent fifty-fathom void below your body, the will-power is going to lose a lot of steam. But if you bring in the subconscious to work *for* you, it means the imagination will be programmed in, and in place of a lead weight you've got yourself a propeller. Feed it the key image 'shore' and you're there already, prone as a log and coughing up water, but safe and alive.[3]

The activity of exam-taking is rather less dramatic than Hall's example, but the principle is identical. '*Si tu veux, tu peux*': if you want to, you can. Establish the right attitude and the worst is over before you even sit down. You are ready for anything they can reasonably throw at you, and you are positively looking forward to it. Such an approach won't guarantee success; but it will guarantee an absence of dry-up, panic, mental blocks, and that sudden sense of not being equal to anything you're asked.

Summary: Exam phobia – authentic or phoney?

Some students experience genuine, deep-rooted problems in exams. Their minds 'go blank', they get the shakes, their hands go numb, and they suffer from any number of sudden disabilities. Such cases need careful and caring help, and I hope I'd be the first to be sympathetic. But the vast majority of so-called 'exam phobes' are not of this order. In all my years as a teacher, I have come across only about half a dozen authentic cases. The rest are simply nervous, in a normal and healthy way. The trouble is, they don't *regard* it as normal and healthy. They aggravate their nerves by talking about it with their friends and colleagues, swopping horror stories and exaggerations in a kind of masochistic game.

I use that last word advisedly: a great number of students *enjoy* getting 'het up' about exams. Up to a point, this is both harmless and amusing; once it takes root, however, it becomes a neurosis that can't be fully controlled. If you're such a student (and you'll know if you are), then try to act on some of the ideas and approaches I've outlined. They certainly won't do you any harm, and they may allow you to wrench yourself out of a pointless and damaging prejudice.

As I said at the outset, exams are a perfectly rational, if imperfect, method of assessment. The major problem is that student unease about them is nearly always *irrational*. For a number of reasons and via a number of routes, student anguish about exams acquires a pathological dimension, ranging in intensity from anxiety to semi-hysteria. Such sudden lack of confidence and calm is, in the overwhelming majority of cases, quite unjustified. And it's as if the sufferers somehow know this – hence the way their irrational fears are quickly rationalised in the form of ostensibly intellectual objections to exams as 'cruel', 'unfair', and so on. But the process shouldn't be allowed to fool anybody. Nearly all objections to exams are based on a gut response rather than a reasoned appraisal, and once you look clear-sightedly at what an exam sets out to do, and at your own abilities, I think you'll find that your gut returns to normal, de-shrunk and calm!

Now it's time to move on from contextual discussion and matters of attitude to detailed questions of technique, in terms of both preparation and the exam itself.

Chapter 10

Preparation tips

> It's not escaped my notice that the last few grains of the sands of
> time are already slipping through the egg-timer of fate.
>
> (Humphrey Lyttelton)

Preliminary

For many, perhaps most, students, the run-up to an exam is a time
of great pressure and considerable anxiety. Even the best and most
confident can feel alarm that time is fast running out and that, like
some renegade Horseman of the Apocalypse, the day of reckoning
is galloping towards them. In short, they wouldn't think Humphrey
Lyttelton's above gag[1] remotely amusing, finding it a complacent
and insensitive understatement.

Such a mind-set may be understandable but it is both unfortunate and unnecessary. Yes, it's a pressured time; yes, there's a lot
at stake. However, more than at any other stage of your course *you
are in charge*. There's nobody to tell you what to do or when to do
it; there are no classes or lectures to attend; it is entirely up to you
how you organise your time. And so I would make a fundamental
principle of something I implied during Chapter 3:

**Try to regard your revision period as a 'working
holiday'.**

- Enjoy the respite from regular classes. No matter how much
  you may have valued your lessons or how well you have got
  on with your teachers, it's nice not to have to turn up to Room
  X at point Y on day Z any more. As the old idiom has it, 'A
  change is as good as a rest', and this new freedom ought to
  refresh and energise you.

- Don't try to revise too much or work all the time. I address this in full shortly, but it's important that from the start you have some rest and have some fun. Your stamina is about to be tested as well as your knowledge; for that you need to be fit and serene. So you should turn off and 'get away from it all' regularly and without shame or worry.

In Chapter 3 I introduced the principle of *RAYL – Review As You Learn* (pages 60–3). Even if you have followed it only fitfully, you should find that you know a great deal more than your darkest moments lead you to imagine. But however secure most of your knowledge and ideas may be, you will of course need to do some further work, and that will be all the better for being sensibly thought-out and scheduled.

Revision strategy and timing I: Basic principles

I've discussed this already in 'Taking the misery out of revision', page 65. But a number of points are worth repeating, and there are others to make as well – the first of which is of paramount importance, not least because so many students ignore it:

Revise in shortish bursts of 30 to 40 minutes at most.

I stress this partly because, as we saw in Chapter 1, half an hour represents the normal optimum concentration span. But I do so also because revision is – or should be – by definition a *second*[2] look at material you're pretty familiar with. As a result, your mind will be working far faster than was the case when you first perused it, and half an hour's work will be both highly productive and quite tiring: you'll *need* a rest before going on to the text topic, subject or task.

At the start of your revision period, make a careful and detailed list of everything you feel you're least strong on.

These areas should be tackled right away. Not only are they urgent anyway, but if you 'crack' them early on, your sense of confidence and pleasure will receive a major boost.

In addition to that overall strategy, you should:

Start each revision session with your weakest topic.

That's the same advice in miniature: get your worst and least plea-surable task out of the way when you're fresh. That is both sensible and subsequently pleasant, for it allows you to go on to stronger areas with a sense of real achievement and earned respite.

Take plenty of breaks, and give yourself little rewards on completion of each task.

More negatively, but no less important:

If you get bored with something, *stop*.

It never makes sense to push a tired and resistant brain too far anyway, and that is particularly true when revising. If tedium is your main reaction, very little of what you're doing will register, let alone stick.

Finally:

Have a good time between working periods.

A happy student who's having plenty of fun is very likely to be more efficient when s/he comes to work than one who is doggedly joyless. As always, you've got to be tough and honest about this: if your revision period degenerates into a series of riotous binges, you've got the balance wrong! But there is no need to work all the time:

***Quality* of revision is more important than quantity.**

That quality is likely to be more forthcoming if the student is rested, contented, and therefore – who knows? – actually quite eager to return to important work.

Revision strategy and timing II: Subtler considerations

At various stages in this book, I've suggested that the more you can bring your own experience – including that of your five senses – into your work, the more effective it will be. I would therefore suggest that:

> **If possible, you should visit and inspect the place where you'll be sitting the exam.**

Memory relies partially on environment: if you can arrange to do some of your revision in the exam centre, that could prove an important bonus. But even if that facility is not available, such a visit is still worthwhile. It will reduce – perhaps remove – the disagreeable awe you feel when entering the place on the exam day, and the consequent familiarity will enable you to relax and think more efficiently.

Self-evidently, a great deal of your revision work will be *reading*, although I'll shortly be looking at written tasks that you might think of doing. But now more than ever you don't want to emulate a sponge, important though reinforcement of what you've learnt undoubtedly is. And so:

> **Look over your past work *critically*.**

Seek to improve it as well as absorb it more deeply. You are a better student and mind now than when you first did that work: use that development as fiercely as you can. Correlate your teachers' marginal comments with your own revised judgments; make notes and take action accordingly. Log your discoveries and plug any gaps. This increases your knowledge, your control and your awareness of how far you've developed.

> **Try to ensure that you do some writing – other than note-taking – every day.**

One reason for this is purely mechanical. You (literally) need to 'keep your hand in': all exams make formidable demands on your wrist and finger muscles, and regular daily writing will ensure that they are supple and acclimatised. But there are other reasons too. Writing will reinforce and sharpen lessons learnt from your reading, and also make your brain more active, more in command.

What you write is a tricky matter. The standard advice offered by teachers and commentators is to 'mainline' on past papers; I'm not entirely convinced, for reasons I now explore.

Past papers: Advantages and limitations/dangers

Needless to say, all examinees should be thoroughly schooled in the *format, requirements and structure* of every paper that they will take, and that the most effective way of ensuring that is to peruse the syllabus and attendant past papers with concentrated care. It also goes without saying that *exam practice* is essential. There is a big difference between doing a fine essay or an exquisitely-answered mathematical problem in your own time and doing it under timed conditions, and it is highly probable that the latter part of your course has featured such practice more and more intensively.

During private revision, however, 'overkill' becomes a real possibility. As a wise ex-colleague of mine put it:

> **In the end, and beyond a certain point, doing past papers makes you good at one thing only – *doing past papers*.**

That punchily epigrammatic remark embraces these tough, perhaps unpalatable truths:

> **No matter how diligently you do a practice paper, you are always aware that it *is* a practice.**

There can be no substitute for 'the real thing', and while you can polish technique and consolidate knowledge, there is a limit to how accurate a guide your performance will be in such circumstances. Furthermore . . .

> **When you attempt a past question as a revision exercise, you almost certainly will have prior knowledge of it: that is to say, you've chosen it to fit your needs of the moment.**

Nothing wrong with that in itself, naturally. But you don't get to choose the topics/questions in the exam: the most you can do is select from those set – one from two, four from six, whatever. Again, 'the real thing' is crucially different: not necessarily worse, but different.

They can become addictive, persuading you that *this* is the way, when in fact other methods might prove much more fruitful.

It's very easy to get into a past-paper 'trap' whereby you're convinced that your every sentence is enhancing your readiness and authority. In fact, you're more likely to dull both, because you're not addressing your subject in full, only 'angles' on it.

There is a distinct danger of becoming bored or sated.

If you do too many past questions, your pleasure and interest in the topic can be put at serious risk. Of all the things you want to avoid, the chief one is arriving at the exam centre bored by the subject you're about to sit, all its stimulus and challenge ground out of you.

All that said, past papers do have their value, provided you regard them as useful adjuncts and servants rather than elixirs and masters. But I would advise against undertaking *full* essay-form answers, unless you feel your style is in need of a stringent work-out. Instead:

Choose some questions/topics, and do an outline answer for each.

Talk these over with your peers/friends – with your teachers too if they're still around and available. In addition, look them over a couple of days later (perhaps after doing some further reading and noting on the topics concerned) and then ask yourself:

1   How many good points have you made?
2   How many more could/should you have made?
3   Did you actually answer the question?
4   Are there any irrelevancies/things best omitted?

5   Could your answer have been clearer/better designed?
6   How easy is a stranger going to find your handwriting?!

All those questions are excellent revision aids and spurs to even greater command – and you don't need to have done a complete answer in continuous prose to make the discoveries you need. You thus save time and energy, and you also avoid the boredom factor that at this stage especially can be your deadliest enemy.

Summary

Some of my chapter summaries have turned out to be quite lengthy: not this one. All I want to say in conclusion is:

> **However you go about your revision, try above all to enjoy it, or at any rate to look on it as the opportunity to prove all those teachers, lecturers, parents, brothers and sisters, friends and Uncle Tom Cobley wrong!**

Revision is the last preparatory lap of your course. Make it the time when you assert yourself fully, when you are in sole control. There is no reason why that experience should not be as pleasurable as it is decisive.

And now on to the biggest crunch of all – the exam itself.

Chapter 11

Skills and techniques

We have nothing to fear but Fear itself.

(F.D. Roosevelt)

Preliminary: The day of the exam

Good preparation from the start is essential.

If the exam is in the morning, all that you need should have been laid out the evening before so as to prevent a last-minute panic. Obviously that means all writing implements, geometrical instruments, calculators and so on; these days it also can mean certain texts or pamphlets that you are permitted – or, in the case of 'open book' literature exams, *require*. Most exam centres can lend you a pen, but they are most unlikely to have a stock of set texts, so be warned!

Get up early enough to leave yourself plenty of time. You may be tempted to get up *really* early for a last, intensive revision session, but I advise against it:

The freshness and energy you lose will not be compensated for by the small amount of knowledge you might gain.

Try to get ready in as leisurely a fashion as you can manage. By all means listen to some music or do something that you know has a relaxing effect, but do make sure you allow plenty of time for any journey that has to be made: a delayed train or bus isn't just irritating if you're on an over-tight schedule. On the other hand, avoid if you can premature arrival at the exam hall. About ten minutes before is ideal: any earlier, and you'll have an empty time in which to panic or expend a lot of nervous energy uselessly; any later, and you'll be rushed and won't have time to compose yourself.

Much of the same advice applies if the exam is in the afternoon. Here, however, a gentle look over a past question or two can be a good way of 'ticking over' in the morning without losing too much energy. If there are some quotations or formulae that you've always found hard to memorise and which you think may be useful, it's worth trying to get them into your short-term memory. But launching into full-scale revision is as unwise now as it would have been in the early morning; besides, if you've followed the advice in the previous chapter, it won't be necessary!

In the exam hall: Before writing

Compose yourself

As noted, get there with about ten minutes to spare. Try to relax as much as you can: those meaningless conversations are a *good* idea, however inane – if only because they ease your mind by revealing that others are just as nervous as you! If you prefer to be alone and silent, then take a crossword puzzle or something similar to fill those few minutes: it will 'warm up' your brain without the risk of it focusing grimly on the approaching 'crunch', which is unpleasant anyway and can induce panic.

Nerves

For a start, don't *worry* about being nervous. You are about to perform: any performer – actor, footballer, musician, politician, TV weatherman – should be nervous just before starting. Indeed, experienced performers are only worried when they're *not* nervous: it suggests they are too laid-back, or simply uninterested. A sharp, heightened sense of being alive is admirable – what we call being 'keyed-up'. Adrenalin will charge you up perfectly and naturally, and ensure that you are at your most alert. Nobody else can do it for you, and you certainly can't get it out of a bottle of *any* shape!

The first few minutes

Once at your desk, you'll have a few moments while people settle and so on. *Use* this time. Get properly comfortable; look around you and banish that inevitable sense of strangeness; set out your pens for easy access; jot down any reminders you feel like making; and try to relax – deep breaths and muscle tensing-and-relaxing exercises may help.

The exam paper

When you are instructed to open your paper:

Take it easy for at least two minutes.

Read it; and then read it again. Don't try to frame answers right away: just let the questions sink into you naturally. The brain will register most of the essential information without you having to push it in anyway. You're under time pressure, yes, but a frenzied charge at it from the absolute outset makes no sense at all. 'Festina lente' is a wise Latin saying:[1] your speed will be much the more efficient for having first settled into a relaxed groove.

Understanding the questions

Be quite sure you've fully digested all the instructions – including the questions' *precise* wording. As an (I hope) amusing and instructive way of showing how important this is, how dangerously easy it is to 'understand things too quickly', please try the 'Intelligence test' opposite. You will find the answers on page 198 overleaf, but don't cheat!

The spoof test light-heartedly dramatises the fact that any fool can *read* a question; understanding its exact requirements is another matter entirely. Therefore:

Never start writing – or even planning – an answer until you are *100 per cent* sure you've 'decoded' the question.

All exam boards 'advertise' such vital matters – word-limits, numbers of examples to be included, methodological instructions and so on – by the use of bold type, but it is still a good idea to highlight them further by circling them in red biro or whatever

Intelligence test

You have three minutes to complete this test

1 Write your name in the square provided. [_____]

2 How many of each species did Moses take on the Ark? _____

3 Divide thirty by half and add ten. _____

4 What was the highest mountain in the world before Everest was discovered? _____

5 If you drove a bus leaving London with 40 passengers, dropped off seven and picked up two at Watford, then stopped at Heathrow Airport, dropped eight there and picked up five, then drove on to arrive at Oxford three hours later, what was the driver's name? _____

6 Take two apples from three and what do you have? _____

7 If a doctor gave you three tablets and told you to take one every half hour, how long would they last? _____

8 Which country has the fourth of July, USA or UK? _____

9 What was the Prime Minister's name in 1950? _____

10 Some months have 31 days; some have 30; how many have 28? _____

Intelligence test answers and explanations

1 Your name should appear, as instructed, in the square
  – which is located at the bottom of the page, right hand
  corner – not in the oblong alongside the question.
2 None. The Ark was Noah's enterprise.
3 Seventy. Basic arithmetical terminology and practice,
  this: dividing something by half is the same as multi-
  plying it by two, or doubling it. Thus:

$$30 \div \tfrac{1}{2} = 30 \times 2; \text{ add } 10\text{: } 70$$

4 Everest. It was there before man discovered or named
  it.
5 Whatever your name is – 'you' did the driving.
6 Two apples. It is dangerously easy to assume that you're
  being asked 'what do you have left?' or 'what remains?',
  but you're not! A wonderful illustration of the need to
  read/'de-code' a question properly.
7 One hour. For example, take the first at 12.00; the
  second at 12.30; and the third at 1.00.
8 Both of them. The question says nothing about, nor even
  implies, the date's national significance.
9 Whoever the Prime Minister is when you read this; at
  the time of writing, it is Tony Blair. The Prime Minister
  in 1950 was, as a matter of fact, Clement Atlee, but
  that's not what the question asks!
10 All of them (cf. questions 6, 8 and 9).

method you've found suits you best. Take particular note of all
instructional verbs; indeed, this is so important – even more than
when doing a 'private' assignment – that I repeat here the exercise
included in Chapter 8. You may have attempted it then, but try
it again: you'll be intrigued by how difficult it still is second time
around, and that should further arm you towards a successful
outcome.

What does the question mean?

Below follow fourteen instructional verbs and alongside them four-teen definitions of those verbs. *Can you pair them off accurately?* The answers can be found on page 145.

Verb	Definition
Account for	Give reasons; say 'why' rather than just define.
Analyse	Write down the information in the right order.
Comment on	Item-by-item consideration of the topic, usually presented one under the other.
Compare	Point out differences only and present result in orderly fashion.
Contrast	Estimate the value of, looking at positive and negative attributes.
Describe	Elect features according to the question.
Discuss	Present arguments for and against the topic in question; you can also give your opinion.
Evaluate	Explain the cause of.
Explain	Make critical or explanatory notes/observations.
Identify	State the main features of an argument, omitting all that is only partially relevant.
List	Give the main features or general features of a subject, omitting minor details and stressing structure.
Outline	Make a survey of the subject, examining it critically.
Review	Point out the differences and similarities.
Summarise	Separate down into component parts and show how they interrelate with each other.

As before, do not 'translate' the prime need to work out what you've got to *do* into the treacherous and doomed question, 'What do they want me to *say?*' That is always *your* business and yours alone – and especially in an exam.

There is one final thing to bear in mind before starting, even though it doesn't come into play until you've nearly finished. It is:

Always try to leave yourself ten minutes to read through your answers at the end.

To have a good chance of achieving this goal, you need to 'programme' it into your planning from the outset. You might even – if you have such a thing – set the alarm on your watch to remind you forcibly.

Concerning the advice itself, two observations:

1   I *know* every teacher advises you to do it, and that it's there-fore a boring and predictable remark on my part.
2   I also know that hardly any student actually does it! This is not usually out of defiance or contempt, but because they simply don't remember until it's too late.

The benefits of such a step are considerable, even crucial.

1   If you check ruthlessly for errors, flab, lack of clarity in both expression and handwriting, you will forestall quite a few of what would otherwise be the *examiner's* discoveries, and thus improve your mark.
2   Such correction is in any event a much more fruitful use of that time than the frantic addition of a further paragraph or two to your final answer. Remember that by this stage the examiner's judgment of your material will be more or less formed. Last-minute thoughts are unlikely to affect it very much, but tight-ening and polishing *earlier* answers might well do so.
3   By this stage, also, you are almost sure to be suffering from fatigue, and unlikely anyway to come up with anything too brilliant in the way of a new idea. Mechanical checking makes no demands on your tired imagination, and is the perfect activity for a brain now beginning to wind down.
4   Paradoxically, because you have now begun that winding-down process and are thus a little more relaxed, it is possible that a snappy phrase/the right word/any kind of 'missing link' *will* now occur to you where previously you had neither time nor inclination to 'let it come'.
5   You will almost certainly feel better when 'Time' is called – and if you're doing another paper that same day, such a feeling of well-being is a significant bonus.

Writing your answers I: Elementary strategies

The rudimentary tips which follow are no less important for being obvious.

Answer the easiest, or your strongest, question first.

This boosts confidence, which in turn gives you added energy, or the illusion of it, which in these circumstances amounts to the same thing. It may also leave you extra time to deal with the harder tasks later.

If you answer a question on a topic you haven't prepared, you're taking a gamble.

In my experience, such gambles either come off very well or – much more often – very badly indeed. Unless you feel truly inspired, stick to what you know you know/can do successfully.

In multiple choice papers, don't change your first answer unless you're *positive* that the second decision is correct.

Better still, leave such a decision till the end – those final ten minutes just discussed. Make a note somewhere visible to do just that.

Always pay particular attention to the marks allotted per question.

These are not included on your paper for laughs or even polite etiquette: they are decisive signals about how much time and substance you should devote to each one. I've lost count of the number of times I've examined scripts which lavish twelve lines on a two-mark question and then about fifteen *words* on a ten-mark one: don't fall into that trap.

Don't imagine you need to write – or even think – all the time. If you need a brief break, take it.

Most advanced exams are two hours-plus – an artificial length of time so far as the brain's natural rhythms are concerned (see pages 25–30). If you feel the need to 'down tools' for a minute or two, to yawn cavernously and have a stretch, then do it: your brain's messages to you are rarely wrong, and that goes for an exam as much as any other time.

So far, my advice will probably be familiar to you: you'll have heard most of it before from your teachers. Don't let this familiarity breed contempt: remember that

> **More people fail exams – or do less well than they should – through carelessly ignoring such advice than through lack of ability or preparation.**

Now, however, I'd like to offer some tips that you may not have encountered.

Writing your answers II: Performance strategies

Let's assume that everything is 'set up' soundly. That is to say, you have:

- been adequately taught;
- worked hard;
- settled yourself in the exam room in a relaxed and alert way;
- taken full note of all the rubric and all the requirements of the paper;
- succeeded in banishing panic, and now feel quietly confident.

How can you ensure that you perform at your best?

The first 'performance strategy' hinges on your paper's eventual destination – the examiner's desk.

Bear in mind your examiners' timetable and work rhythms

I have already dealt with that absurd and harmful delusion – the notion that your answer must match what the marker thinks.

However, it is very sensible to be aware of probable examiner *behaviour*, and I can best help you towards a sound working estimate of that with the question:

Roughly how long do you think an examiner will spend reading and marking your script?

I've had answers ranging from '20 minutes' to 'over an hour'. In fact, an experienced marker will look to do an average of five scripts an hour, which means that you have approximately

ten minutes of his/her time to make your quality count.

That isn't meant to frighten you but to help you, as is the additional suggestion that you would be wise to make as good an immediate impact as you can. Nearly all examiners develop an early 'feel' of what an answer is like and worth, and while they will of course read *all* of it with due conscientiousness, in most instances those early intimatons turn out to be confirmed. So:

First impressions count: grab your examiner's attention as early as possible.

Make them sit up and say, 'This one knows what s/he's doing.' It's always a pleasure to mark scripts that have a sense of purpose and clarity, and such qualities nearly always render your *material* cogent and enjoyable too. Let's now look at how you can best achieve this.

Making an Immediate impact

First of all:

Get some ideas down on paper as soon as you can.

On the whole, I *don't* advise you to begin writing the actual answer straightaway. There can be exceptions to this: if, for example, you quickly spot a question you know you can launch into at once, then go ahead – it will boost morale by getting you off to a flying start. But it's more likely that you'll need a brief warm-up first.

So use an 'energising pattern', as described in Chapter 8 (pages 145–9). This will take only a few moments, will ignite your mind fully, and (best of all) will give you a wealth of visual triggers to aid your progression from point to point, stage to stage, and argument to argument.

I have already written at some length on the subject of introductions, and will not weary you with its repetition. All I'll suggest for exam work is this:

> **Map out an introductory paragraph in your head**
> **– *and then abandon it*, or at any rate examine it**
> **ruthlessly.**

Does it really say anything? Are you using your time or merely marking it? For now is the time above all others to remind yourself that

> **A blank sheet of paper is a uniquely frightening**
> **thing.**

The temptation to start filling it up on the knee-jerk-reaction principle can be almost overwhelming. Don't do that: reconsider your planned first sentences as calmly as you can and, if in any doubt, scrap them. Unless you have a particular knack for constructing short, pithy introductions,[2] it is always best – *especially in an exam* – to get right into the substance of your argument/answer. This increases the chance of grabbing the examiner's attention, and it also avoids the danger of making your first remark a paraphrase of the question, which is never a wise way to begin.

There is one kind of question where an introduction *is* essential, however, and we need to look at it at once.

'Stating one's terms'

Sometimes you will need to *define* what is to be the basis or 'angle' of your answer. An example will soon establish what I mean.

A recent English Literature A level paper included this question on Milton:

> **Examine the ways in which Milton's style assists**
> **the argument in *Paradise Lost, Book IV*.**

Incautious students might say to themselves: 'Nice one! It's the banker-question on Milton's use of language – plus the Biblical story, naturally. I *like* it!' Well, partly, yes; but crucially, *no*. It is not a trick question, but it's more subtle than such a breezy reaction recognises.

The thing is, you cannot answer that question properly until you've defined what Milton's 'argument' *is*. Your answer requires a brief introduction, summarising that argument; then, and only then, can you go on to show how his use of *Genesis* and the English language reveals and dramatises that argument.

You might say that this is obvious enough, and you wouldn't be wrong. But it was sobering – and sad – how many quite able students failed to do it. As a result, much of their stylistic analysis was insufficiently locked on to the question's real focus to impress. And by the way, it doesn't matter if your subject is physics or economics rather than English literature: the principle I'm outlining applies to all disciplines:

> **If you need to 'state your terms', do so, clearly and quickly. Otherwise, just get on with it. Beware of confusing *private*, preparatory thinking with *public* performing and arguing: don't offer coy 'appetizers' – hit the 'main course' at once.**

So much for how best to start. Turning to the main body of your exam time, how can you maintain maximum impact and advantage?

Be interesting: Show them you can think

I've addressed this vital matter in earlier chapters: all I want to do here is to emphasise the importance of being fresh and individual in this your final test. You should never despise the obvious, whose importance and value can be decisive; in addition, you must, yes,

- do what you're told;
- answer the question;
- never 'bend' a title to your own whims and in defiance of its own focus;

- jettison altogether any 'prepared' answer unless it matches the question's concerns word for word.

But within those requirements try to produce *your* answer, as opposed to a dull, worthy, featureless consensus. This is especially true if you want more than a mere pass, and here are five tips to help you go beyond that.

1 *Don't be too 'holy'.* If you've got something negative to say, and you genuinely *feel* it, then go ahead and say it. If you pretend to be impressed with something when you're not, it will show – badly.

2 *Never apologise.* Very few people truly object to what an incisive and honest mind has to say in any circumstances, and that is perhaps truest of all in an exam. Trust your responses and present them straightforwardly.

3 *Never 'rave' emptily.* Such remarks as 'Shakespeare's brilliant play is quite wonderful' or 'Turner is a fantastic painter who really turns me on' are not only useless but annoying. I've encountered both those statements in exam papers I've marked, and they strike me as mere crawling waffle!

4 *Equally, avoid arrogant criticism* – that is, snooty and unsupported judgments: they nearly always bounce damagingly back on you. An exaggerated example might be, 'Chaucer's middlebrow wisdom about unimportant and extinct matters renders him merely dull. Besides, he can't spell.' Aim for dignity, politeness and the air of one conducting some kind of *dialogue* with the examiner – a meeting of two interesting and interested minds.

5 Finally, try to *remember that crucial last step* mentioned earlier – always leave ten minutes at the end to check over and correct your work!

Elementary and performance strategies: A summary

When you've perused the exam paper and decided, at least provisionally, which questions you're going to answer, you need each time to address these three things:

- What does the question ask you to do?
- Do you know what you chiefly wish to say?
- How are you going to start?

They are separate, and yet they interlock almost spookily, as these two contrasting formulae illustrate. The bad news is:

Ignore or make a mess of one of them, and the other two will suffer as well.

The good news is:

Solve the first 'problem' properly, and the second will be easier; solve that, and the third one will be.

If you follow all the above strategies, your chances of success will be high. And I hope I've managed to make you feel positive about the whole business of exams. However, my account could never be complete without a hard look at the examinee's worst nightmare.

'Exam block': What to do if stuck

This apparent disaster is often more easily dealt with and solved than the panicky student might think.

The first thing to do is recognise the fact – say to yourself 'I'm stuck'.

The very fact of articulating this should calm you – and *panic* is a deadly enemy to be avoided at all costs. Remind yourself that we all get a mental block from time to time, and that you may just be tired: after all, the examinee's other deadly enemy is *fatigue*.

Do *not* 'rack your brains'.

As noted in Chapter 2, it rarely works anyway, and such frantic mental activity is precisely what you *don't* want/need at this particular moment.

Further to those last two observations, give yourself two minutes to de-fever yourself and amass some 'cool'.

You can probably do with a brief rest in any case, and now is a good as well as necessary time to take it.

Free associate.

Cast your mind back to when you last heard or saw the material you want. What was the book, who was the lecturer? What was s/he wearing, what was the weather like? Where were you? Was there any music going on when you last perused the stuff, and would remembering the tune trigger other recall? Any system like that may well yield the secret you require.

> **If none of the above works, then abandon the point at issue and go on to the next and/or one you're solid on or, ... if necessary, go on to an entirely new question.**

A drastic measure, maybe, but still a much better idea than sitting there in a doubly injurious state of panic and inactivity. Besides, now that you've made an *in-charge* decision, it is distinctly possible that the 'stuck' material may come back to you later. Your brain has relaxed and re-assumed control, and it may yet come up with those missing goods.

Conclusion: Don't be frightened

I've headlined this chapter with a wise remark by one of the greatest presidents of the United States. His words are by now a cliché, but they still have value for anyone who cultivates either excessive modesty or self-induced nervousness – about anything, but particularly about exams. Although arrogance is often warned against, the fact is that very few students ever make *that* error: far more – indeed, far too many – reduce their impact through coyness or needless diffidence.

Above all, stop yourself using fear as an excuse. It is always tempting to do this: it gives you a first-class and apparently unanswerable get-out. But remember: people may be sorry for you if you say, 'I messed up the exam – I was too scared to do myself justice.' They may even believe you. But they won't *admire* you – how can they? You've had your chance, and now you've blown it. As I've admitted, on a few occasions such an event will be a genuine injustice; far more often, however, it'll be nobody's fault but the candidate's.

I'm not trying to preach. If you've followed some of the advice in this book, you'll be aware of how able you can be, and that exam success is realistically – and enjoyably – within your grasp. Good luck to you; but, if you've studied well (and I hope this book has helped you to do that) then you don't need luck:

Just *do* it! You are in charge.

Reading novels and creative literature

It is, I think, obvious why my six-point speed-reading programme (pages 122–5) is unsatisfactory for works of literature. Novels, plays, and poetry cannot be dealt with in this manner – not because there's anything 'holy' about them, but because it simply doesn't work. If you dart through a novel or a play by Shakespeare employing the first four 'points' I suggest, you end up precisely where you started, and annoyed to boot. The main reason, of course, is that literary works don't have summaries, graphs, illustrations or even chapter headings. And their introductory and concluding sections work in a different, less straightforward, way.

So how can you increase your rate of coverage if the central part of your course is literature? To come to terms with a major play takes a lot of time. Even more arduous is a text the length of *Jane Eyre* or *Our Mutual Friend* (both frequent choices for A level and undergraduate courses). When you remember that reading the text is only the first stage – you've then got to discuss, analyse and absorb it – the task can seem forbidding.

One answer is to cultivate 'skip-reading', which I've looked at already. This provides useful 'ignition', which is important; however, it won't do much more than get you started, especially if you're missing out 20 pages at a time. By all means use it to kick you off; but you need something else as well.

Letting the book do the work

In Chapter 6 I did not mention the simplest kind of 'speed-reading' of all – that of reading a book very fast, without pausing to mull anything over, and not being concerned about the bits that make no sense. I have found this method consistently valuable ever since

I started A levels 40 years ago. When I read in this way, I don't *consciously* ignore anything, as I would if 'skip-reading'. This method is more passive. I make no decisions, no choices, no clever short-cuts. I let the book do the work, not me – I let it wash over me, leaving the book to determine which bits 'stick'.

Time for an example – and a hefty one at that. My favourite novel is Leo Tolstoy's *Anna Karenina*.[1] One of its major features is *length* – over 850 pages in my Penguin edition. It is doubly daunting to pick up such a tome knowing it to be not only very long but also one of the greatest aesthetic achievements of all time. How on earth are you going to cope?

When I first read the novel at the age of 17, I covered it in two days. I positively *belted* through it, determined to get to the end as quickly as I could. This was not because I disliked it: quite the reverse. I was hoping to acquire, as fast as possible, a sense of its majesty, and a kind of 'skeletal' idea of its plot, style and characters. And I believe I achieved this. I had an at least basic knowledge of the plot (or rather, the *plots*) and some sense of how these separate narrative strands were interwoven. I knew something about all the major characters; and I had an awed awareness of the grandeur of the writing. I could see, however vaguely, that Tolstoy was equally masterly whether describing the subtlest emotions, the most vigorous physical activities, or the feel of the ever-changing landscape. In short, I knew something of what the book was about, and a little bit about why it has such a reputation.

I've read *Anna Karenina* probably twenty times since then. I still don't feel I 'know' it really well, and I imagine I won't feel that even when I've read it a further twenty times – it's that kind of book. And that is very much the point. As I said at the start of this chapter, *any* significant work of literature (and it's unlikely you'll be asked to centre your studies on anything less) has a richness and variety that will continue to yield new pleasures on the tenth, twentieth or umpteenth reading; and nobody will expect you to plumb all its depths in a mere two or three years. With this in mind, a tearaway first reading is perfectly sensible, and will very probably encourage you to make an early and more sober return to the text. The alternative – plodding haltingly through it over a period of weeks – is unlikely to be more efficient in terms of retention. Your response will be less vibrant if you plod, and you may end up hoping to God you never have to open the book again. Not a very productive attitude for a student faced with a set text.

Think of a novel as a painting or a piece of music

When we first look at a painting, we take in a general, overall impression. We note the subject, the colour, the size, the 'feeling' it radiates. Later, returning to it, we start to notice details: the *blending* and *number* of colours, the way the eye is drawn this way and that by the *picture's line*, the perspective, and other subtler things. Still later, we may see evidence of particular techniques, acquire a full sense of the picture's structure, and be able to say with some authority and analytic prowess what the picture *does* and why it is impressive.

Similarly with a piece of music. At first we will merely be aware of tunes, the instruments used, and the 'atmosphere' engendered. Subsequently, we will start to realise how the tunes relate to each other; precisely how the composer deploys the various instruments and why; how he uses dynamics and even silence. Eventually, our appreciation will grow to include grasp of structure, and a familiarity with its themes/tunes that makes proper sense of individual phrases.

A novel can be approached in much the same way. First time round, you will get an overall sense of its structure and subject, plus a general ideal of its style, pace, and characters. Just as the painting and the music are not *studied* in detail at first, so should you 'glance' at your novel, establishing a pleasant, undemanding acquaintance. The study comes later – when you're in shape for it.

Works of art are complex, profoundly intricate things. No one, however clever, can understand them quickly. People who expects to achieve adequate mastery through one laborious 'go' at a novel not only understand nothing about how literature works: they know very little about how their own minds operate. By now I hope you are not such a person! So read as fast and as 'superficially' as you like: the detailed digging that has to be done later will be all the easier and more successful as a result.

Literary analysis

A strategy

Preliminary

Chapter 8 advocates the three-point plan for purposes of analysis
– all analysis, regardless of discipline, even the the latter material
does include a specific literary example (see page 159). The strategy
explored here is closely allied to that method, but it differs in two
respects. First it assumes *choice*. Some assignments and exam questions specify absolutely the poem(s) or extracts that you must tackle;
others allow or indeed require you to select your own examples.
Second, it addresses *five* considerations rather than three – chiefly
because at the time of writing the UK's A level system lists five
Attainment Objectives in English Literature, as does the International Baccalaureate's English A1, a wholly literary course. As
a final introductory point, I would stress that although my remarks
centre on the critical analysis of a poem, the criteria and techniques examined apply equally to all genres and to all aesthetic
analysis.

I Choice

Following a programme of study of a poet or a number of poets,
coursework or non-examination students are almost always able
to choose which poems feature in their essay. I usually advise
junior students (i.e. pre-16) to start by answering, albeit quite
briefly, one or all of these questions:

- Why did you choose this poem rather than another one?
- What makes it special to you?
- What might make it special to others?

Doing so gives both writer and reader an immediate, personal focus that is mutually beneficial. Sixth formers and beyond might think that a more sophisticated start is preferable: in keeping with my warnings about unmuscular introductions, they may well feel such things don't need addressing at all! Nevertheless:

> **It is essential to answer this question *for yourself*, even if it does not graduate onto your script.**

That is a variant of the principle established in Chapter 8:

> **The question 'Why?' should be the first word on any and every essay plan.**

If *you're* not clear why you've picked this poem, it's most unlikely that the reader will know either – and that kind of vagueness will do neither party any favours. So even if you don't make it explicit, be sure that clarity of reason and purpose is there: it will establish the foundations of a good essay.

2 Theme/subject matter

This criterion is also best elucidated by a simple question:

> **What is the poem about?**

'Simple' it may be, but it isn't *easy*: incautiously tackled, it can in fact become very dangerous. Answering it

> **absolutely does *not* mean you have to spell out the obvious.**

If, for instance, you are addressing the poetry of World War I, it is starkly evident that virtually *all* such poems are about the ghastliness of war. To draw even brief attention to that might cost momentum; to do so at any length would be useless, boring and invite ridicule: not a great combination! What would be needed instead is a more precise focus on the *particular* ghastliness or misery which this or that poet addressed (for example, disablement, boredom, madness, futility, so forth).

Similarly and further: *never explain things for the sake of it.* To take a ludicrous example: if you came across the sentence

The cat sat on the mat

you would both waste your readers' time and enragingly patronise them by then writing:

In this line, the writer draws our attention to the fact that a domestic feline pet is in a prone position on a small carpet.

Pompous rubbish that does nobody any good, least of all the writer!

So when *should* you explain 'what is it about?' Well, I've found this an excellent rule-of-thumb:

If something caused *you* difficulty, the chances are high that your *readers* will be finding it similarly problematic.

That's when you explain.

3 How does it work/What techniques does the writer use?

This will, almost certainly, form the main body of your analysis. Look at:

- The length of the poem; length of the stanzas; regularity (or otherwise) of those stanzas. If it's a decent poem[1] these decisions on the poet's part will be significant.
- Rhyme scheme – or lack of it. If the poet employs one, why does s/he do so? How does it assist meaning and impact? Or if it does *not* so assist, why not? If the poet includes *no* rhymes, why might that be? What is the poet looking to bring about via such an absence?
- Punctuation, flow, rhythm and line length. Decent poets (let alone great ones) devote enormous attention to these things – just as much as to the words themselves. So how do such features work and assist the reader's understanding?

- Imagery, metaphors, choice of phrasing. Why does the poet choose this word or phrase rather than that one? Does this poetic language please or trouble you? (Don't be dismissive, but don't be *too* humble either: if you don't like a phrase, there's probably a good reason for it if you're being sensible.)

4 Anything else you want to say not covered by the above?

Younger students should not worry about this too much unless they really have got something extra they want to examine. But sixth formers should regard this strand as an ideal opportunity to bring in comparisons with *other* texts, to place the poem in a historical and cultural context, and (paradoxically, in view of the previous point) to show why the poem is in some important way *timeless* – hence our twenty-first century study of it.[2]

5 Do you like it and/or what effect does it have on you?

This is, crucially, different from Point 1 above. You may have a very good reason for having chosen poem *x*, but at the end of your study that does not necessarily mean you have to *like* or *approve of* poem *x*. In truth, it is quite unlikely that there will be a big gap between your responses to Points 1 and 5, but it is certainly possible, and if it occurs, address it.

Whether you end up approving wholeheartedly of the poem or having significant reservations about it, be careful how you express yourself. I have stressed throughout this book that you should be honest in your response and unapologetic about it: *you are in charge.* But on the one hand don't *gush* and on the other don't be emptily rude: both are equally disagreeable, and damaging, in their different ways.

A brief note on quotation

Any reader requiring an extensive guide to the art of quotation – and it *is* finally an art, not a skill – might care to consult Chapter 10 of my *Write In Style*.[3] Here I would like simply to make four observations that I hope prove helpful

- No A level candidate gets much credit for trotting out a quotation *per se* – especially in 'open book' exams, when s/he hasn't even had to memorise it!
- A quotation *never* speaks for itself: you need to indicate what it proves and/or why you've chosen it.
- A quotation must be grammatically complete, whether standing alone or as part of a sentence of your own. That is not mere syntactical pedantry: if the quotation doesn't make full sense, neither can the argument you seek to build out of and around it.
- Make sure the quotation and the point you're advancing *match*, and match fully. You'd be surprised by how often this does not apply, even in very good essayists (including professional critics).

An ICT glossary/some useful websites

Compiled by Jon Down

Glossary

ADSL Asymmetric digital subscriber line. The most common 'Broadband' technology that delivers high-speed Internet access.

Apple Mac A desktop computer that runs the Apple Mac operating system. Strictly speaking an Apple Mac is a personal computer but this term has been hijacked by IBM-compatible computers.

Broadband Any communication line that delivers high-speed Internet access, where high speed means connections of 128kbps (kilobytes per second) or faster.

Byte A keyboard character such as a letter or number uses exactly one byte of memory.

CD writer Part of a computer or a peripheral that copies files onto a CD-RW.

CD-ROM Compact disc read-only memory. A CD containing a computer program.

CD-RW A compact disk that, like a floppy disk or tape cassette can be used over and over again.

Database A software program that holds tables of information, such as an address book or a membership list. The most common is *Microsoft Access*.

Desktop PC A standard, non-portable computer.

Dial-up Shorthand for using a modem and a telephone line to connect to the Internet.

Email An electronic way of sending messages from computer to computer.

Floppy disk A magnetic disk onto which data can be copied from a computer. Has largely been superseded by CDs and DVDs.

Gigabyte 2^{30} bytes or a thousand million bytes.

Hard disk   Also known as a hard drive. Part of a computer that stores data. Unlike a floppy disk, a hard disk cannot easily be removed.

Hardware   The physical devices such as PCs, printers, scanners and the like.

ICT   Information and communications technology – computers, peripherals, networks and devices to aid communication.

Internet   A worldwide network of computers. Anyone can join the Internet.

Internet technology   Allows computers of different and incompatible types to be used on the same network.

Intranet   A private network, sometimes in one building, sometimes just one company at many sites, sometimes many companies at many sites.

ISDN   Integrated services digital network. A communication line that delivers a connection to the Internet of up to 128kbps.

ISP   Internet service provider. A company which provides an Internet connection for whom your computer. The most well-known include Freeserve and America On-Line (AOL).

IT   Information technology. Computers and peripherals.

List server   A list of email addresses used to send messages to groups or forums, usually about a particular topic.

Megabyte 2^{20} bytes or 1 million bytes.

Modem   A device that connects a computer to a telephone line in order to connect to the Internet.

Online   Connected to the Internet.

Operating system   A program that enables the user to tell the hardware what software to run. Windows is the most well-known operating system.

PC   An IBM compatible personal computer, the computer most widely used in offices and in the home. Most PCs run the Windows operating system.

Printer (ink jet)   Cheap printers usually used at home.

Printer (laser)   More expensive but fast. Usually only prints in black and white.

RAM   Means and measure of computer memory.

Scanner   Enables pictures (and hard copy text) to be copied and used by a computer.

Software   Programs, such as word-processing, that run on the hardware.

Spreadsheet   A software program used for financial and mathematical calculations. The most common is *Microsoft Excel*.

Upgrade   Either a fix for software that didn't work properly or an attempt to persuade users to throw out perfectly good older software.

URL   Uniform resource locator. An Internet address which usually starts with 'www'.

World Wide Web (WWW)   How the collection of files set up on special 'web servers' around the world has come to be known.

Some useful websites

Note: Given the speed and frequency with which websites change and move you may find that by the time you read this several of the references may not be accurate.

Websites mentioned in the text

dictionary.oed.com/entrance.dtl	*The Oxford English Dictionary.*
rmc.library.cornell.edu	Cornell University.
uk.yahoo.com	One of the best-known search engines.
www.bbc.co.uk/learning/	The BBC learning website.
www.blackpresence.co.uk	Black Presence in Britain.
www.eb.co.uk:180	*Encyclopaedia Britannica.*
www.google.co.uk	One of the best-known search engines.
www.learndirect.co.uk	The largest government-funded provider of e-learning courses and opportunities.
www.pro.gov.uk	The Public Record Office.
www.sanger.ac.uk/HGP	The Human Genome Project.
www.statistics.gov.uk	Office for National Statistics.
www.tate.org.uk/home/default.htm	The Tate Gallery.

Resources and information on adaptive technologies

www.abilitynet.org.uk
www.ace-centre.org.uk
www.rnib.org.uk

Other useful sites

www.infoville.org.uk/internet/ internet_isplist.htm	Help on finding and choosing an ISP.
www.searchenginewatch.com	A good guide to varieties of search engine.
www.sophos.com/	One of the leading producers of anti-virus software and a mine of anti-virus information.
www.virusbtn.com/	Independent anti-virus advice.

Appendix IV

Some simple relaxation and fitness exercises

There are few things more maddening than being blithely told to 'Relax!' when you're feeling like an over-wound watch-spring. It usually seems about as sensible and tactful as telling someone who's depressed to cheer up! Nevertheless, there are ways in which you can reduce *physical* tension at least, and that can often ease the mind's jangling as well. So here's a simple routine that you will find calms you down quite effectively and pleasantly.

1 Lie down on your back, or sit in a chair which fully supports your back.
2 Close your eyes.
3 Think about your head. Feel the forehead muscles relaxing. Relax your eyelids, and let your jaw go slack. Let your tongue fall to the bottom of your mouth. Start to take deep breaths.
4 Now move down to your shoulders. Let them go loose, and allow your arms to go limp.
5 Relax your neck: let your head roll gently until you find an agreeable position.
6 Let your stomach go slack. It is probably the tensest part of you in such circumstances, so take your time. Concentrate on smoothing away all the creases that seem to line it inside.
7 Tense and relax your right arm, several times. Then tense it once more and slowly relax it from the top of the shoulder to the fingertips.
8 Do the same with your left arm.
9 Tense and relax your right leg several times. Then tense it once more and slowly let the tension go, from hip down to toes.
10 Do the same with your left leg.

11 Now listen to any sound from within your body – heartbeat, breathing, stomach. Pick one such sound and focus on it. Block out all other sounds and thoughts.

12 Tense and relax your whole body at five-second intervals. Do this twice more. Then, slowly open your eyes and sit upright. Take a long, slow stretch.

You can even use these at an exam desk, and certainly anywhere else. They soften tension through being physically pleasant; and for a valuable five minutes they reduce all that mental 'buzzing' – or at any rate reduce your anxious concentration on it.

Everyday fitness exercises are also good for sharpening your muscle tone and general alertness. If in doubt about your physical state, consult your doctor first, but I wouldn't imagine these will over-tax many of you.

1 Toe-touching: try touching each foot with the opposite hand. Keep your legs straight, or as straight as you can bear!

2 Press-ups: excellent for toning you up and controlling the breathing. Women sometimes find these hard, and should be prepared to improvise.

3 Sit-ups: lie on your back, and if possible hook your toes under something solid (i.e. unlikely to move). Clasp your hands behind your neck; and then haul yourself up to a sitting position. Real masochists can try to bring their head down to meet their knees! Repeat 5–10 times, or until the stomach muscles lodge a formal protest.

4 'Cycling': lie on your back; raise your legs about two feet; then 'pedal' as smoothly as you can. Regulate pace according to taste/pain level.

5 The straight-leg lift: lie on your back, legs together. Raise them six inches. Hold that position for 5 seconds. Lower. Repeat 5 times. Then repeat, but, after raising, splay each leg to the side, maintaining a 6-inch distance off the ground. Do this three times, then return to together-position and lower.

Of course, if you're keen to get truly fit in a more athletic sense, these would qualify only as warm-up exercises. But for the less vigorous, they will keep your body quite freshly tuned at an outlay of about fifteen minutes a day. And the better you feel physically, the more alert and 'bright' you will be in your study.

Notes

1 Attitudes, assets and achievement

1 All that said and meant, I would urge great care over study aids. Some of them are frankly terrible, and a great many others, while far from disgraceful, are not worth your money, in that you can do a much better job if you trust your own brain and that of those who teach and confer with you (as in B 9 a, b and c on page 7). If you must buy them or have them bought for you by anxious, hysterical or insane relatives, use them as occasional back-ups, as *servants*: they must never be your masters.

2 I am well aware that some students only have option b, private work, available, and nobody should make light of the feelings of deprivation that inevitably steal over them from time to time. However, these *distance learners* enjoy one or two surprising advantages over their more orthodox counterparts. The independence and strength of mind essential to survive such isolated study very often shine through in written argument. The absence of 'discussion' puts a greater premium on dedicated reading and research – which is always a private affair, whoever and wherever you are. They also work when they want to, or when they can – which in the case of the determined distance learner amounts to the same thing. That means they are invariably focused when addressing their tasks; it also means that they don't have to sit through lessons or lectures which are only marginally useful – and every teacher delivers those, no matter how brilliant s/he may be!

3 Even the sad few who need to think about whether they should tick it will end up doing so: I've yet to meet anyone who is happy to plead guilty to the charge of humourlessness!

4 I.e. between *c.* 1.1 and 1.4 kilos.

5 Tony Buzan, *Use Your Head* (London: BBC Books, 1971, p. 13).

6 Not only does silence distract me (I've never been able to work for any length of time in a library, for example), but also in my experience true silence is extremely rare. Dogs bark, children play, cars drive past and aeroplanes fly overhead: music helps to shut out those sudden and frequent sounds that are beyond my control. Besides, it makes me happy and thus increases both my pleasure and my energy – excellent bonuses when working!

7 That sentence is not a bad definition of a concept I cited on page 4 – the 'pleasure principle'. The term was coined by Sigmund Freud in the early 1900s but, as is evident (and as he knew), the truth it enshrines has been fundamental to human life from its very beginnings.
8 If in any doubt about this, check with your doctor. I would not like to be accused of causing you cardiac arrest – especially in court.
9 There are further observations about these matters in Chapter 5, 'Other sources and resources' (page 92ff).

2 Memory

1 Though not yet the police!
2 William James, *Principles of Psychology*, Vol. 1 (1891, p. 662).
3 James, ibid., p. 663.
4 If you are interested in these, consult the bibliography (page 230), which gives a list of books that offer detailed information on the topic.
5 While I stick to my insistence that mnemonics are best devised by each individual, you might find these further two favourites of interest and exemplificatory value.
   In the mid-eighteenth century the Swedish naturalist Karl Linnaeus devised a classification of all living things which, in descending order of 'size', runs:

Kingdom/Phylum*/Class/Order/Family/Genus/Species/ Variety

To recall that I use the mnemonic sentence:

<u>K</u>indly <u>P</u>lace <u>C</u>over <u>O</u>n <u>F</u>resh <u>G</u>reen <u>S</u>pring <u>V</u>egetables

I also very much like this explanation of the Equals sign (=), which was invented by Robert Recorde and which appeared in his *Whetstone of Witte*, 1557. He chose the symbol because 'noe 2 things can be more equal'.
   * A *phylum* is a sub-kingdom; tribe or race of organisms.
6 They are also seldom watertight, especially if they address the minefield that is English spelling! The mnemonic is flawed, for the different reason that it's not always true – as witness words like 'weird', 'foreign' and 'seize'.
7 I.M.L. Hunter, *Memory* (Harmondsworth: Penguin, 1957, p. 310).
8 It doesn't matter if the logic is clear only to you: after all, it's *your* mnemonic!

3 Review

1 The phenomenon also cropped up in an episode of the BBC 1 thriller, *Spooks*, that I watched the evening before I wrote these words! It was very well done, but my point stands: work, not magic, is the answer.

2   For this table, and the account of Ebbinghaus's work that it illustrates,
    I am indebted to Ian M.L. Hunter, op. cit., pp. 126–8.
3   Hunter, op. cit., pp. 141–2.

4   ICT and the knowledge revolution

1   *Julius Caesar*, Act I, Scene ii, 140–1.
2   This piece of (mild) jargon simply denotes 'the printed version'.
3   I should point out that these tips apply specifically to Microsoft Word
    and some will not necessarily be available in less sophisticated word-
    processing packages.
4   Powerpoint is a Microsoft presentation package.
5   Not that this has ever happened to me, you understand!
6   It often seems to me that Internet time and earth time are two entirely
    different measures. You can be surfing the Internet for just a couple
    of minutes, look up for a moment, and find that several hours of your
    life have disappeared. If you pay your telephone bill through some sort
    of price plan, make sure you can include calls to the Internet on it.
7   For example: once any instance of plagiarism is confirmed, The Inter-
    national Baccalaureate not only disqualifies the culprit from the paper
    in question *but the entire Diploma*. Sometimes the offending candidate is
    barred from re-taking the Diploma at any future time.
8   Put simply, an intranet is a *private* part of the Internet.
9   [*Richard Palmer* adds] I like it! For my own assessment of this ghastly
    practice, see page 162, 'Pleasing your reader'.

5   Other sources and resources

1   I will never forget asking, as an undergraduate, for a copy of the
    medieval masterpiece *Piers Plowman* – a set text for over four hundred
    Cambridge students – and being asked in return, 'Which of his books
    did you want, sir?'!
2   There are also some institutions which cultivate a distance between
    teacher and taught without, it must be said, any noticeably deleterious
    consequences. Not many such are to be found in the UK or USA,
    however: that ethos is more prevalent in certain European countries,
    notably France.
3   Those remarks assume you have a choice. Some students do not, being
    hundreds or even thousands of miles away from the nearest teacher,
    school or college. That kind of 'dire necessity' brings its own will-power
    and hungry concentration which can often inspire great success: see
    above, Note 2 to Chapter 1. Other, less 'geographically challenged'
    students should look on their teachers – even the indifferent ones! – as
    a key resource.
4   As noted in earlier chapters, it is sensible in such circumstances to take
    a break anyway, as rest can prompt a sudden subsequent clarity. This
    may occur the following morning at breakfast, on the bus, when you're
    ambling between lessons, and so forth; whenever it happens – and it
    often does – it is all the more wonderful for being so unexpected.

5 To be fair to Shaw, the remark is given to the hero of his *Man and Superman*, John Tanner, a man more distinguished for would-be *bon mots* than for any real sense or achievement.

6 Having said that, if you are unlucky enough to get a teacher who is interested neither in you nor the subject, there is only one sensible thing to be done – transfer to another class. I am well aware of how embarrassing and difficult this can be, but it's the only way, ultimately. If you're getting nowhere under his/her guidance (or lack of it), it makes no sense to remain miserable and uninstructed; and perhaps it's only right that others should know.

6   Eyes right: Effective reading

1 That may damage your *mind* with its plastic corn, but your eyes will be okay!

2 Discounting, that is, the possibility that they're doing the wrong course!

3 This is one reason, incidentally, why a 'photographic memory' is almost always an illusory concept.

7   Creative doodling: Note-taking for fun and profit

1 'Intelligible' simply denotes something *you* will understand when you return to the notes in an hour/day/week.

2 G. Orwell, 'Politics and the English Language', in *Inside the Whale* (London: Penguin Books, 1946, pp. 143–57).

3 N. Mailer, 'Totalitarianism', in *The Presidential Papers*, (London: Deutsch, 1964, pp. 181–6).

4 In view of all the techno-advice offered by Jon Down earlier, you might care to avail yourself of laptops, palm-tops or any other gizmos to refresh and amend your note-taking during any of those six stages. However, it's worth recalling that for all preliminary noting and planning, and some other occasions too, he advocates good old-fashioned pencil and paper! See pages 70–71.

8   Crunch time: Essay planning and writing

1 It is probably true that scientists will do fewer essays, as such, than those studying other disciplines. However, the number of written tasks they have to perform is hardly negligible; in addition, *all* students pursuing the International Baccalaureate – a fast-growing cohort – are required to submit a 4,000-word extended essay as well as various coursework assignments.

2 In case you can't, I look further at the controversy in Chapter 9.

3 The same holds true if – like so many students nowadays do – you're using a PC rather than a pen. The word-processing facilities standard to every modern PC greatly enable the 'scissors-and-paste' approach I've just been advocating, and by all means avail yourself of them – they're fun as well as efficient and fast. The fact remains that many students behave in a fashion highly analogous to how I've characterised

their pen-toting peers. Instead of editing text properly – moving it around, amending it, looking fiercely for and acting on mistakes or clumsinesses – they simply fool around with fonts, spacing and other toys, adding little if anything to their draft. The final version will, it's true, be rather more polished. But the only thing you can polish is a surface – and the final version of an essay needs to go a bit deeper than that.

4 Those wanting a more detailed discussion of the five issues just outlined are referred to Chapter 10 of my book *Write In Style* (London: Routledge, 2002). That volume caters primarily for humanities students and anyone for whom clarity and accuracy of expression are central to their professional work; to duplicate such material here would not only have have been somewhat tawdry but inappropriate, since this book looks to serve students of all kinds. That said, *Write In Style* may prove additionally useful to any of you requiring guidance on quotation and reference and essay performance skills; the latter area is also addressed here, in Chapter 11.

5 Those readers in search of guidance on specifically *literary* analysis should consult Appendix II. I would like to repeat my thanks to Andrew Grimshaw Esq. for inspiring much of the material for this sub-section.

6 This can also characterise certain word-processor writers. See pages 163–4.

7 If you're interested, I use Bookman Old Style, point size 12, with 1.5 line spacing. The effect pleases me; it is also (I'm reliably told) pleasant for others to read.

8 They are also likely to find fonts over size 16 irksome (as will most other readers). It is fine to use these for titles, sub-headings and so on, but standard text in anything from size 16 upwards has a 'yelling' effect that rapidly displeases. If my experience is representative, such in-your-face script is a far less frequent option than the use of font 10 or below; nevertheless, it is no less unattractive than its stunted brother to read or – an issue raised in the main text's next paragraph – for the writer-as-reader to *check*.

9 Apart from those who have been finally ambushed by their own ignorance and waffle desperately because they have no idea what they're doing or what they want to say. I don't include you in that number, naturally!

10 If wishing a more detailed discussion of this item and others, I provide that in my *Write In Style* (op. cit.) and *The Good Grammar Guide* (London: Routledge, 2003). You will also find more 'what not to do' advice in these chapters, including Jon Down's.

11 Interview with *Paris Review* (1982); published in *Required Writing*, 73.

9 Psychology and attitudes

1 It can be done, however. See Appendix IV, pages 222–3.

2 Just a week after I wrote those words, the Headmaster of Eton College, Tony Little, referred to GCSEs as analogous to 'Boy Scout Badges' – i.e. juvenile medals commemorating this or that semi-meaningless

hobby. He may have (wittily) exaggerated the case, but plenty of students and teachers would defend its essential cogency.

3 A. Hall, *The Striker Portfolio* (London: Fontana, 1975 p. 71).

10 Preparation tips

1 From the still-running – and wonderful – BBC Radio 4 show, *I'm Sorry I Haven't A Clue* (November 1993).
2 Or preferably a fourth or fifth!

11 Skills and techniques

1 Literally, 'hurry slowly'. An English equivalent might be 'more haste, less speed'.
2 This is an unusual quality, and you'll know/have been told if you possess it – in which case you can ignore my advice!

Appendix I: Reading novels and creative literature

1 Hardly a startling choice: most lovers of literature would consider it among the greatest works ever written.

Appendix II: Literary analysis

1 It's extremely unlikely you'll be given any true rubbish, either by your teachers or the exam boards!
2 Such issues are fundamental to Attainment Objectives 2 and 5.
3 R. Palmer, *Write In Style*, op. cit.

Bibliography

When I wrote *Brain Train* (the original incarnation of this book) in 1984, the field of study skills was a rapidly expanding one. It is now colossal: anything approaching a comprehensive bibliography would probably be twice the size of this volume. Furthermore, I have no desire to send readers in the direction of the many tawdry and frankly damaging publications that abound, chiefly in the form of those thrice-accursed 'study aids'. Instead I offer a selective bibliography of books I admire, have found helpful and know that students have benefited from.

General

Nicholas Alchin (2002) *Theory of Knowledge*, London, John Murray.
Robert Barrass (1984) *Study!* London, Routledge.
Tony Buzan (1974) *Use Your Head*, London, BBC Books.
Tony Buzan (1993) *The Mindmap Book*, London, BBC Books.
Guy Claxton (2002) *Wise Up: The Challenge of Lifelong Learning*, London, Bloomsbury.
Edward de Bono (1982) *de Bono's Thinking Course*, London, BBC.
Graham Gibbs (1981) *Teaching Students To Learn*, Milton Keynes, Open University Press.
William James (1891) *Principles of Psychology*, [First published 1891]
Michael Lockwood (1989) *Mind, Brain and the Quantum: The Compound 'I'*, Oxford, Blackwell.
Roger Penrose (1989) *The Emperor's New Mind*, London, BBC Books.
Peter Russell (1979) *The Brain Book*, London, Routledge.

Memory

Alan Baddeley (1976) *The Psychology of Memory*, London, Basic Books.
Alan Baddeley (1983) *Your Memory: A User's Guide*, Harmondsworth, Penguin.
Ian M.L. Hunter (1964) *Memory (Revised edition)* Harmondsworth, Penguin.
Frances A. Yates (1969) *The Art of Memory*, Harmondsworth, Penguin.

Writing

Edward P. Bailey, Jr. (1990) *The Plain English Approach to Business Writing*, Oxford, Oxford Universtiy Press.
Bill Bryson (1994) *Dictionary for Writers and Editors*, Harmondsworth, Penguin.
Maeve O'Connor (1991) *Writing Successfully In Science*, London, Chapman & Hall.
Richard Palmer (2002) *Write In Style (Second edition)*, London, Routledge.
Philip Davis Roberts (1987) *Plain English: A User's Guide*, Harmondsworth, Penguin.
O.M. Thomson (1992) *A Matter Of Style* (Third edition) London, Thorn.
Christopher Turk and John Kirkman (1989) *Effective Writing* (Second edition) London, Routledge.

Reading

Manya and Eric De Leeuw (1965) *Read Better, Read Faster*, Harmondsworth, Penguin.
J. Moore (1980) *Reading and Thinking in English*, Oxford, Oxford Universtiy Press.

Grammar and basics

Kersti Börjars and Kate Burridge (2001) *Introducing English Grammar*, New York, Oxford Universtiy Press.
G.V. Carey (1971) *Mind the Stop*, Harmondsworth, Penguin.
Sir Ernest Gowers (1962) *The Complete Plain Words*, Harmondsworth, Penguin.
Sidney Greenbaum (1996) *The Oxford English Grammar*, Oxford, Oxford Universtiy Press.
Philip Howard (1985) *A Word In Your Ear*, Harmondsworth, Penguin.
Richard Palmer (2003) *The Good Grammar Guide*, London, Routledge.
O.M. Thomson (1973) *Essential Grammar*, Oxford, Oxford Universtiy Press.

David Crystal (anything and everything!)

Miscellaneous

This final section has no connecting thread other than my own admiring pleasure in all books cited. However, each is excellent in its own right, and all students are likely to find them valuable

Kingsley Amis (1997) *The King's English*, London, HarperCollins.
Henry Beard and Christopher Serf (1994) *The Official Politically Correct Dictionary and Handbook*, London, HarperCollins.
Ambrose Bierce (1990) *The Enlarged Devil's Dictionary*, Harmondsworth, Penguin

John Carey (1987) *The Faber Book of Reportage*, London, Faber & Faber
Rebecca Corfield (1990) *Preparing Your Own CV*, London, Kogan Page.
R.W. Holder (1989) *The Faber Dictionary of Euphemisms*, London, Faber & Faber.
David Lodge (1986) *Write On*, Harmondsworth, Penguin.
Jonathan Smith (2000) *The Learning Game*, London, Little Brown.
Christopher Turk (1985) *Effective Speaking*, London, Routledge.

See also Chapter 5, pages 93–6, where a number of invaluable works of reference are listed and discussed. And Jon Down's survey of *Useful Websites* (Appendix III) should also prove highly profitable.

Index